EASY PIANO

the
DEFINITIVE *jazz* COLLECTION

This publication is not for sale in
the EC and/or Australia
or New Zealand.

ISBN 0-7935-3591-3

HAL•LEONARD™
CORPORATION
7777 W. BLUEMOUND RD. P.O. BOX 13819 MILWAUKEE, WI 53213

the DEFINITIVE *Jazz* COLLECTION

AFTER YOU'VE GONE

Words by HENRY CREAMER
Music by TURNER LAYTON

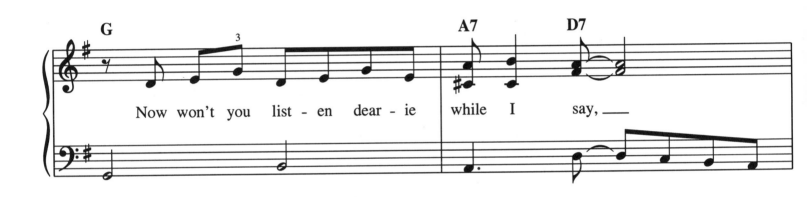

Now won't you list-en dear-ie while I say, ___

How could you tell me that you're goin' a - way? ___ Don't say that

we must part, ___ Don't break my ach-ing heart; ___

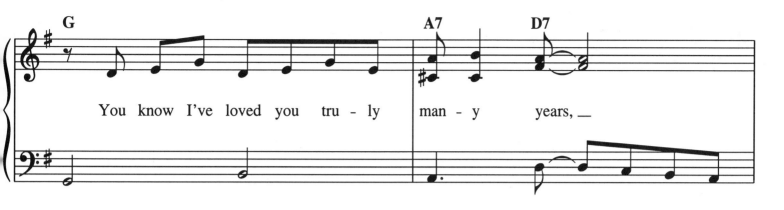

You know I've loved you tru – ly man – y years, —

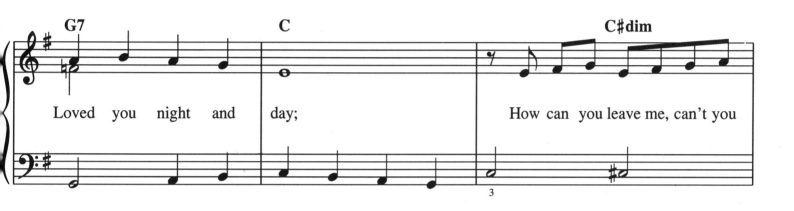

Loved you night and day; How can you leave me, can't you

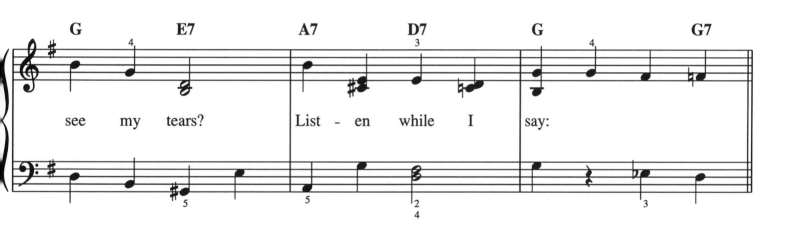

see my tears? List – en while I say:

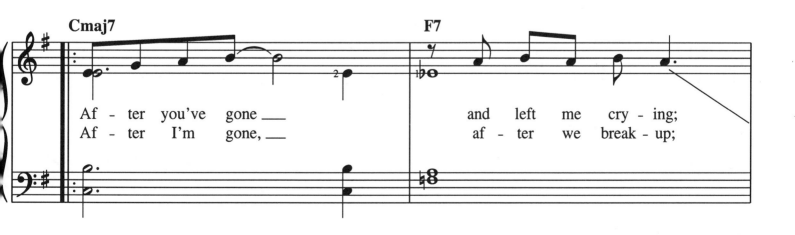

Af – ter you've gone ___ and left me cry – ing;
Af – ter I'm gone, ___ af – ter we break – up;

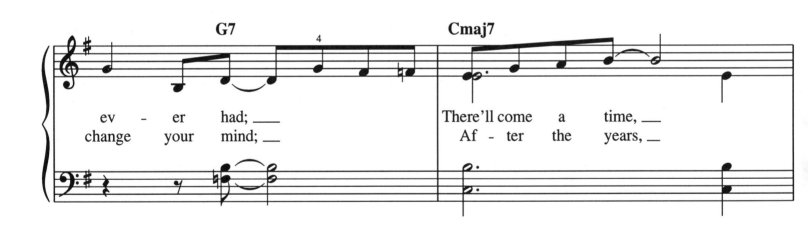

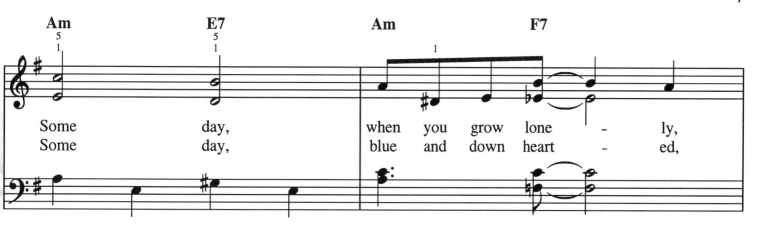

Some   day,   when you grow lone -   ly,
Some   day,   blue and down heart -   ed,

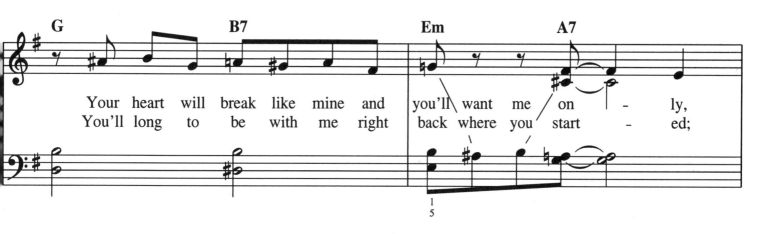

Your heart will break like mine and you'll want me on -   ly,
You'll long to be with me right back where you start -   ed;

Af - ter you've gone,   Af - ter you've gone a -   way.
Af - ter I'm gone,   Af - ter I'm gone a -

way.

AIN'T MISBEHAVIN'
(From "AIN'T MISBEHAVIN'")

Words by ANDY RAZAF
Music by THOMAS WALLER and HARRY BROOKS

I'm thru with flirt-in', it's just you I'm think - in' of. Ain't mis-be-hav-in',

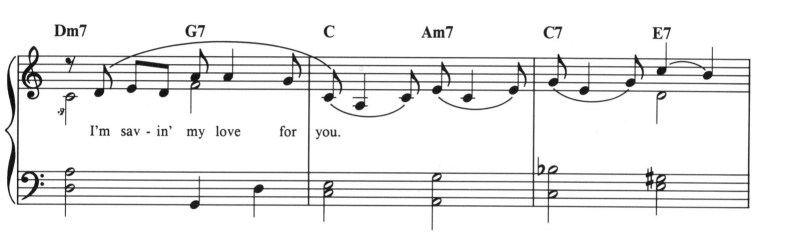

I'm sav-in' my love for you.

Like Jack Hor-ner in the cor-ner, don't go no-where,

what do I care. Your kiss-es are worth wait-in'

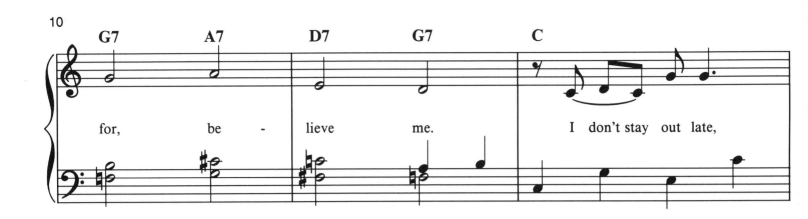

for, be - lieve me. I don't stay out late,

don't care to go, I'm home a - bout eight, just me and my ra - di - o.

Ain't mis - be - hav - in', I'm sav - in' my love for you.

you.

ALL OF ME

Moderately

Words and Music by SEYMOUR SIMONS
and GERALD MARKS

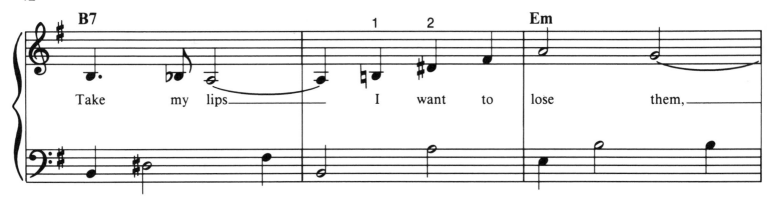

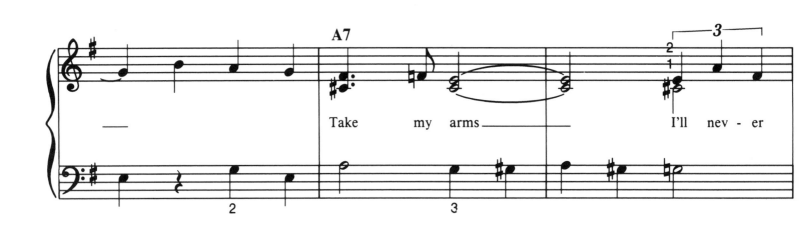

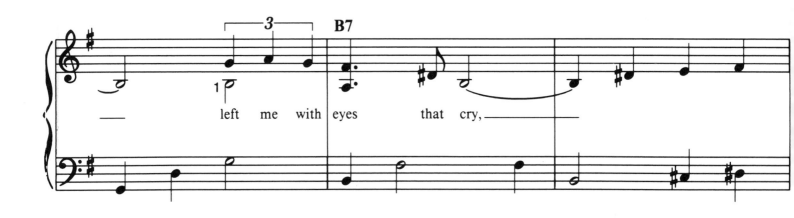

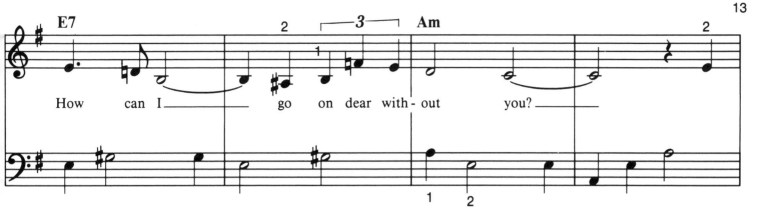

How can I ___ go on dear with-out you? ___

You took the part that once was my

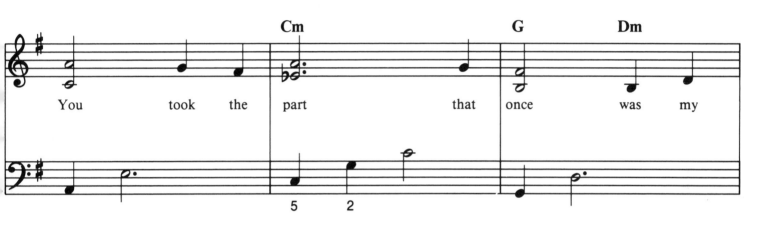

heart. So why not take all of

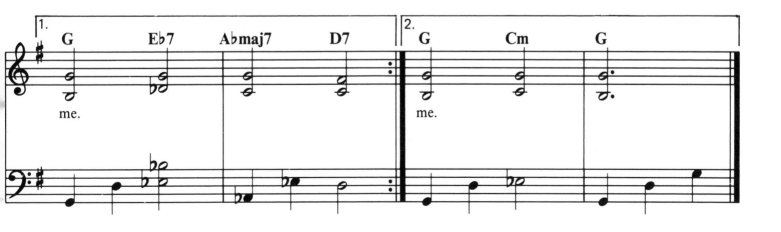

me. me.

ALL THE THINGS YOU ARE

(From "VERY WARM FOR MAY")

Lyrics by OSCAR HAMMERSTEIN II
Music by JEROME KERN

Freely

Verse

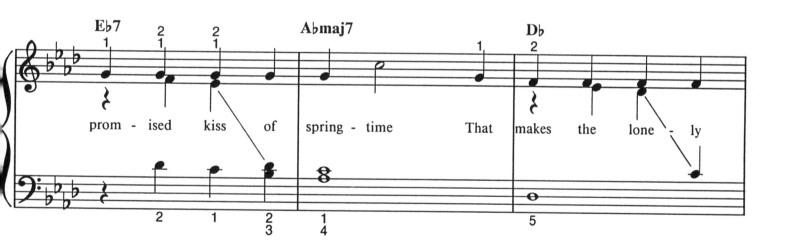

Slowly
Burthen*

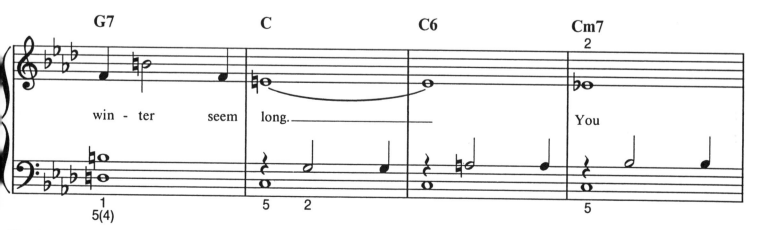

*Burthen is another word for chorus.

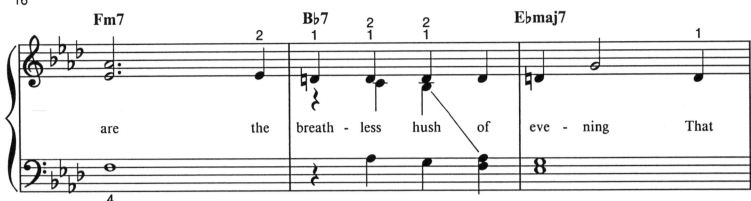

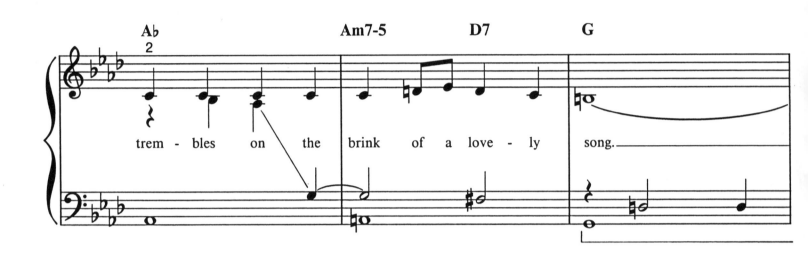

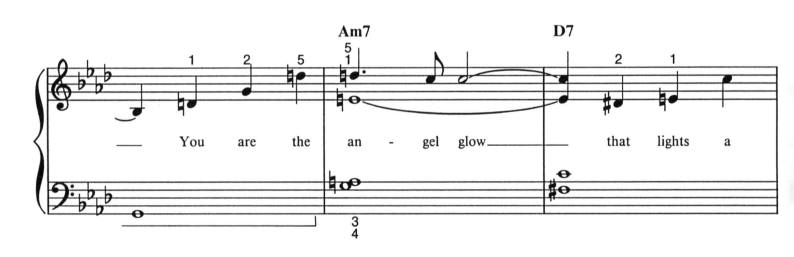

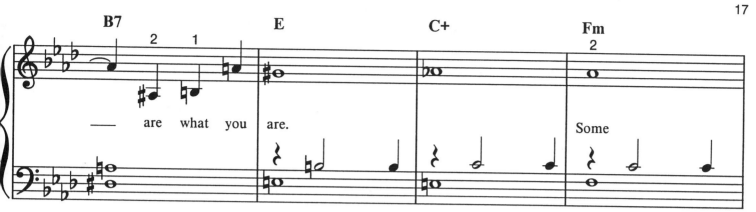

B7 — are what you are. **E** **C+** **Fm** Some

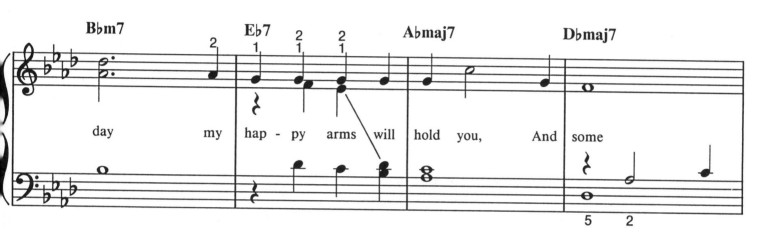

Bbm7 day **Eb7** my hap - py arms will **Abmaj7** hold you, **Dbmaj7** And some

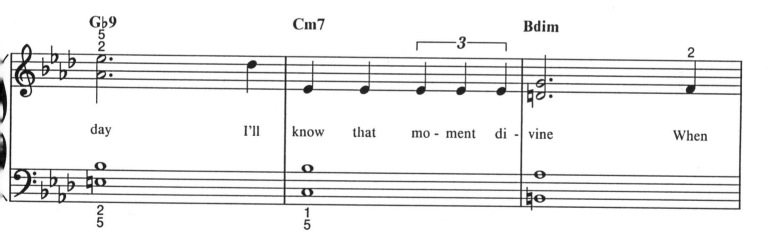

Gb9 day **Cm7** I'll know that mo - ment di - vine **Bdim** When

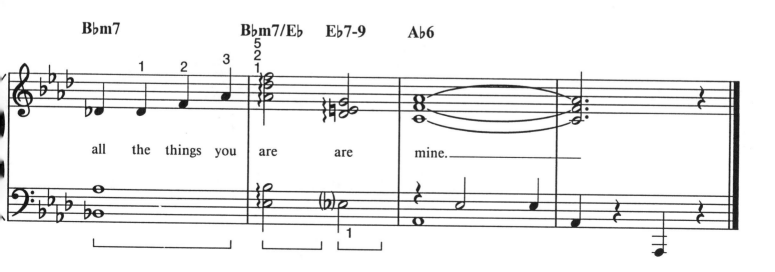

Bbm7 all the things you **Bbm7/Eb Eb7-9** are are **Ab6** mine.

BERNIE'S TUNE

Words and Music by BERNIE MILLER,
MIKE STOLLER and JERRY LIEBER

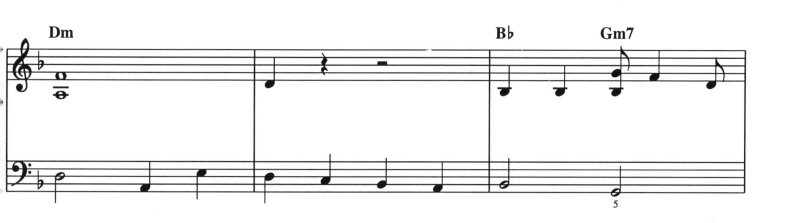

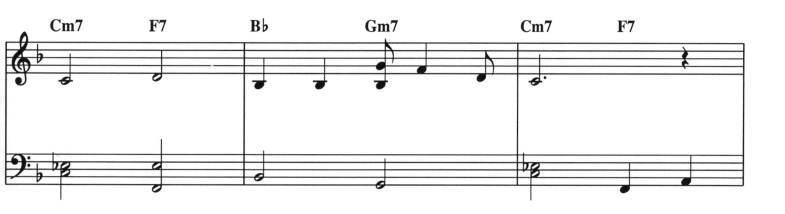

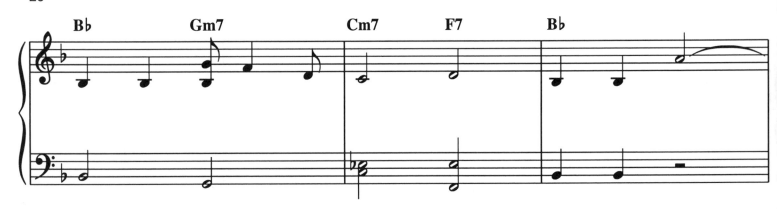

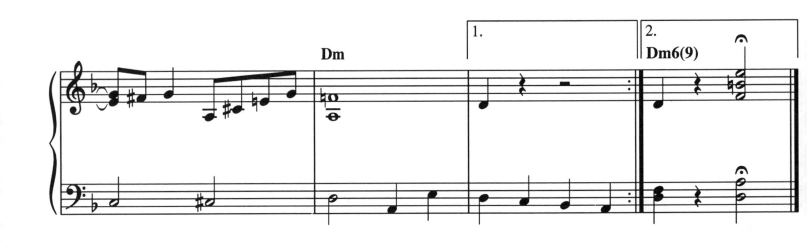

BIRDLAND

Music by
JOSEF ZAWINUL

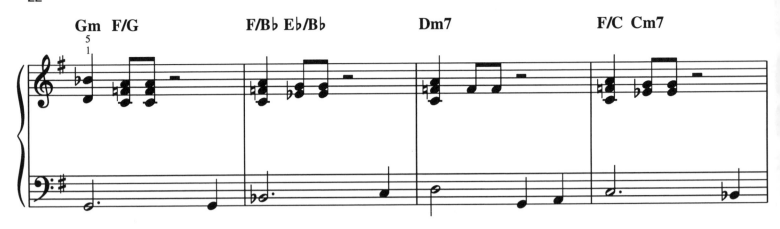

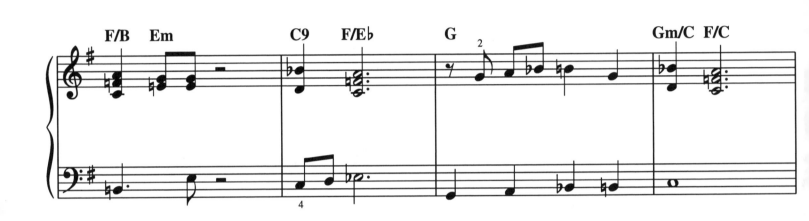

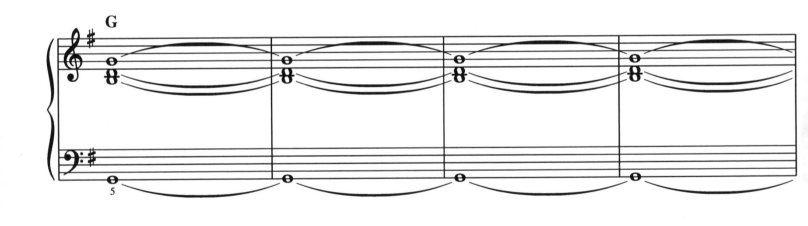

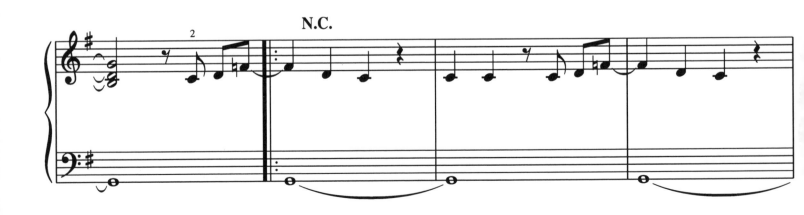

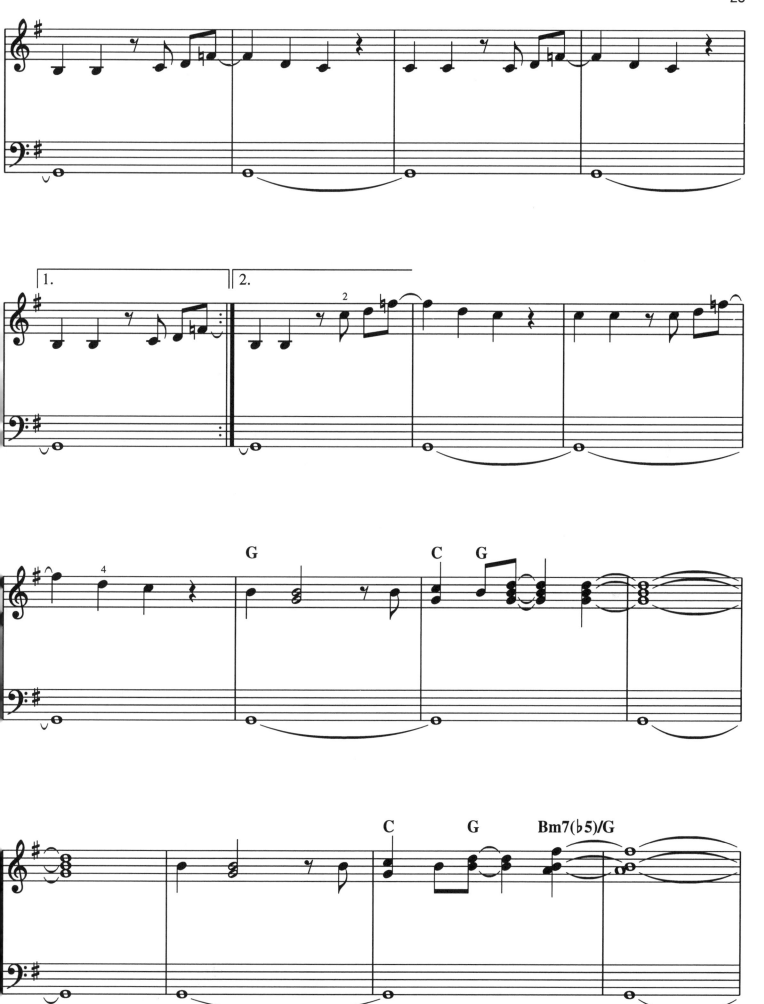

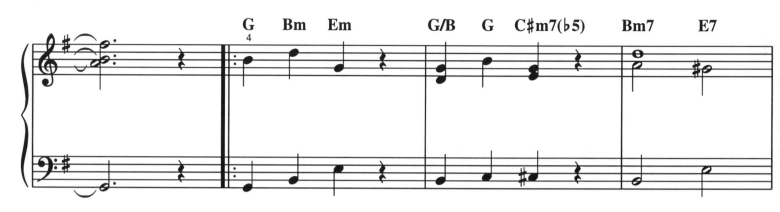

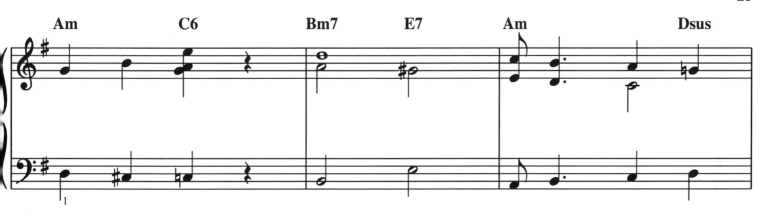

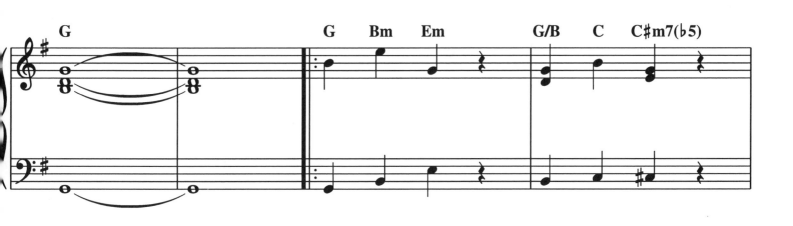

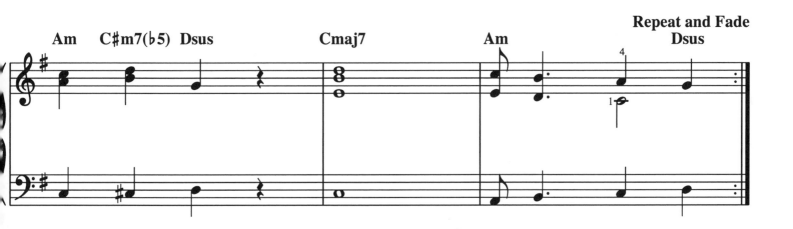

BLUESETTE

Words by NORMAN GIMBEL
Music by JEAN THIELEMANS

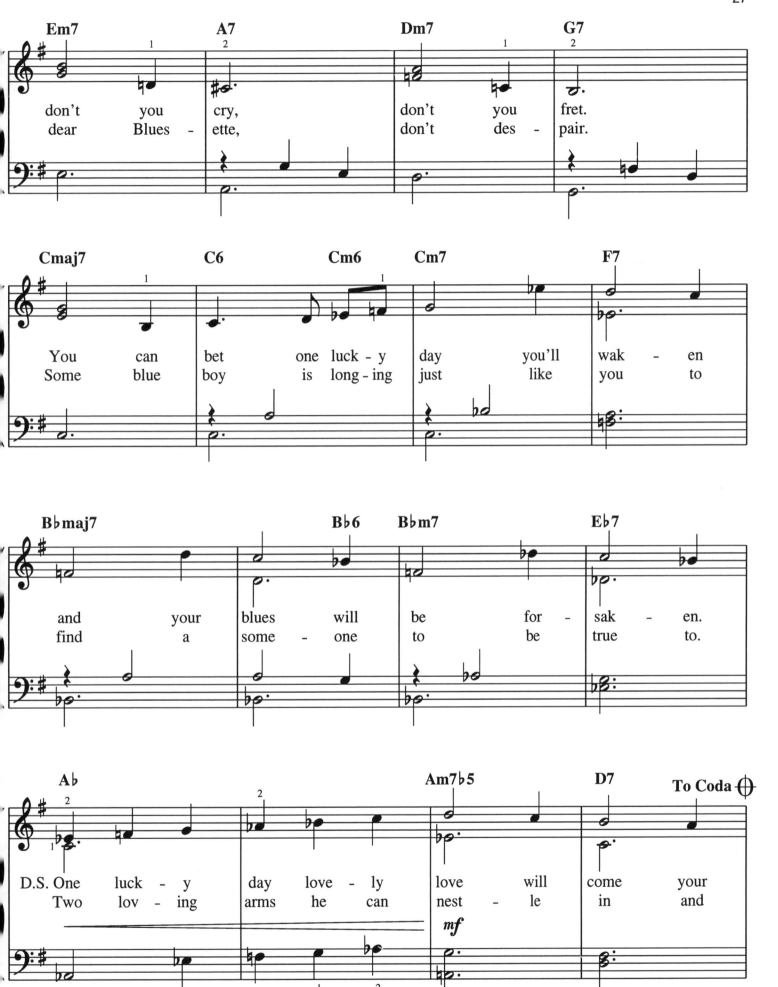

28

30

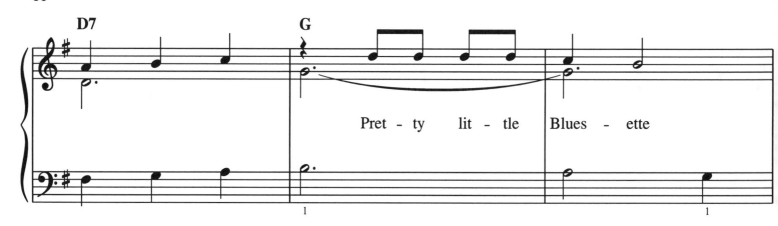

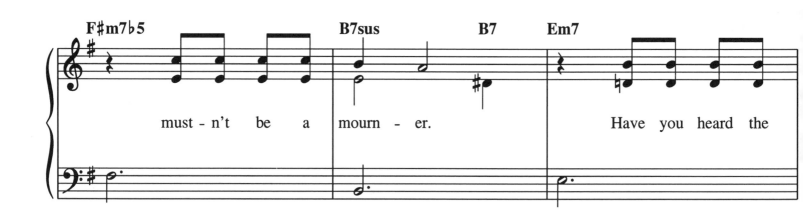

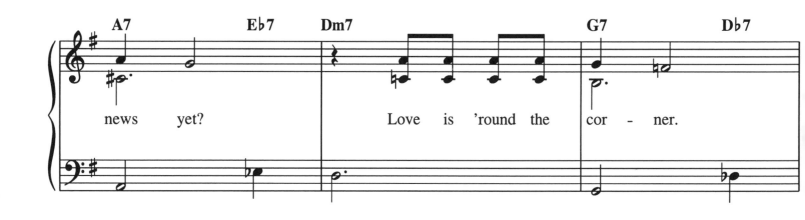

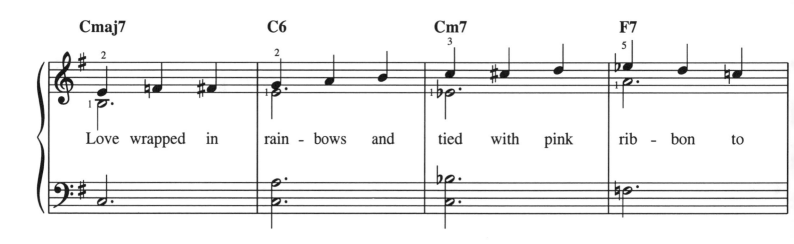

BUT NOT FOR ME

Music and Lyrics by
GEORGE and IRA GERSHWIN

Moderately

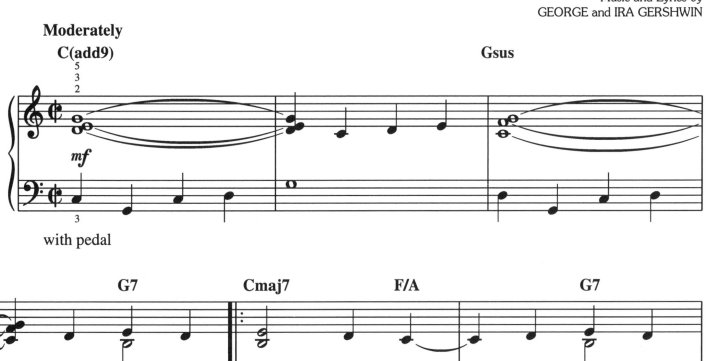

with pedal

They're writ - ing songs of love, _____ But not for
on a door, _____ But not for

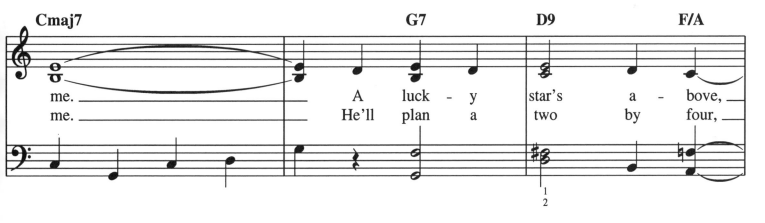

me. _____ A luck - y star's a - bove, _____
me. _____ He'll plan a two by four, _____

But not for me. _____ With love to
But not for me. _____ I know that

34

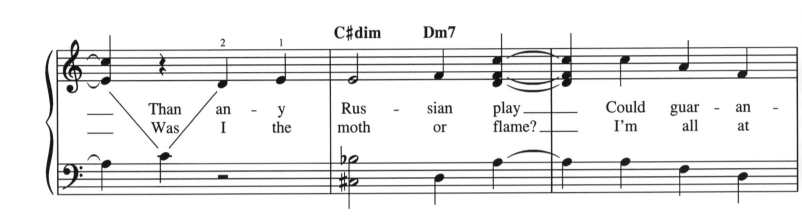

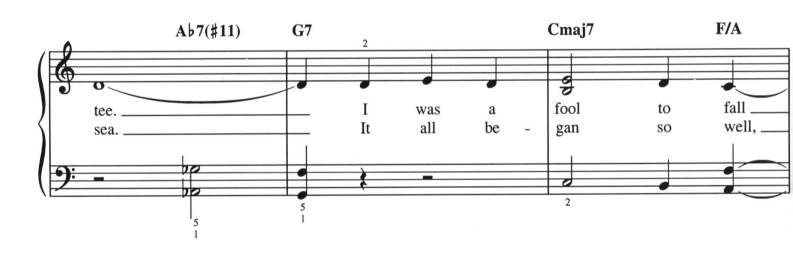

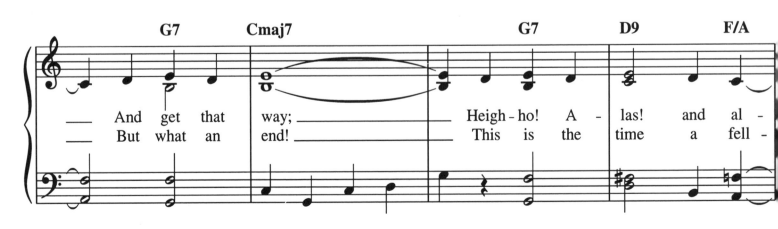

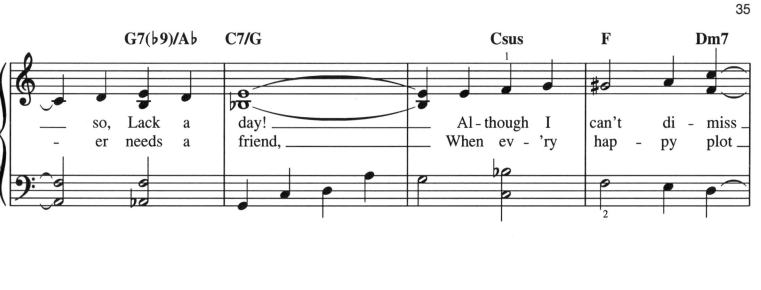

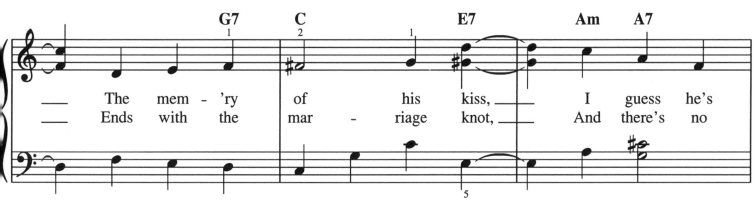

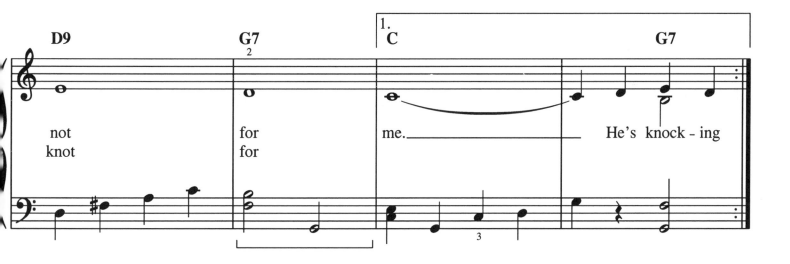

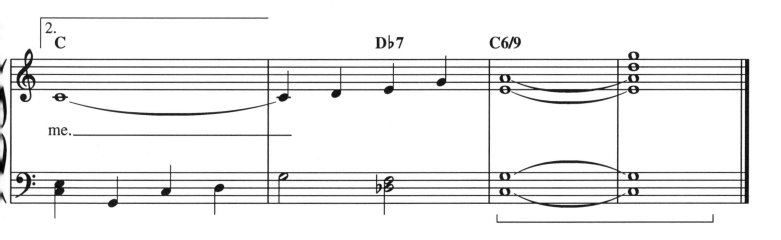

BODY AND SOUL

Words by EDWARD HEYMAN, ROBERT SOUR and FRANK EYTON
Music by JOHN GREEN

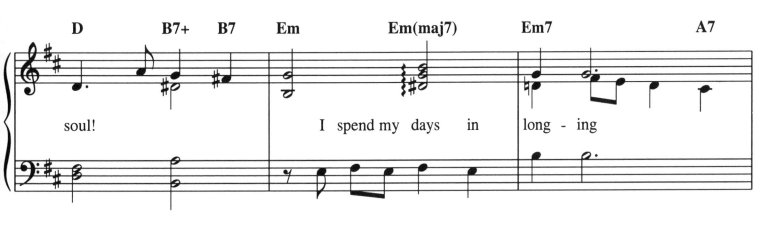

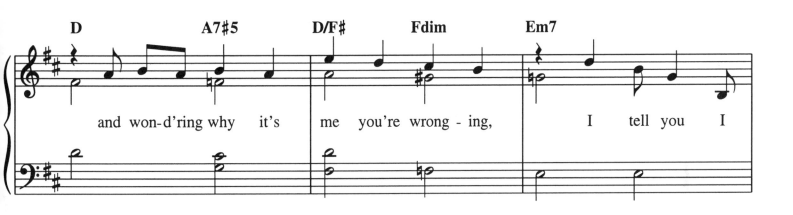

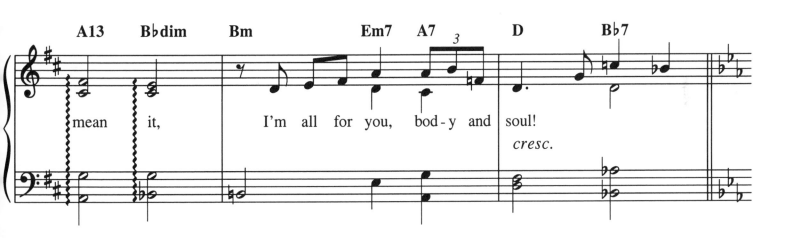

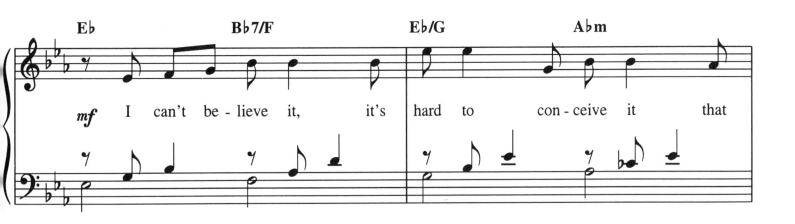

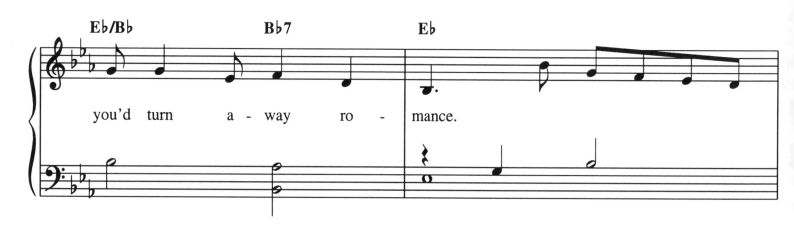

you'd turn a - way ro - mance.

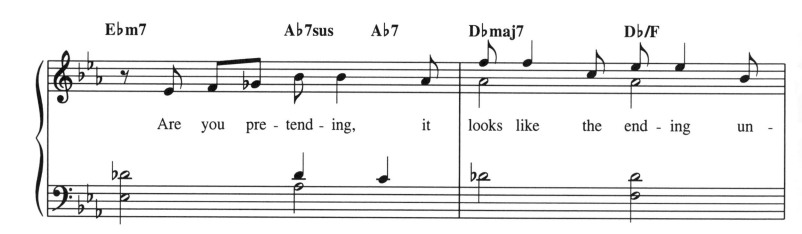

Are you pre - tend - ing, it looks like the end - ing un -

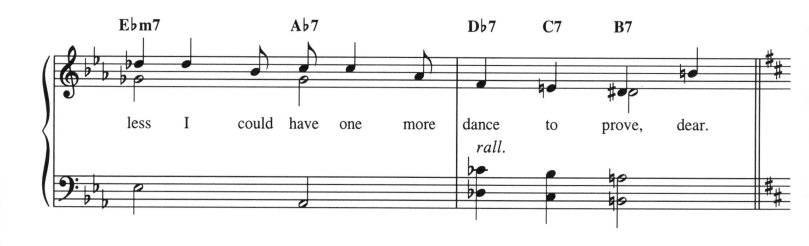

less I could have one more dance to prove, dear.

rall.

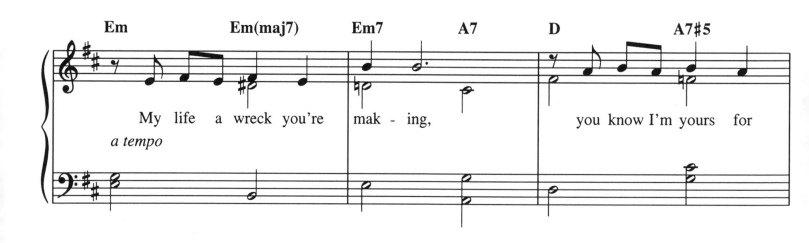

My life a wreck you're mak - ing, you know I'm yours for

a tempo

COME RAIN OR COME SHINE

(From "ST. LOUIS WOMAN")

Words by JOHNNY MERCER
Music by HAROLD ARLEN

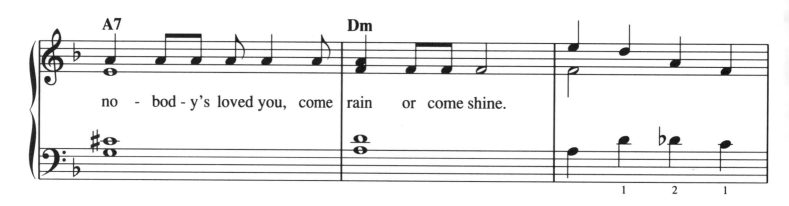

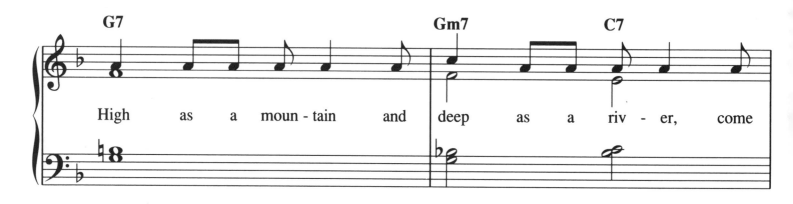

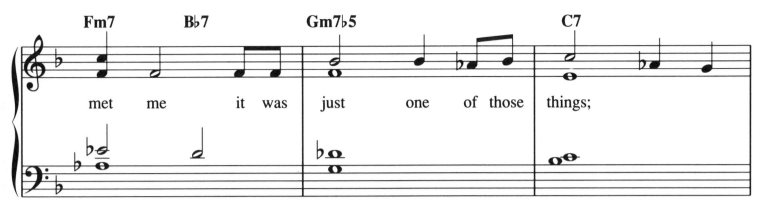

met me it was just one of those things;

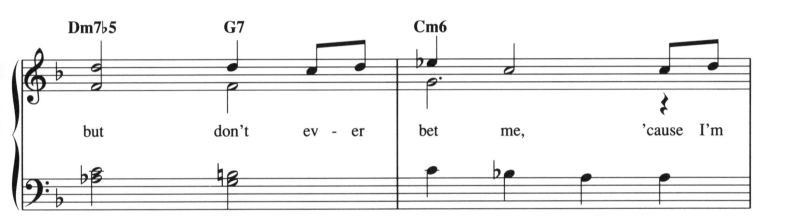

but don't ev - er bet me, 'cause I'm

gon - na be true if you let me. You're gon - na love me like

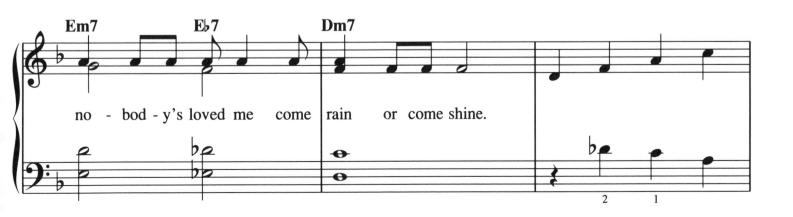

no - bod - y's loved me come rain or come shine.

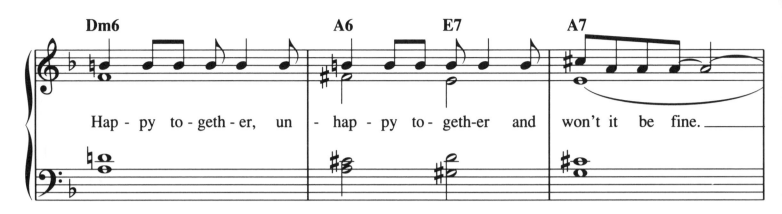

Hap - py to - geth - er, un - hap - py to - geth - er and won't it be fine. ___

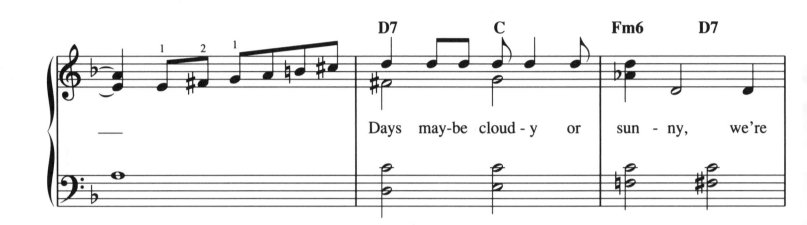

___ Days may-be cloud - y or sun - ny, we're

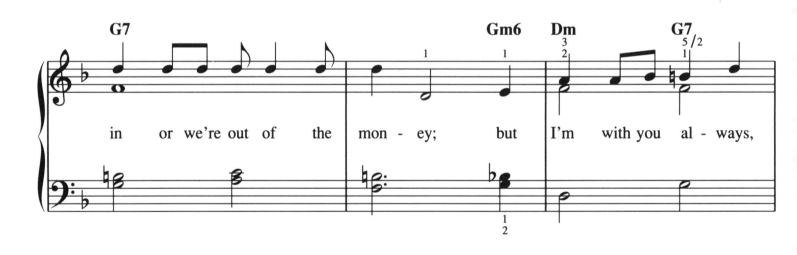

in or we're out of the mon - ey; but I'm with you al - ways,

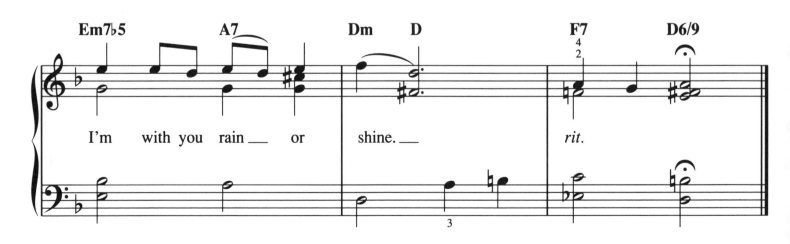

I'm with you rain ___ or shine. ___ *rit.*

CRY ME A RIVER

Words and Music by
ARTHUR HAMILTON

Now_____ you say you're lone- ly,_____
Now_____ you say you're sor - ry_____

You cry the whole night for be- in' so un -

thru._____ Well, you can cry_____ me a riv- er,
true._____ Well, you can cry_____ me a riv- er,

cry__ me a riv- er,
cry__ me a riv- er,

I cried a riv- er o- ver you.
I cried a riv- er o- ver

44

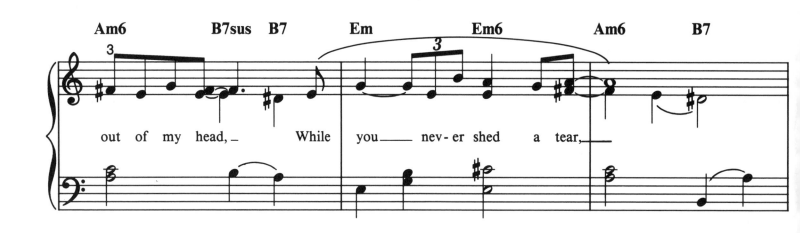

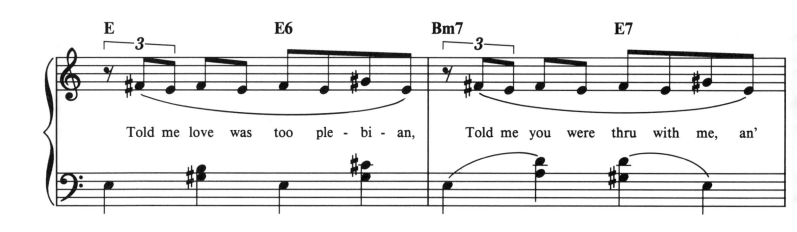

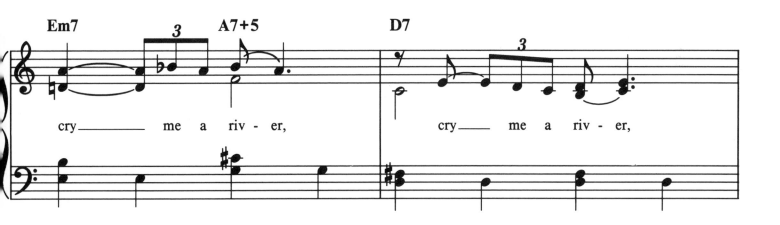

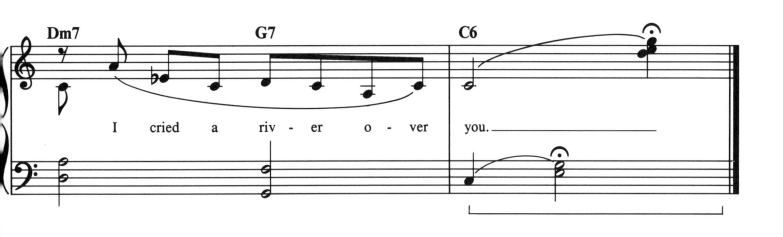

A DAY IN THE LIFE OF A FOOL
(Manha De Carnaval)

Words by CARL SIGMAN
Music by LUIZ BONFA

Moderately

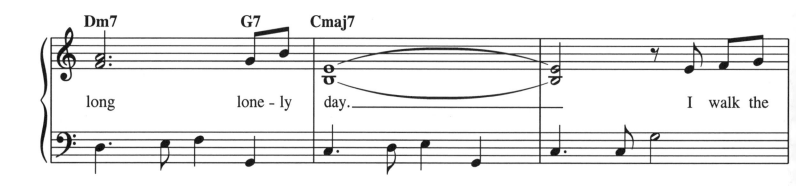

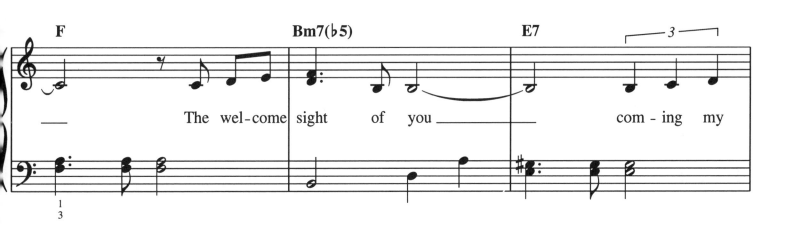

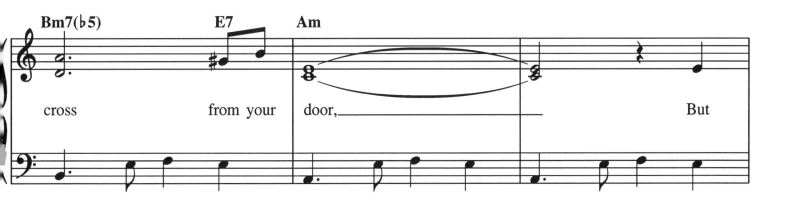

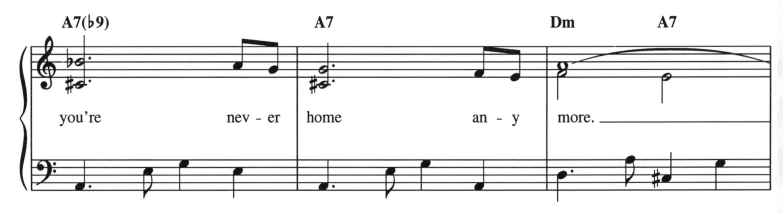

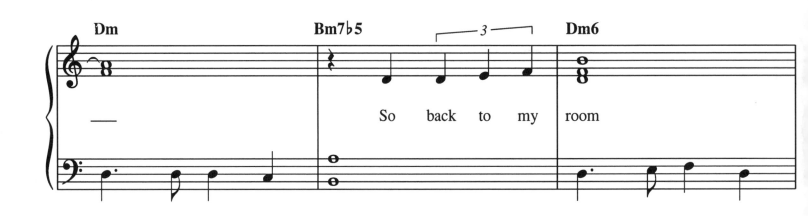

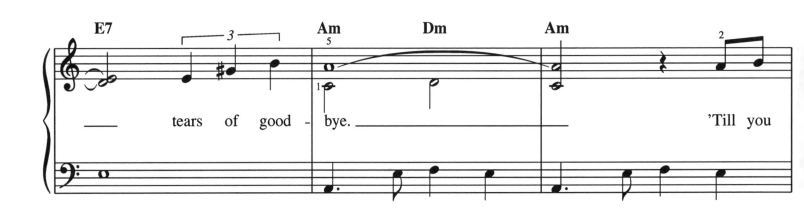

come back to me, that's the way it will be ev - 'ry

Add pedal

day in the life of a fool.

No pedal

DO NOTHIN' TILL YOU HEAR FROM ME

Words and Music by BOB RUSSELL
and DUKE ELLINGTON

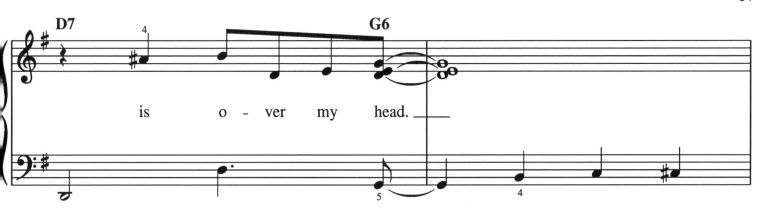

is o - ver my head. ___

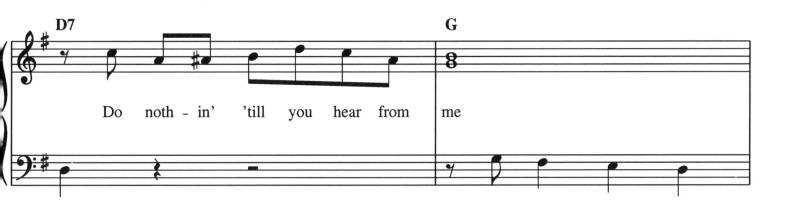

Do noth - in' 'till you hear from me

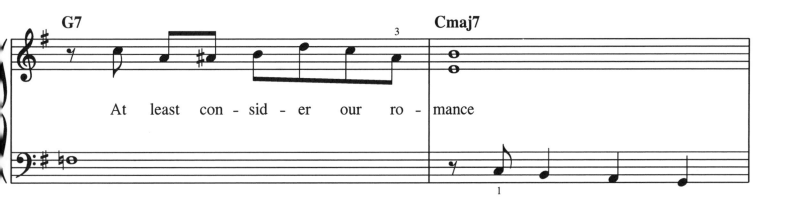

At least con - sid - er our ro - mance

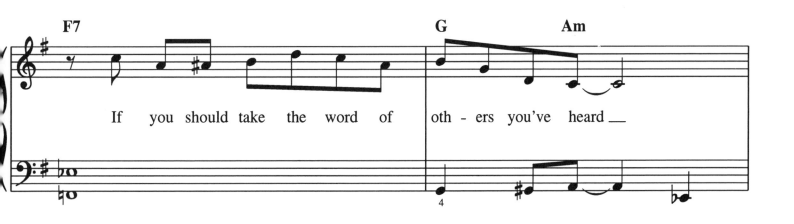

If you should take the word of oth - ers you've heard ___

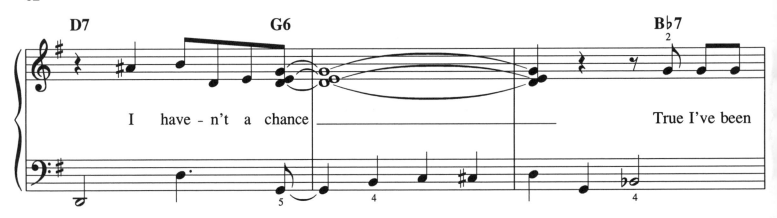

I have-n't a chance _____ True I've been

seen with some-one new __ But does that mean

that I'm un-true _ When we're a-part the words in my heart __ re-

veal how I feel ___ a-bout you. Some kiss may cloud my mem-o-

ry

And oth - er arms may hold a

thrill

But please do noth - in' till you

hear it from me ___

And you nev - er will. ___

1.

Do noth - in' till you hear from

2.

DON'T GET AROUND MUCH ANYMORE

Words and Music by BOB RUSSELL
and DUKE ELLINGTON

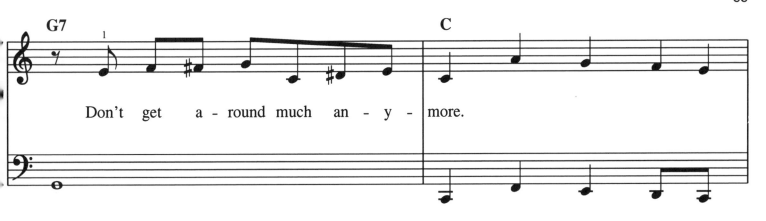

Don't get a - round much an - y - more.

Thought I'd vis - it the club   Got as far as the

door   they'd have ask'd me a - bout you __

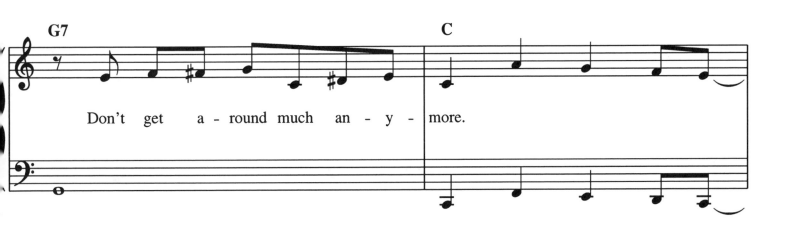

Don't get a - round much an - y - more.

F6   Bb9

Dar - ling I guess my

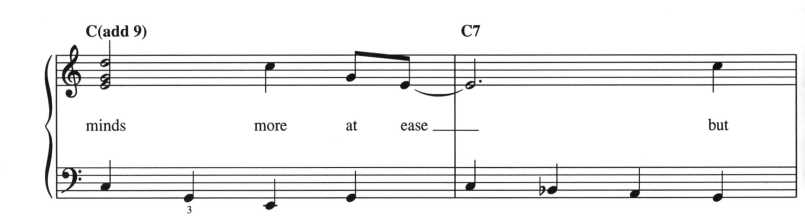

C(add 9)   C7

minds more at ease ___ but

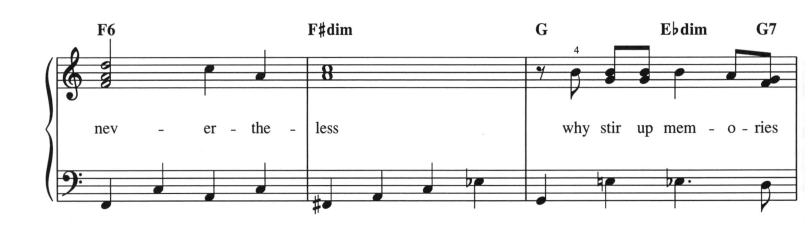

F6   F#dim   G   Ebdim   G7

nev - er - the - less why stir up mem - o - ries

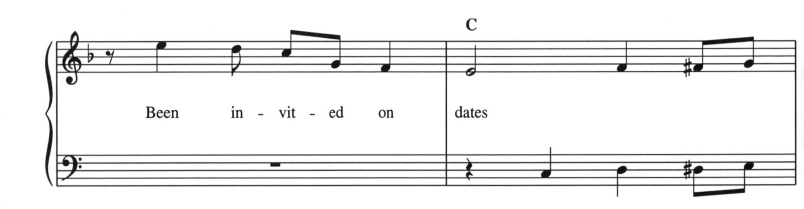

C

Been in - vit - ed on dates

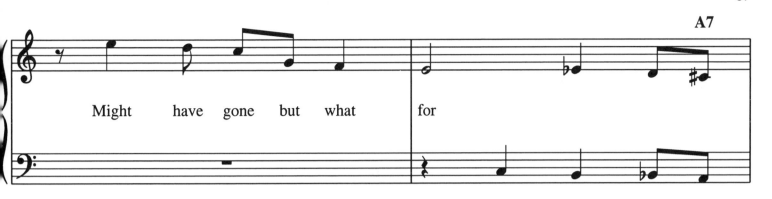

A7

Might have gone but what for

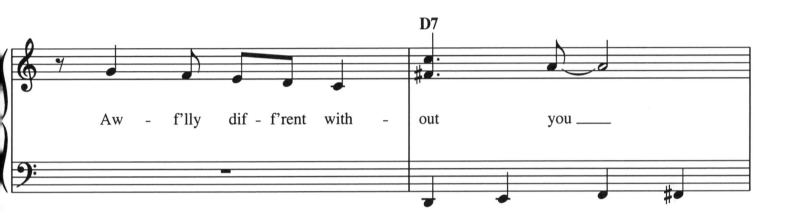

D7

Aw - f'lly dif - f'rent with - out you _____

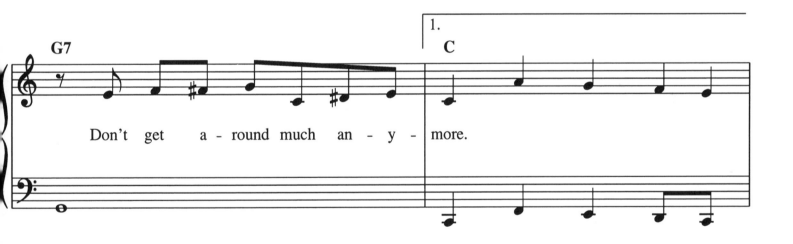

G7

1.

C

Don't get a - round much an - y - more.

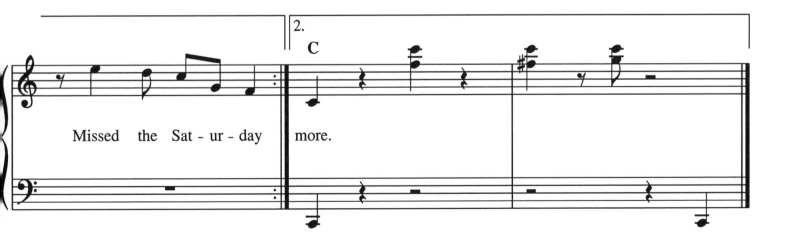

2.

C

Missed the Sat - ur - day more.

EARLY AUTUMN

Words by JOHNNY MERCER
Music by RALPH BURNS and WOODY HERMAN

59

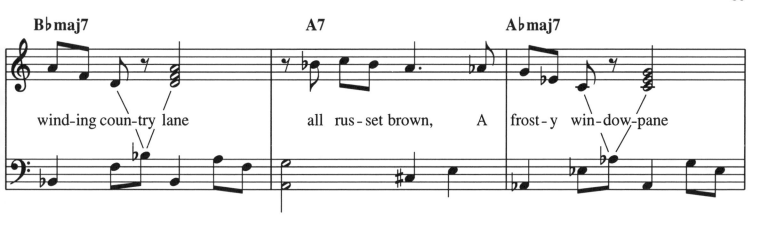

wind-ing coun-try lane　　　all rus-set brown,　A frost-y win-dow-pane

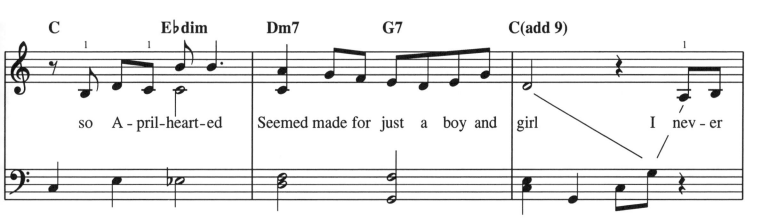

shows me a town　grown lone-ly.　　　That spring of　ours that start-ed

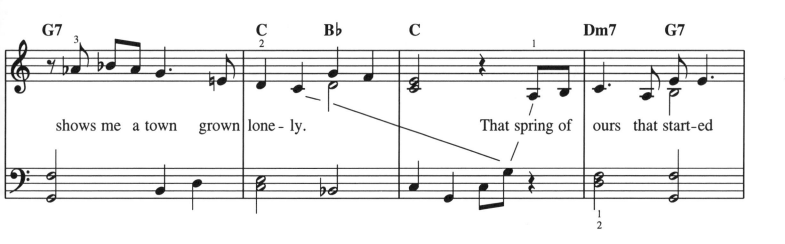

so A-pril-heart-ed　Seemed made for just a boy and girl　I nev-er

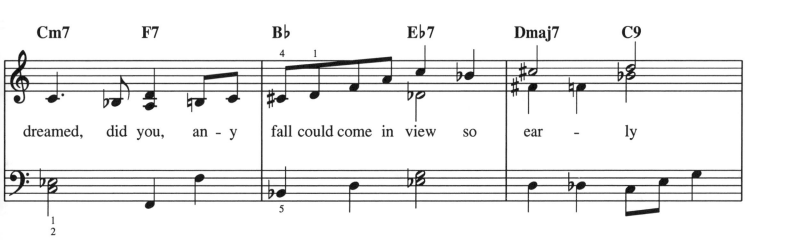

dreamed,　did you,　an-y　fall could come in view　so　ear - ly

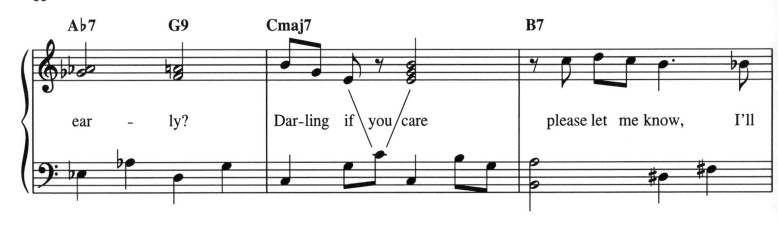

ear - ly? Dar-ling if you care please let me know, I'll

meet you an - y-where I miss you so, Let's nev-er have to share

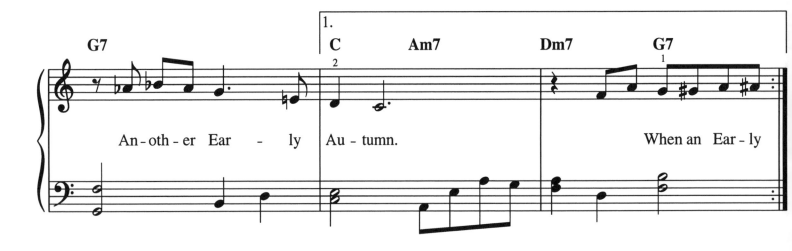

An-oth-er Ear - ly Au - tumn. When an Ear - ly

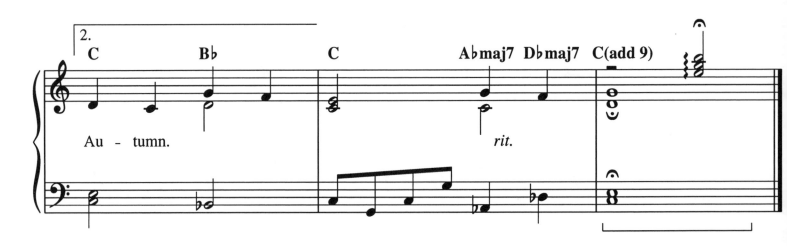

Au - tumn. *rit.*

FEVER

Words and Music by JOHN DAVENPORT
and EDDIE COOLEY

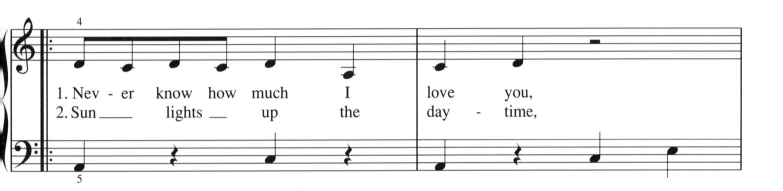

1. Nev - er know how much I love you,
2. Sun ___ lights ___ up the day - time,

nev - er know how much ___ I care.
moon ___ lights ___ up ___ the night.

When you put your arms a - round me, I get a
I ___ light ___ up when you call my name, and you

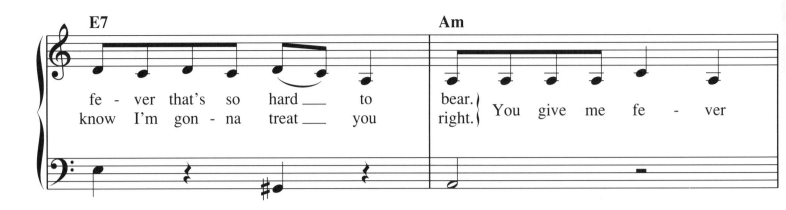

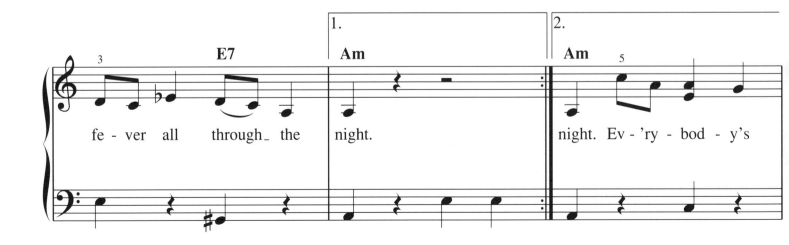

got the fe - ver, that is some - thing you all know.

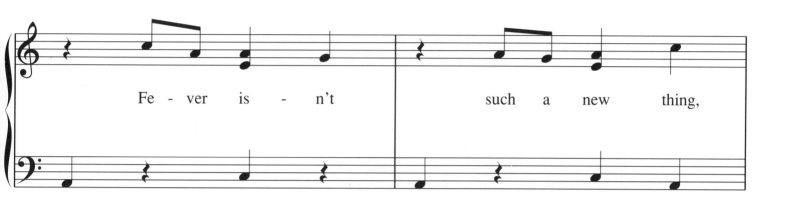

Fe - ver is - n't such a new thing,

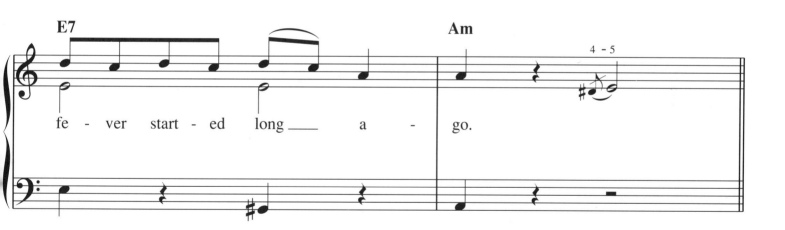

E7   **Am**

4 - 5

fe - ver start - ed long ____ a - go.

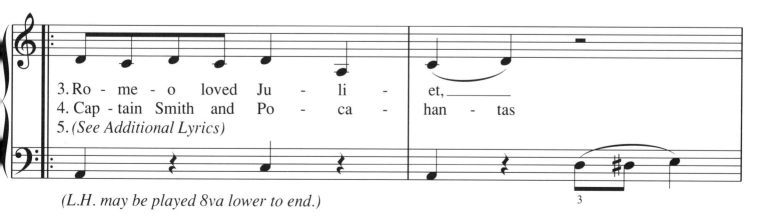

3. Ro - me - o loved Ju - li - et, _____
4. Cap - tain Smith and Po - ca - han - tas
5. *(See Additional Lyrics)*

(L.H. may be played 8va lower to end.)   3

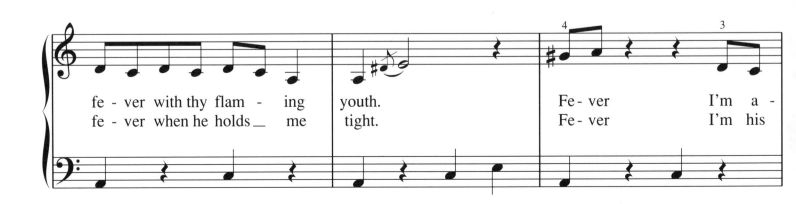

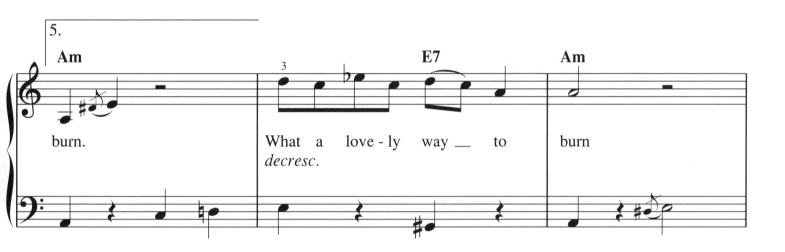

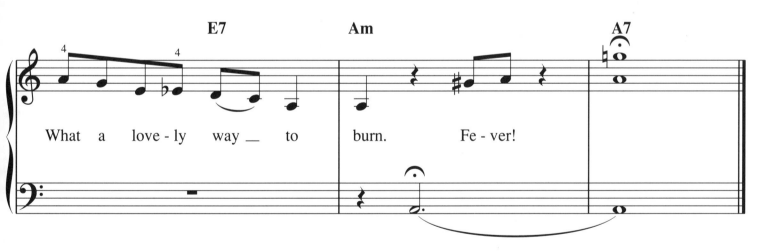

Additional Lyrics

5. Now you've listened to my story,
   Here's the point that I have made:
   Chicks were born to give you fever,
   be it fahrenheit or centigrade.

   They give you fever when you kiss them
   fever if you live and learn.
   Fever - till you sizzle,
   What a lovely way to burn.

FLY ME TO THE MOON
(IN OTHER WORDS)

Words and Music by
BART HOWARD

darling kiss me!

Fill my life with song and let me sing for - ev - er

more; You are all I long for, all I

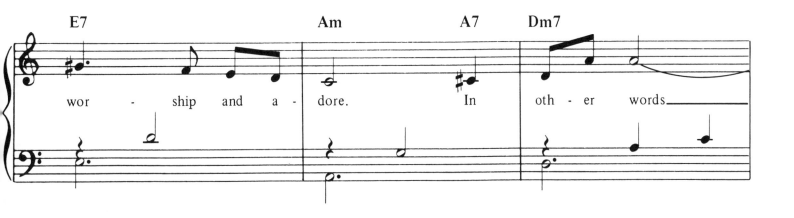

wor - ship and a - dore. In oth - er words____

68

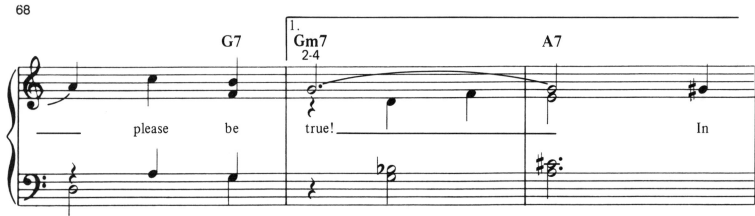

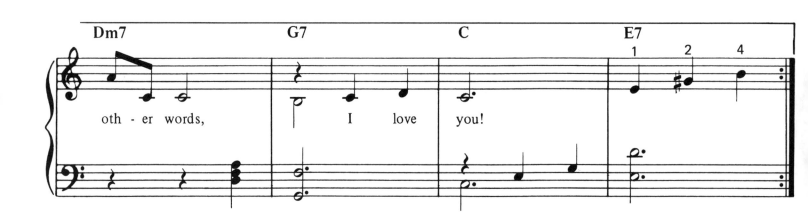

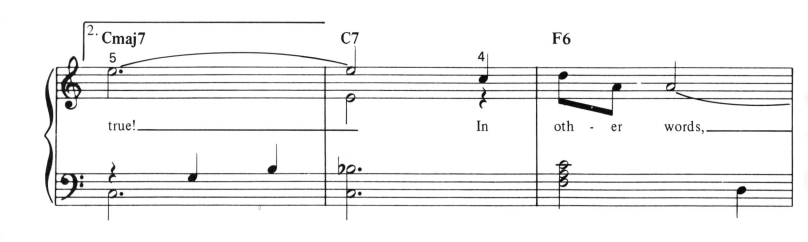

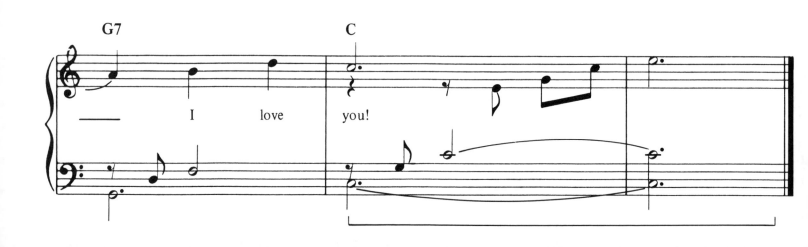

A FOGGY DAY
(From "A DAMSEL IN DISTRESS")

Music and Lyrics by GEORGE GERSHWIN
and IRA GERSHWIN

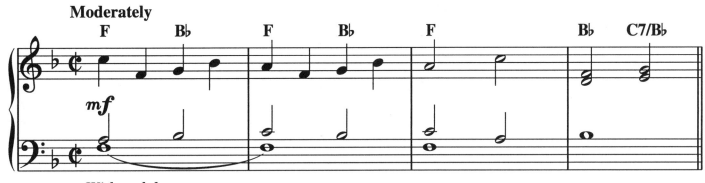

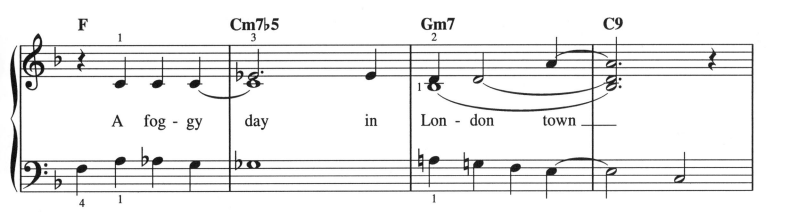

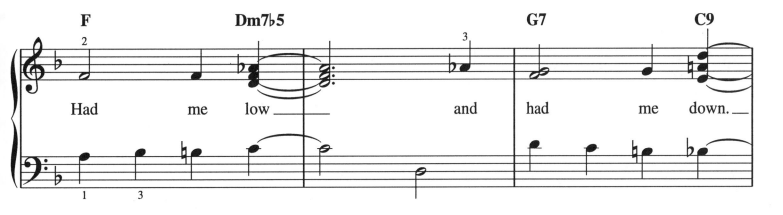

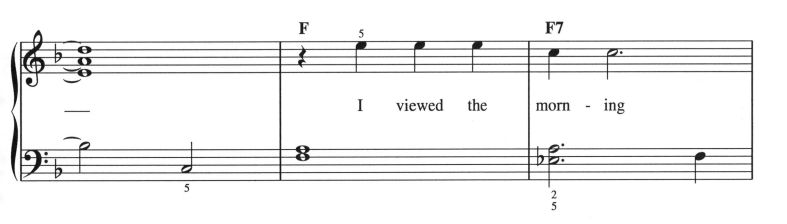

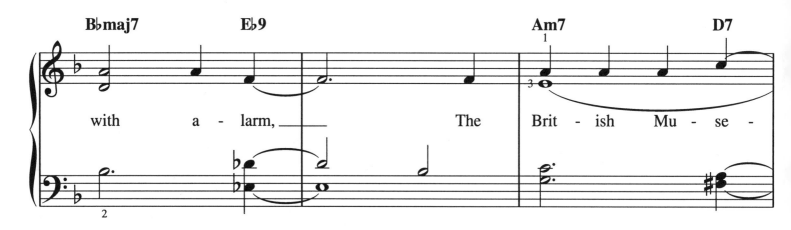

with a - larm, _____ The Brit - ish Mu - se -

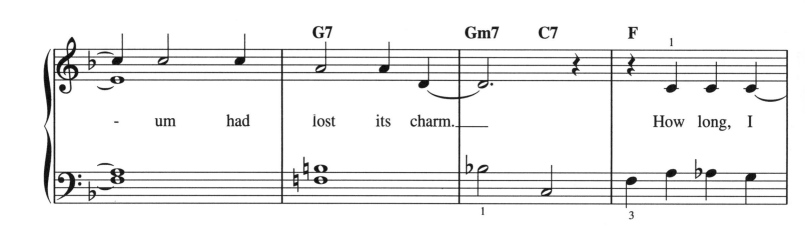

- um had lost its charm. _____ How long, I

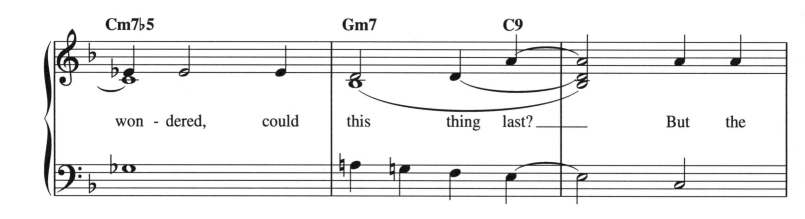

won - dered, could this thing last? _____ But the

age of mir - a - cles had - n't passed, _____

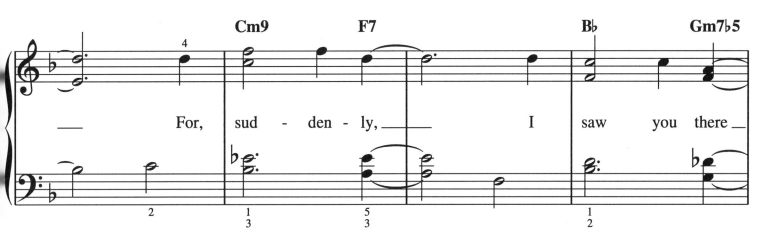

For, sud - den - ly, I saw you there

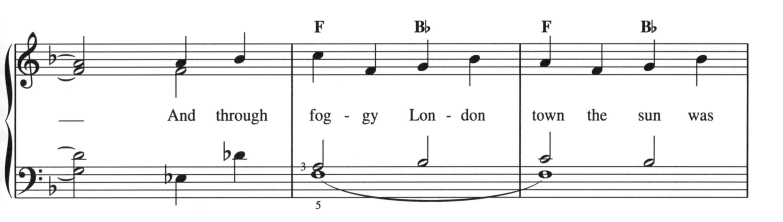

And through fog - gy Lon - don town the sun was

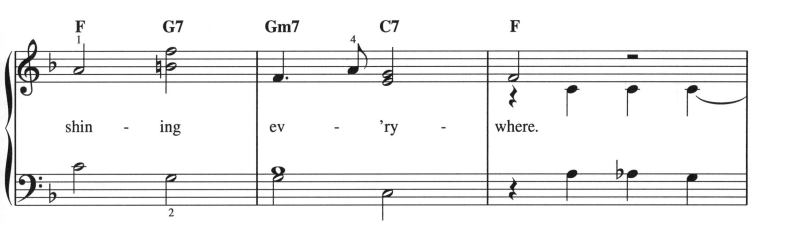

shin - ing ev - 'ry - where.

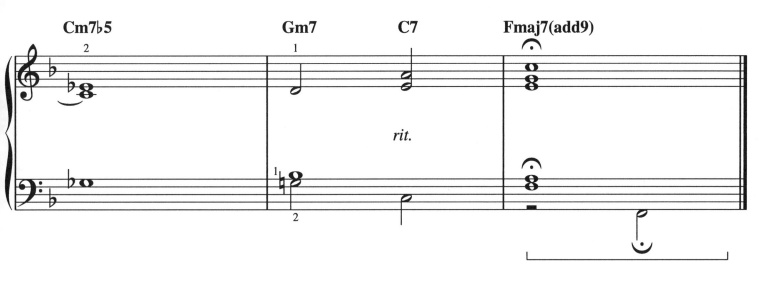

rit.

FROM THIS MOMENT ON
(From "OUT OF THIS WORLD")

Words and Music by
COLE PORTER

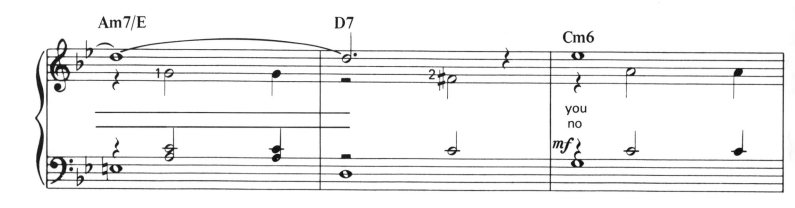

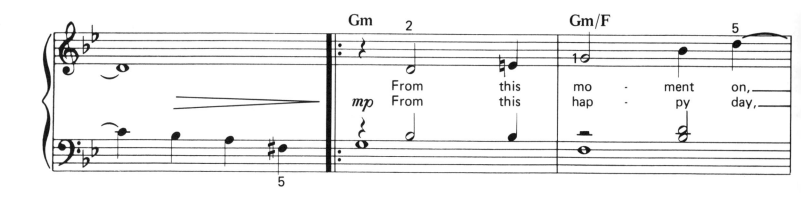

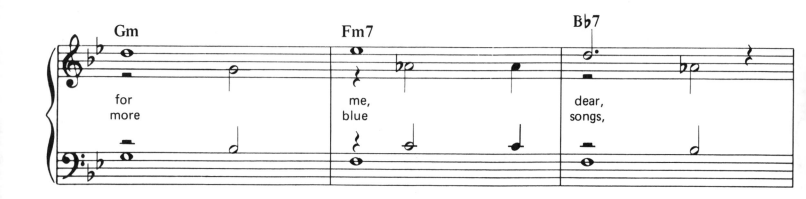

on - ly ___ two for tea,
on - ly ___ whoop - dee - doo

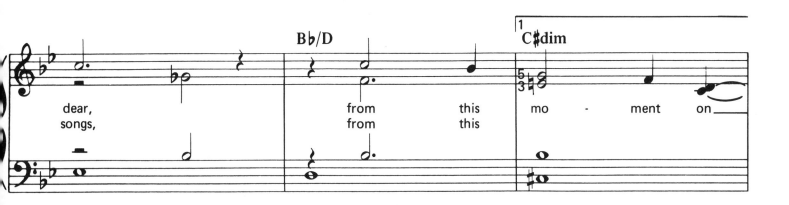

dear, from this mo - ment on ___
songs, from this

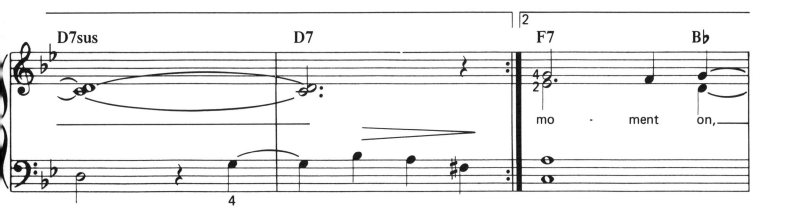

mo - ment on, ___

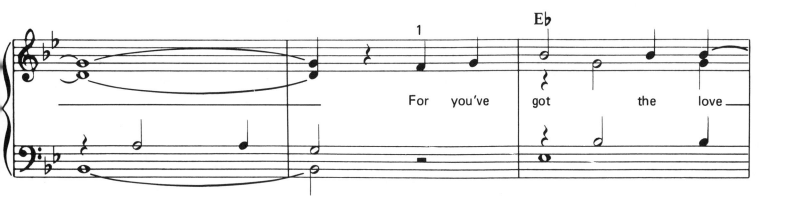

For you've got the love ___

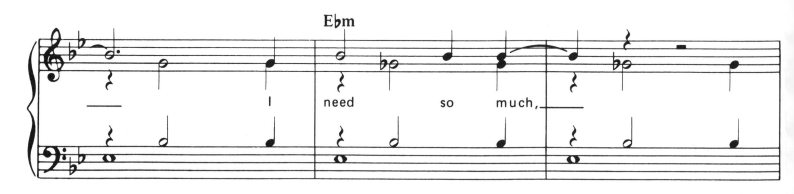

I need so much,

Got the skin   I   love to touch

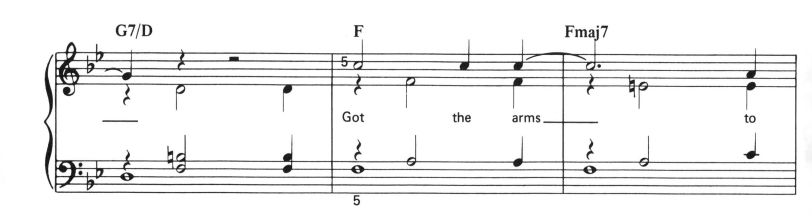

Got the arms   to

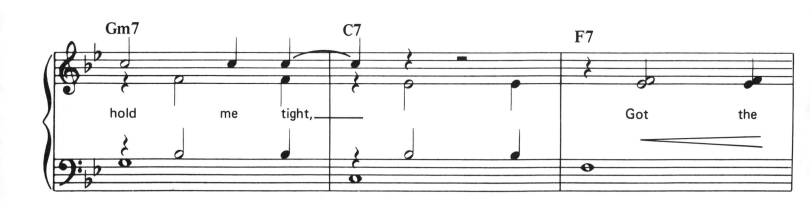

hold me tight,   Got the

sweet lips to kiss me good - night,

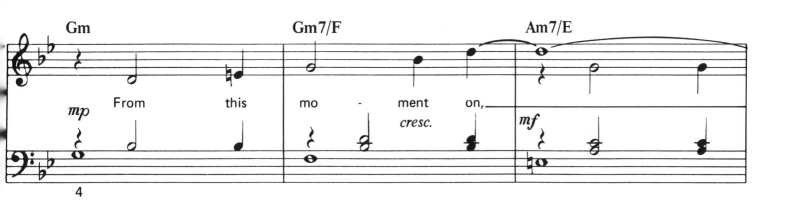

Gm   Gm7/F   Am7/E

From this mo - ment on,

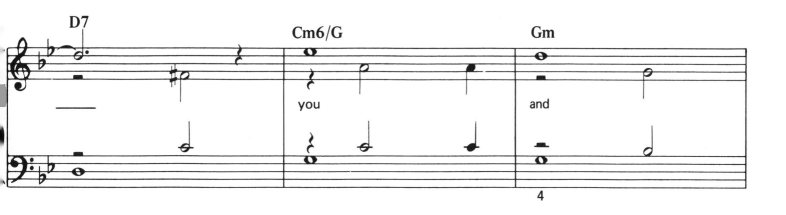

D7   Cm6/G   Gm

you   and

Fm7   Bb7/F   Eb

I,   babe,   we'll   be

75

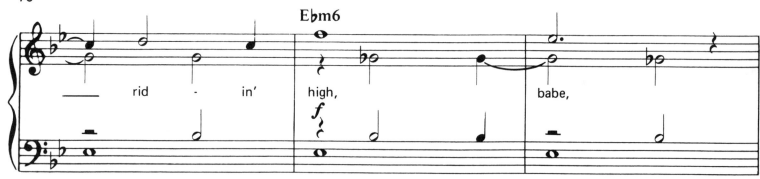

rid - in' high, babe,

Ev' - ry care is gone

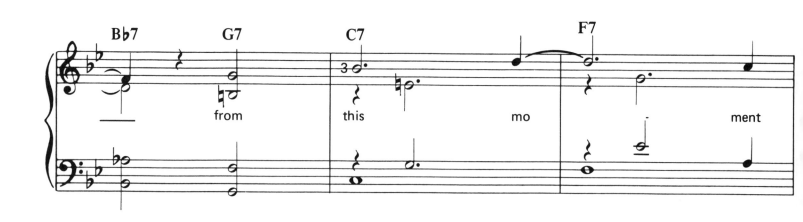

from this mo - ment

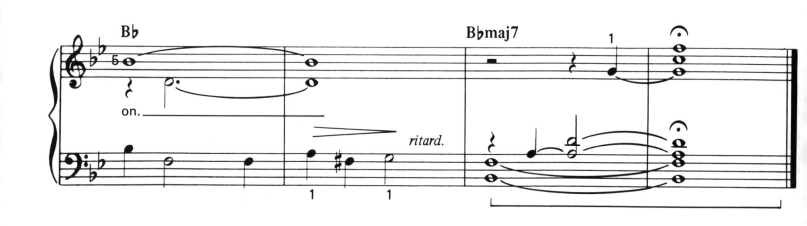

on.

THE GIRL FROM IPANEMA
(GARÔTA DE IPANEMA)

Original Words by VINICIUS DE MORAES
English Words by NORMAN GIMBEL
Music by ANTONIO CARLOS JOBIM

MCA music publishing

78

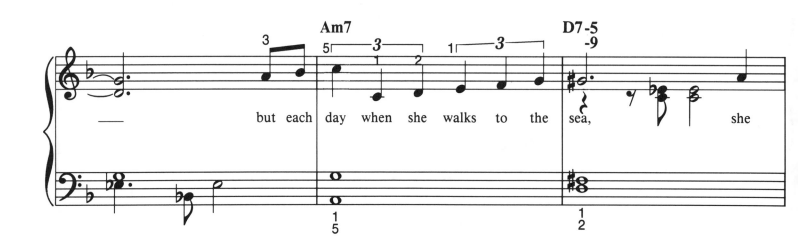

looks straight a-head not at me. Tall and tan and young and love - ly, the

girl from I - pa - ne-ma goes walk - ing, and when she pass-es I

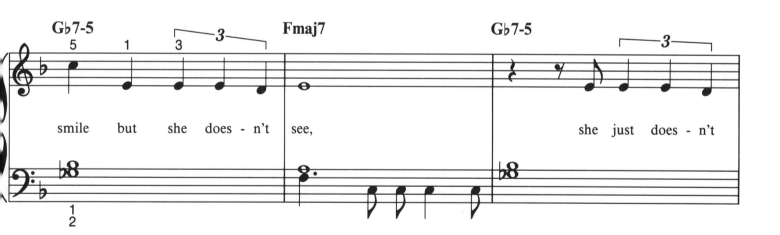

smile but she does-n't see, she just does-n't

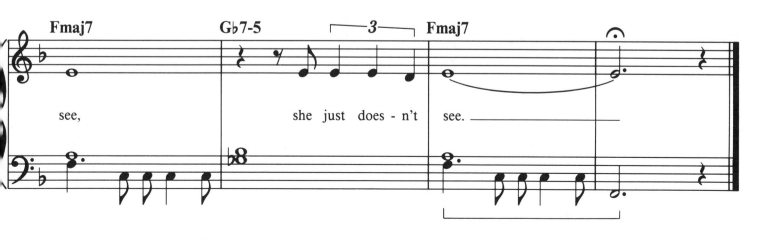

see, she just does-n't see. _____

GIVE ME THE SIMPLE LIFE

(From the Twentieth Century-Fox Picture "WAKE UP AND DREAM")

Words by HARRY RUBY
Music by RUBE BLOOM

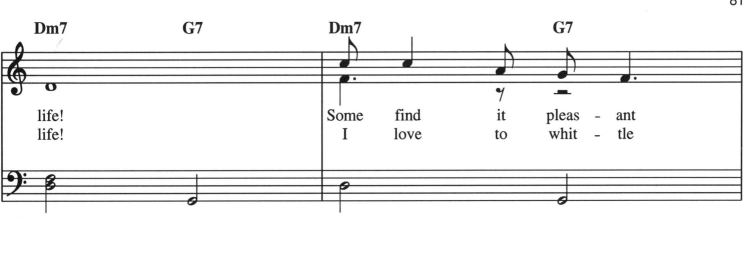

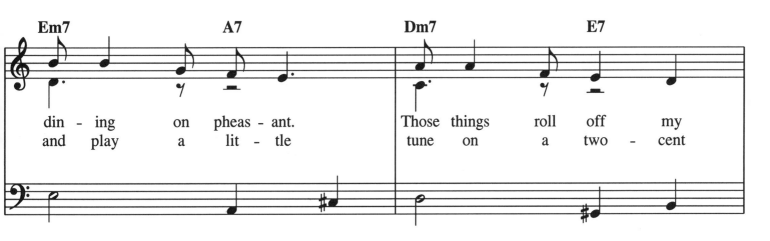

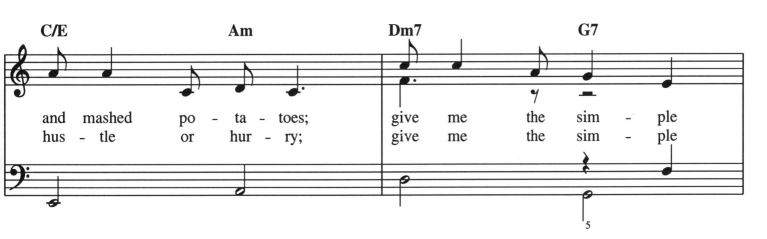

82

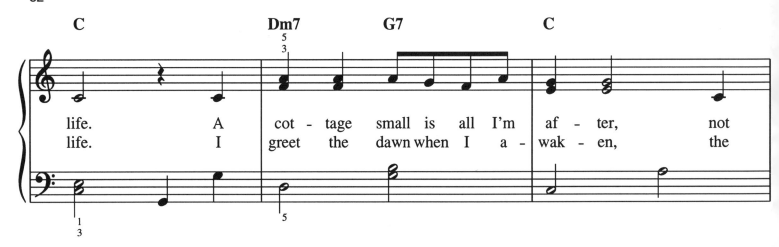

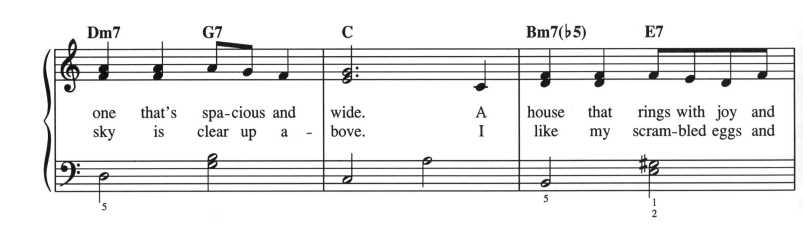

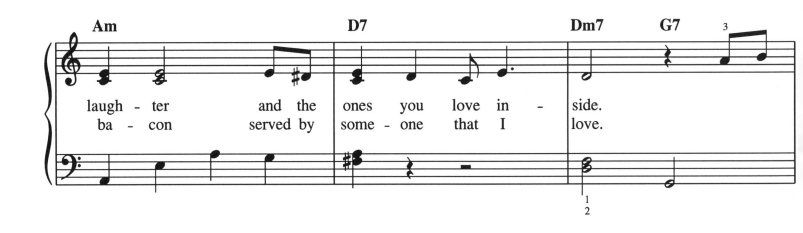

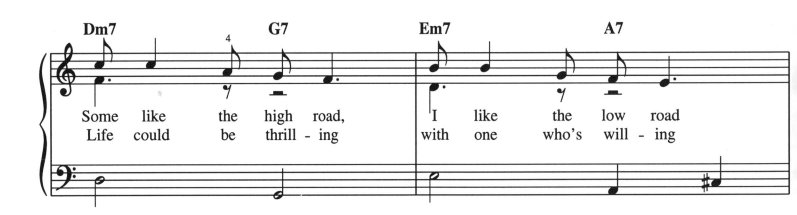

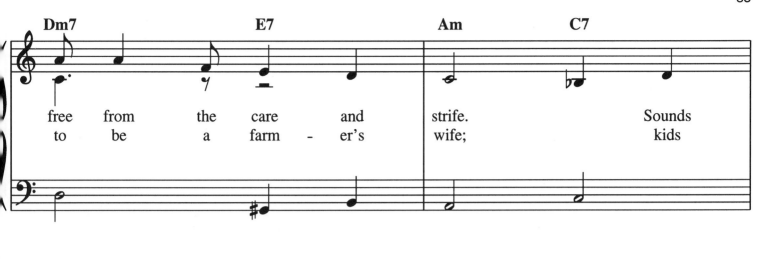

free from the care and strife. Sounds
to be a farm – er's wife; kids

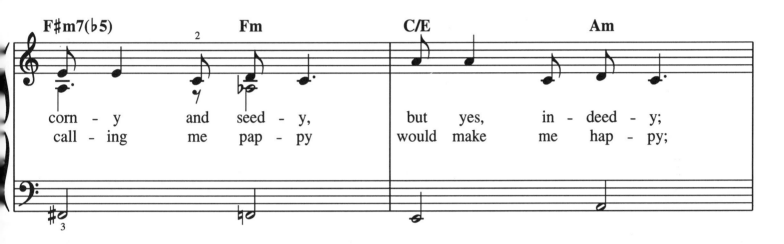

corn – y and seed – y, but yes, in – deed – y;
call – ing me pap – py would make me hap – py;

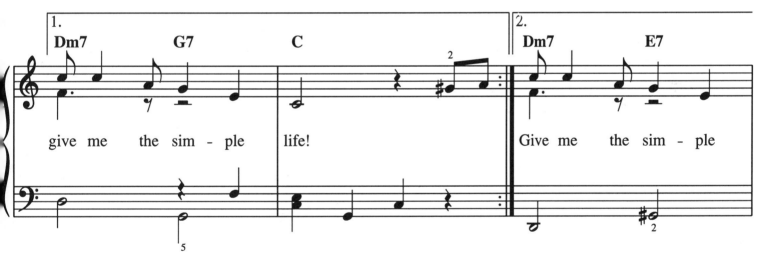

give me the sim – ple life! Give me the sim – ple

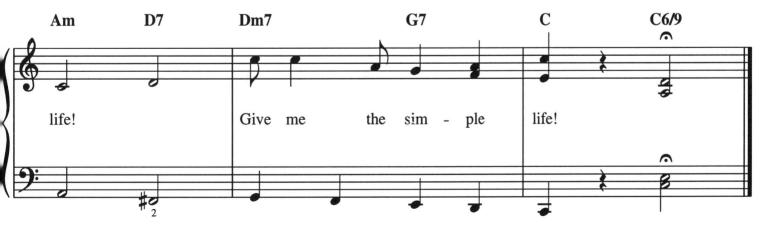

life! Give me the sim – ple life!

GOD BLESS' THE CHILD
(From "LADY SINGS THE BLUES")

Words and Music by ARTHUR HERZOG JR.
and BILLIE HOLIDAY

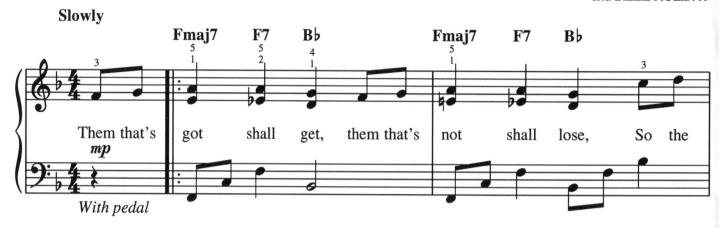

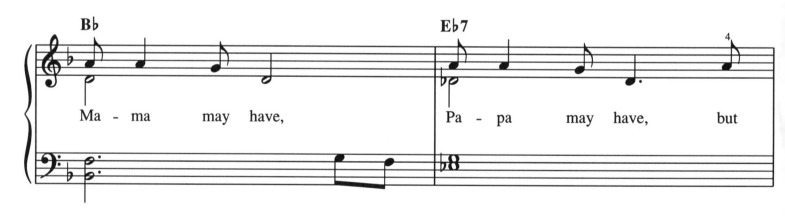

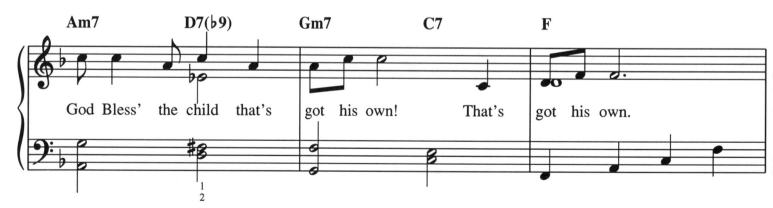

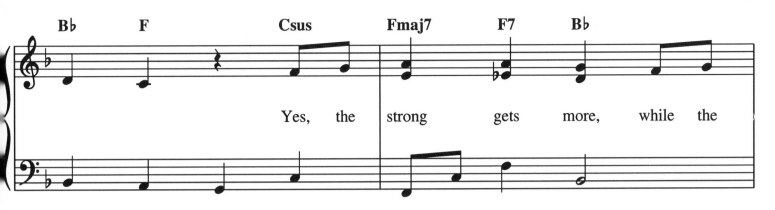

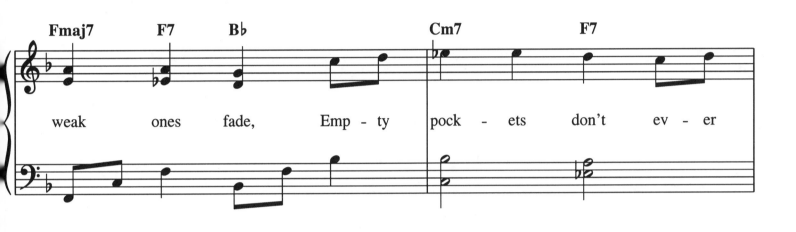

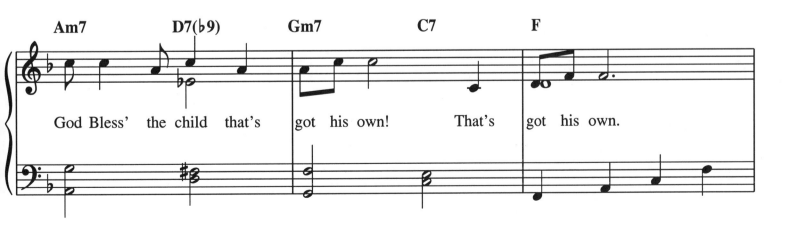

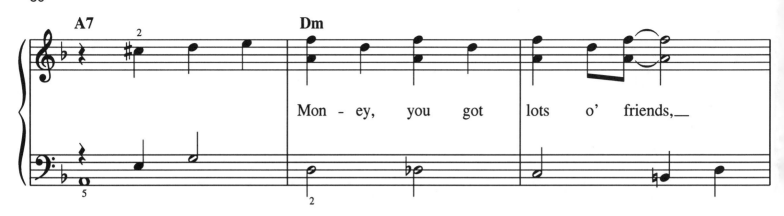

Mon - ey, you got lots o' friends,___

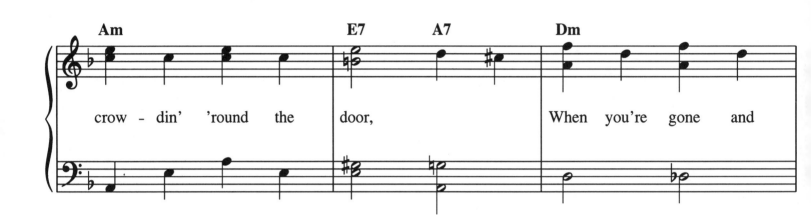

crow - din' 'round the door, When you're gone and

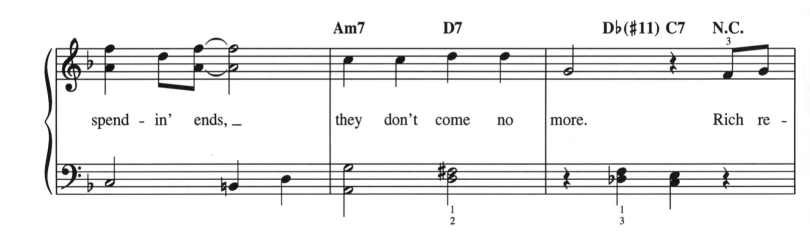

spend - in' ends, ___ they don't come no more. Rich re -

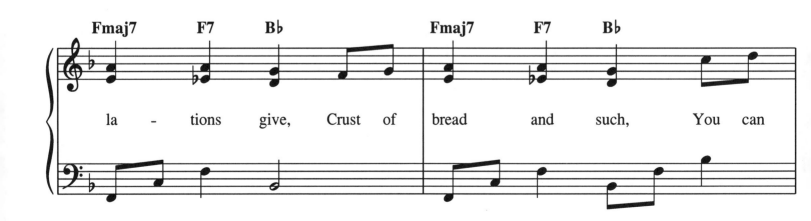

la - tions give, Crust of bread and such, You can

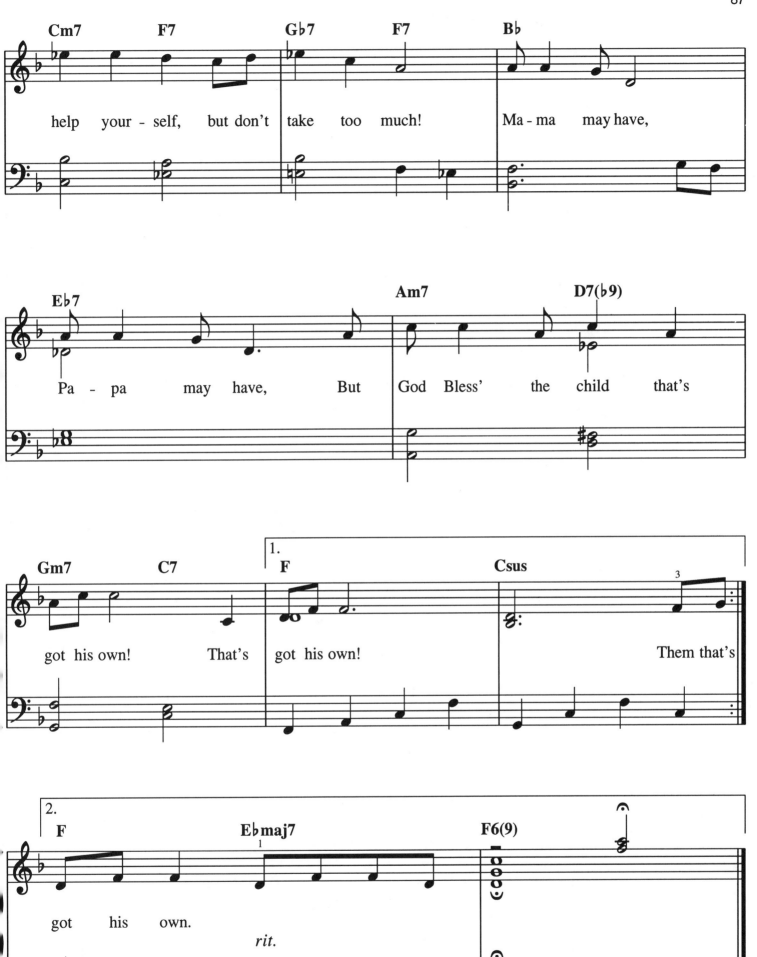

GUESS WHO I SAW TODAY

Words and Music by MURRAY GRAND
and ELISSE BOYD

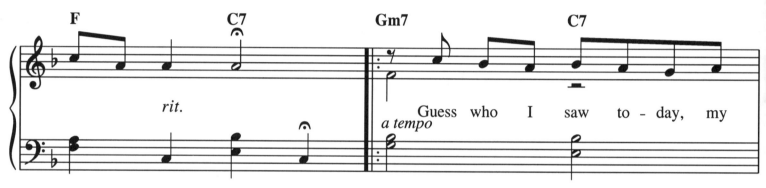

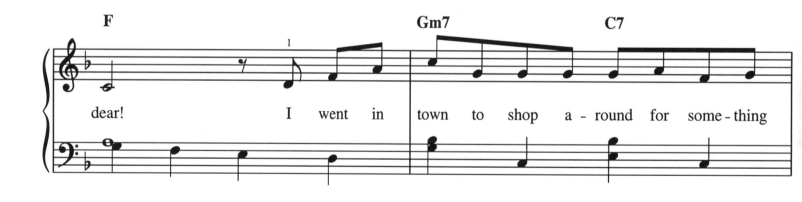

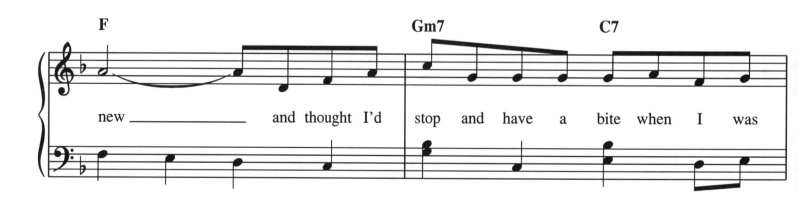

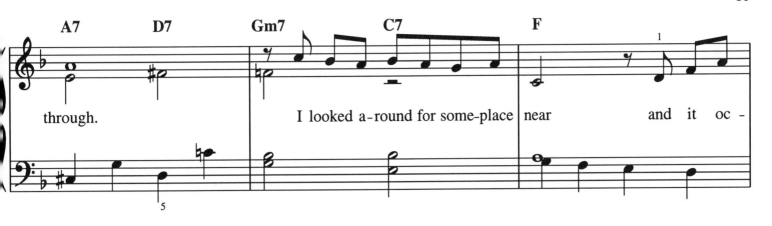

through. I looked a-round for some-place near and it oc-

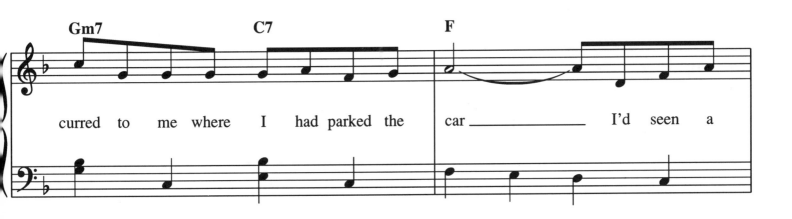

curred to me where I had parked the car _____ I'd seen a

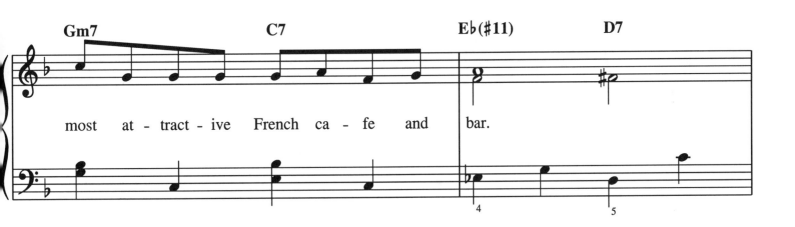

most at - tract - ive French ca - fe and bar.

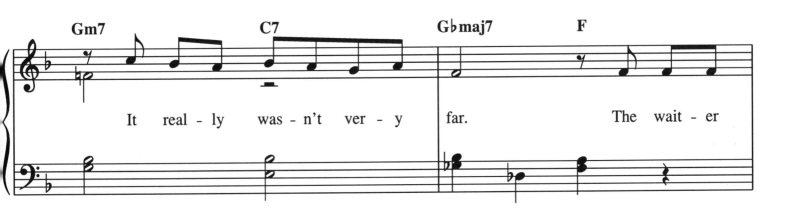

It real - ly was - n't ver - y far. The wait - er

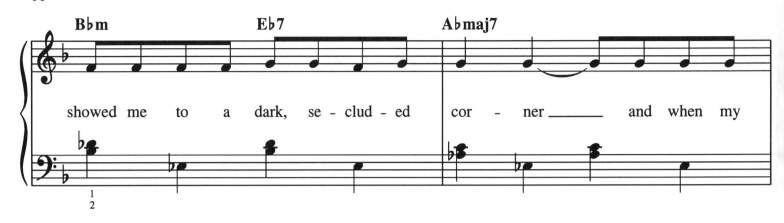

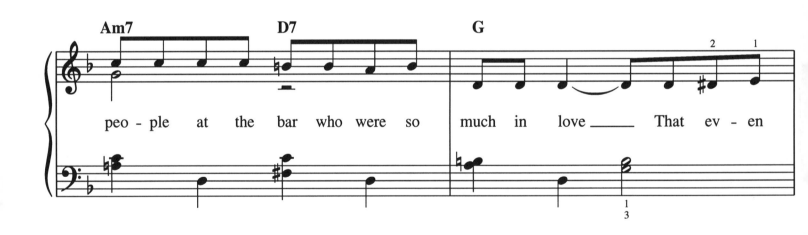

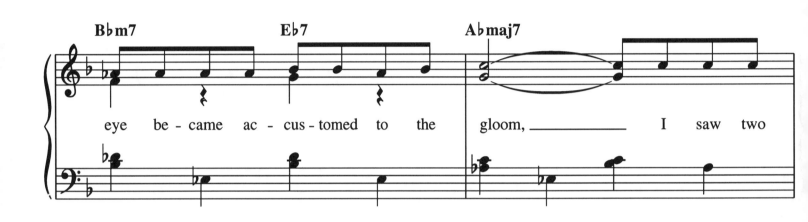

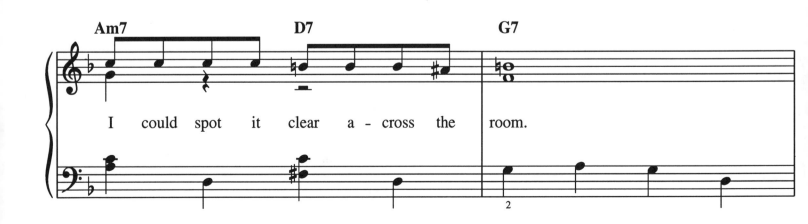

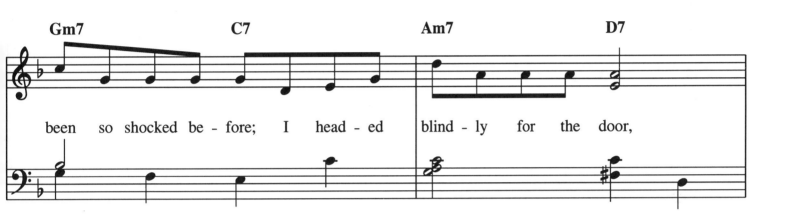

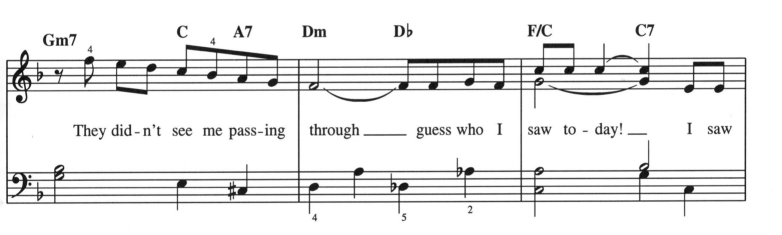

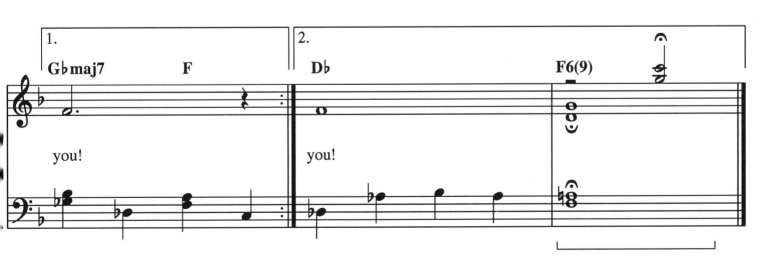

GONE WITH THE WIND

Words and Music by HERB MAGIDSON
and ALLIE WRUBEL

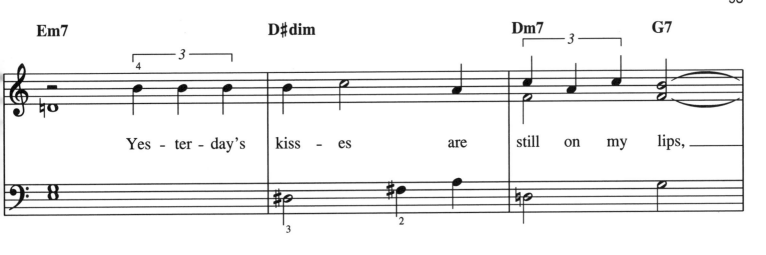

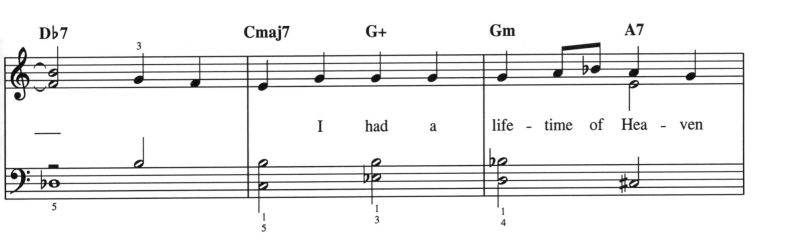

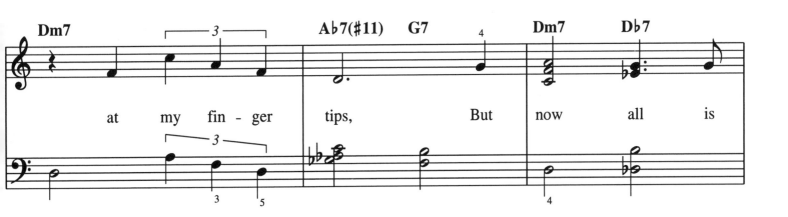

Gone with the wind. _____ The glad-ness that filled my heart,

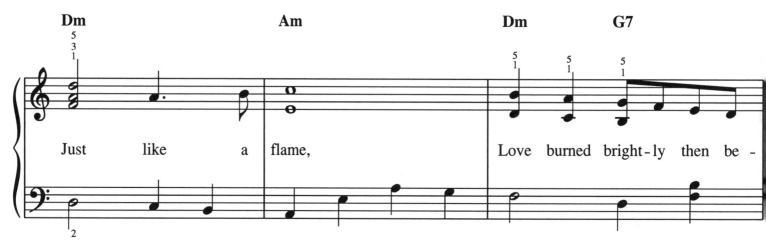

Just like a flame, Love burned bright-ly then be -

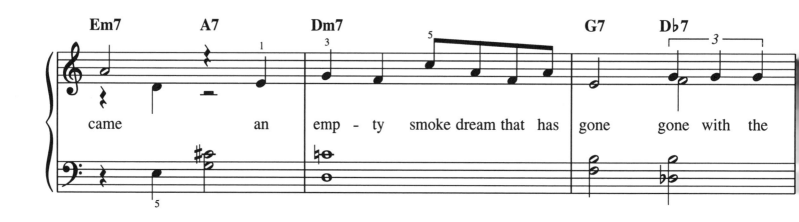

came an emp - ty smoke dream that has gone gone with the

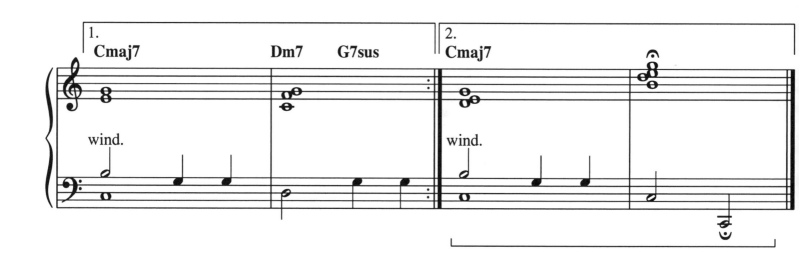

wind.

wind.

HERE'S THAT RAINY DAY

Words by JOHNNY BURKE
Music by JIMMY VAN HEUSEN

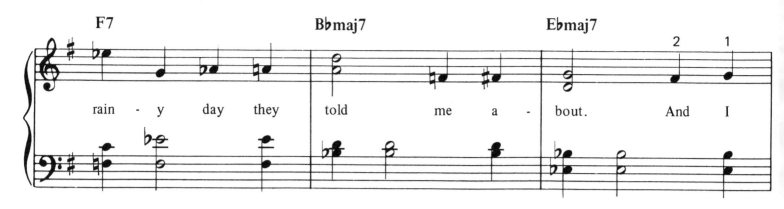

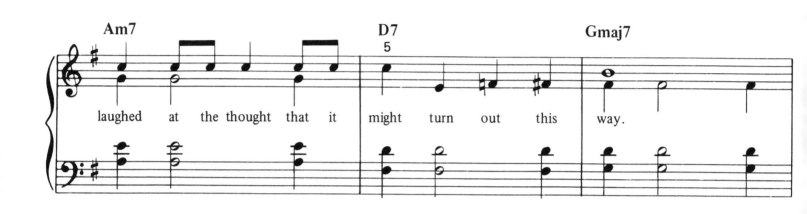

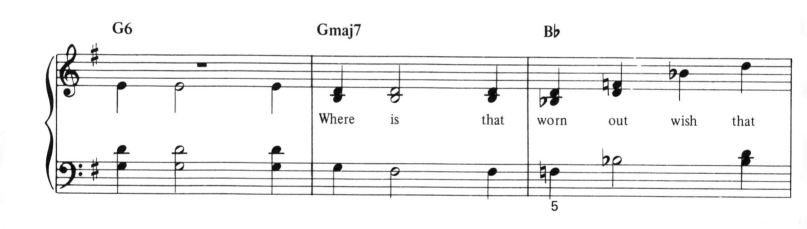

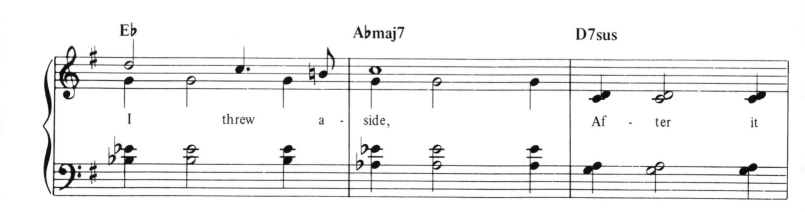

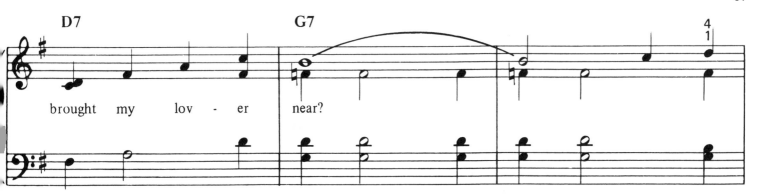

brought my lov - er near?

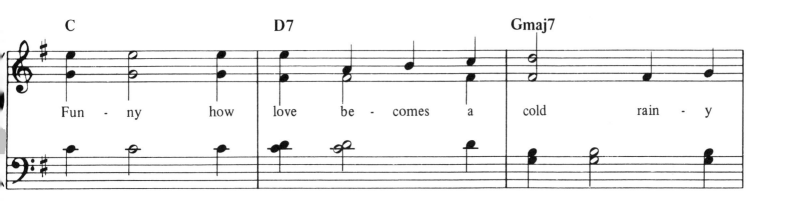

Fun - ny how love be - comes a cold rain - y

day. Fun - ny, that rain - y day is

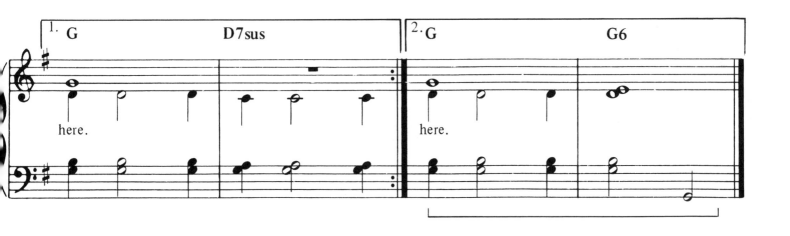

here. here.

HONEYSUCKLE ROSE
(From "AIN'T MISBEHAVIN'")

Words by ANDY RAZAF
Music by THOMAS "FATS" WALLER

you just __ have to / touch my cup. __ / You're my

sug - ar, / it's sweet _ when you / stir it up. __ / When I'm tak-in' sips

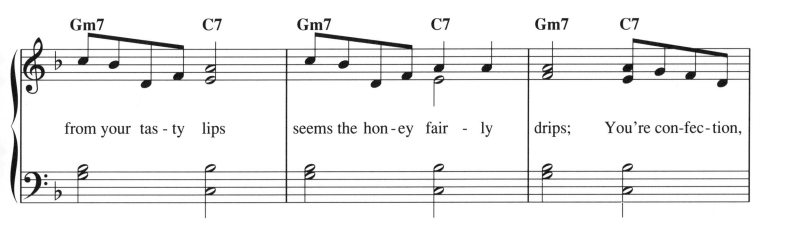

from your tas - ty lips / seems the hon-ey fair - ly / drips; You're con-fec-tion,

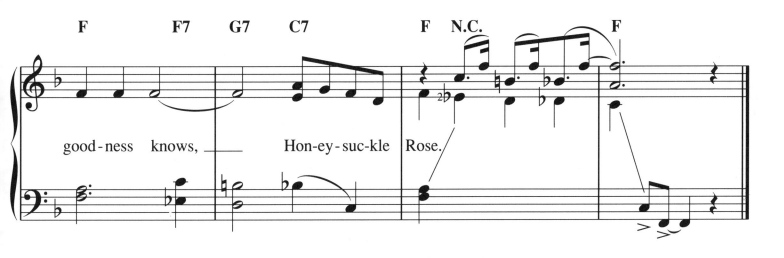

good-ness knows, ___ / Hon-ey-suc-kle Rose.

HOW HIGH THE MOON

(From "TWO FOR THE SHOW")

Words by NANCY HAMILTON
Music by MORGAN LEWIS

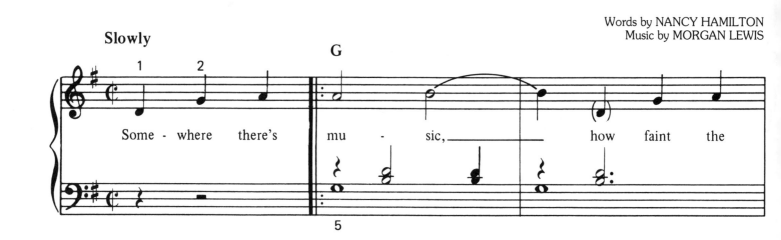

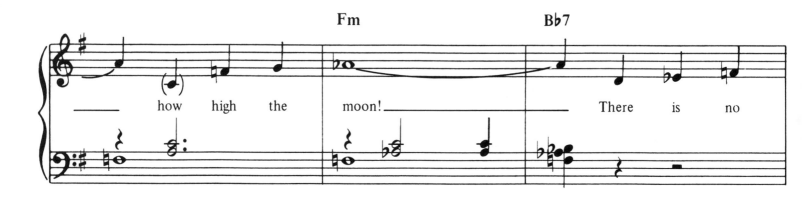

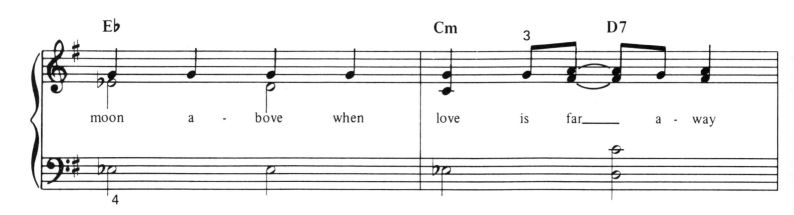

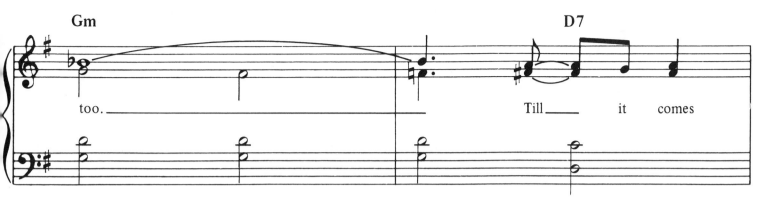

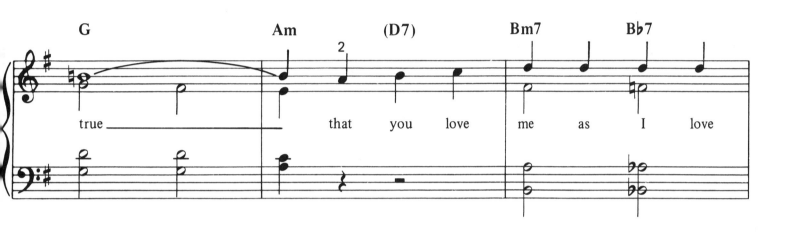

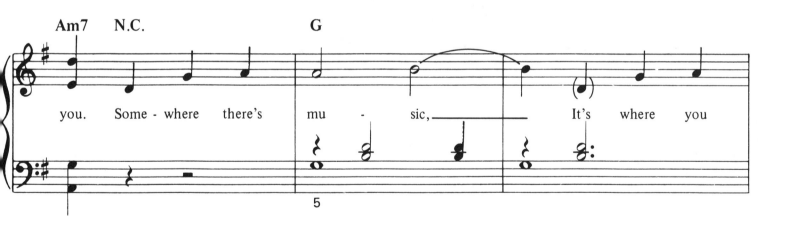

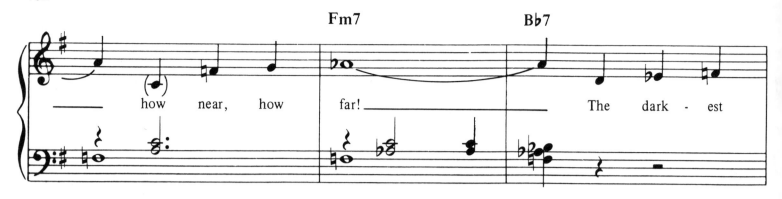

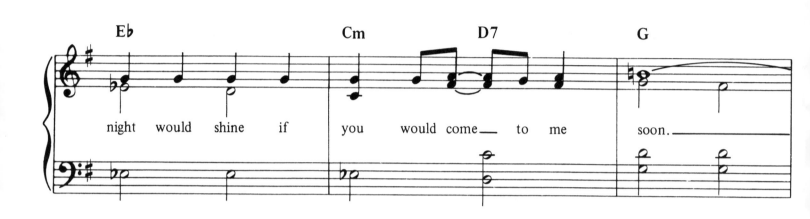

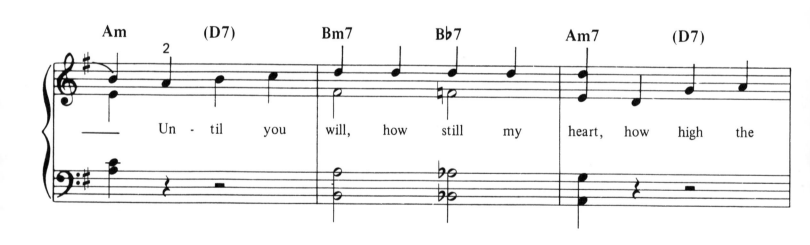

HOW INSENSITIVE
(Insensatez)

Original Words by VINICIUS DE MORAES
English Words by NORMAN GIMBEL
Music by ANTONIO CARLOS JOBIM

Moderately

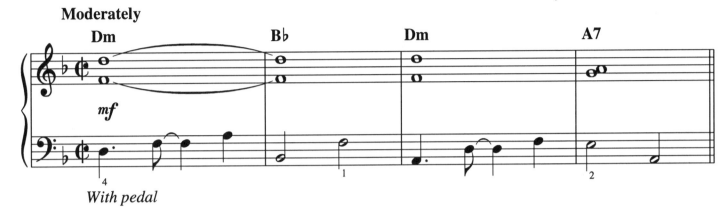

With pedal

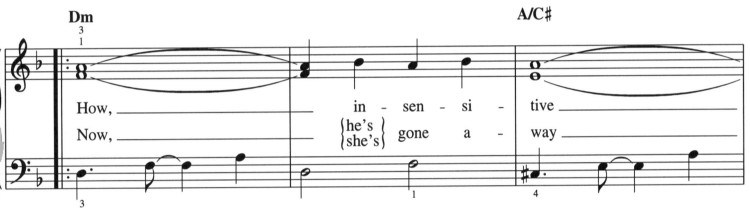

How, _____ in - sen - si - tive _____
Now, _____ {he's she's} gone a - way _____

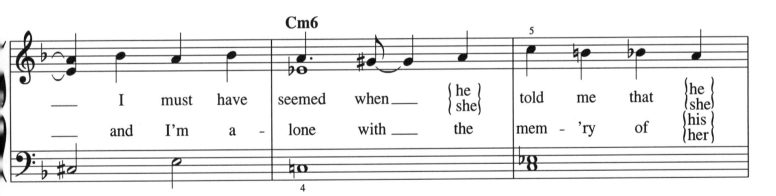

____ I must have seemed when ____ {he she} told me that {he she}
____ and I'm a - lone with ____ the mem - 'ry of {his her}

loved _____ me. _____ How _____
last _____ look. _____ Vague _____

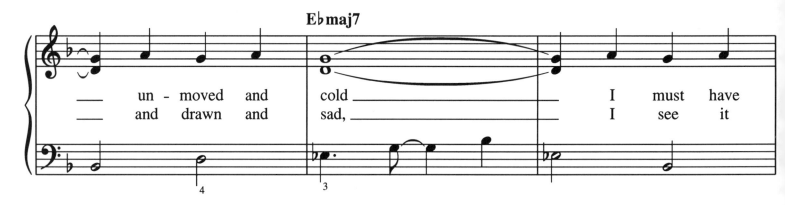

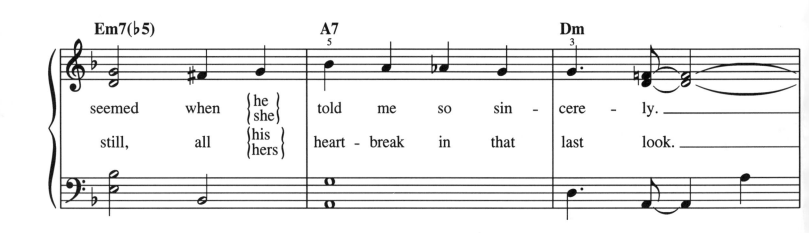

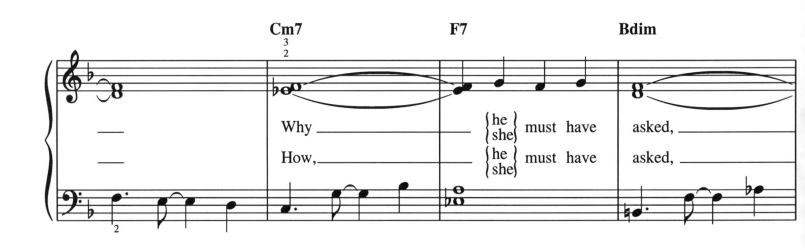

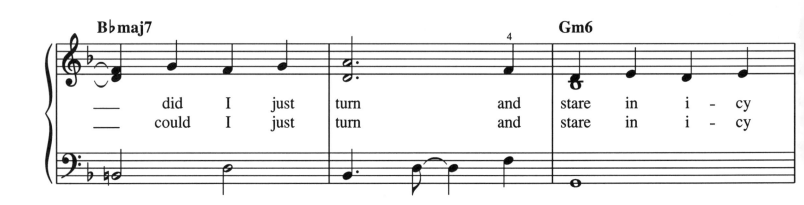

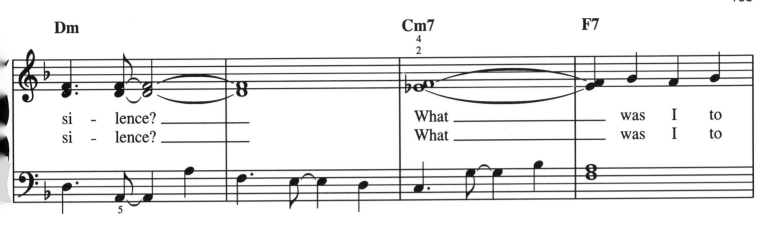

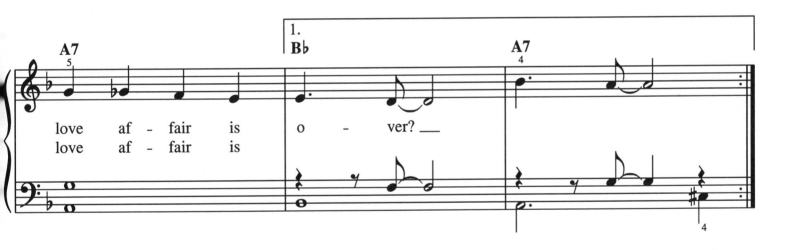

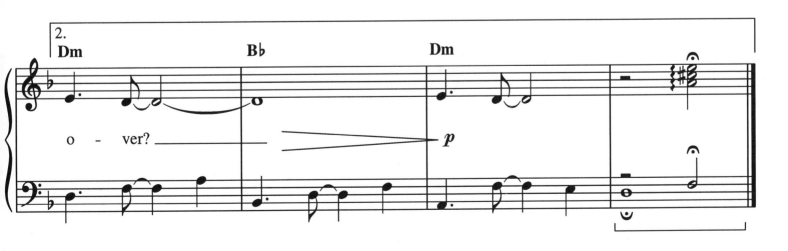

I'LL REMEMBER APRIL

Words and Music by DON RAYE,
GENE DE PAUL and PAT JOHNSON

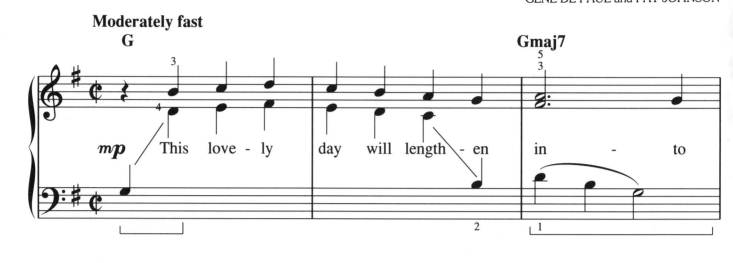

This love-ly day will length-en in-to

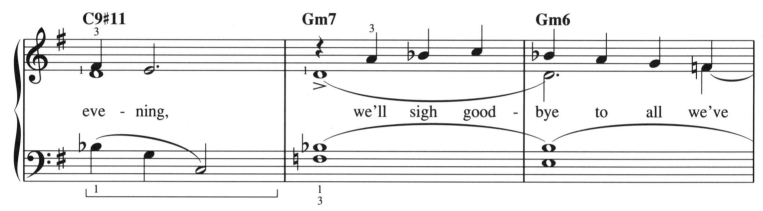

eve - ning, we'll sigh good - bye to all we've

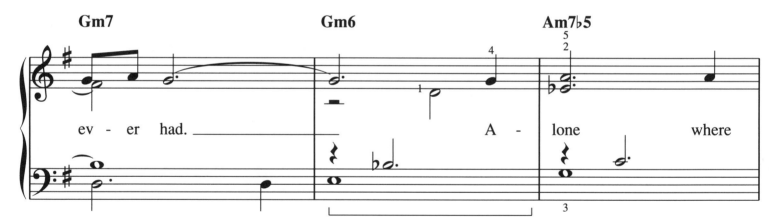

ev - er had. ____ A - lone where

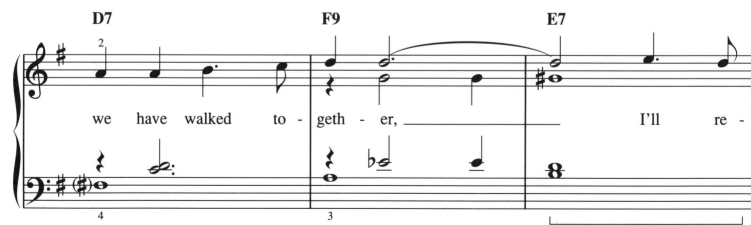

we have walked to - geth - er, ____ I'll re-

MCA music publishing

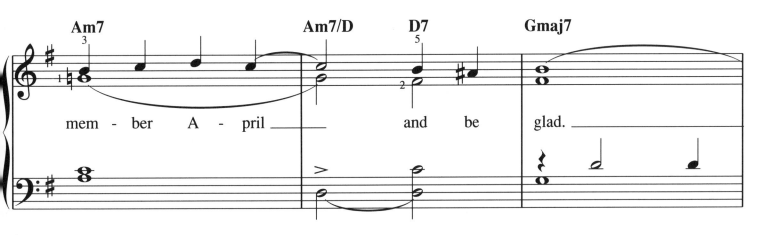

mem - ber A - pril _____ and be glad. _____

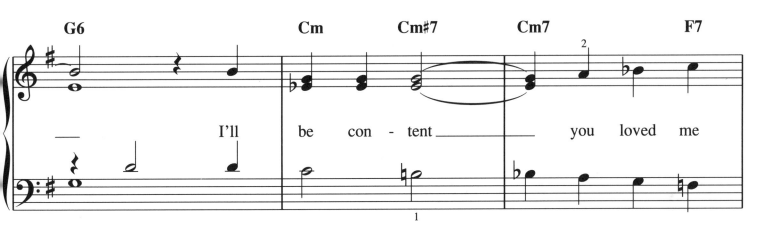

_____ I'll be con - tent _____ you loved me

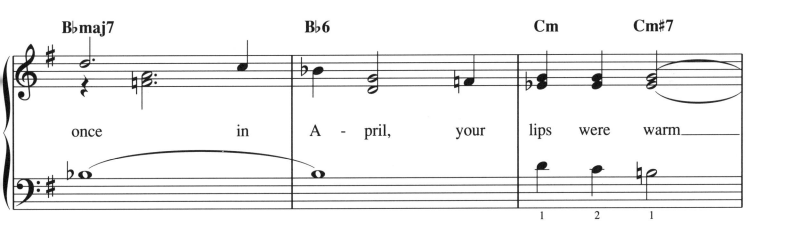

once in A - pril, your lips were warm _____

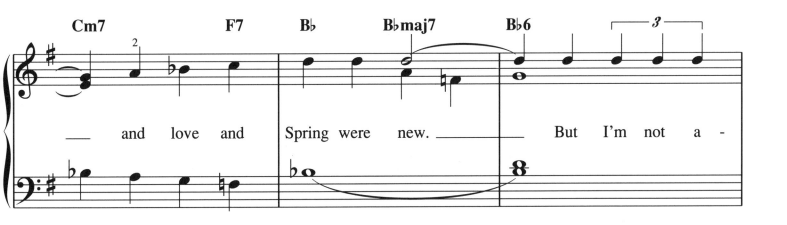

_____ and love and Spring were new. _____ But I'm not a -

108

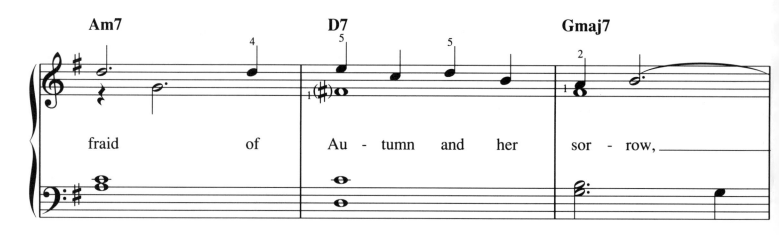

fraid   of   Au - tumn and her   sor - row,____

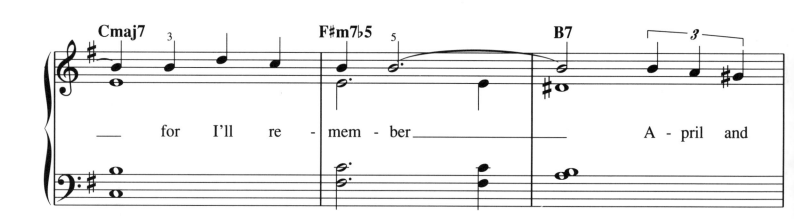

____ for I'll re - mem - ber____   A - pril and

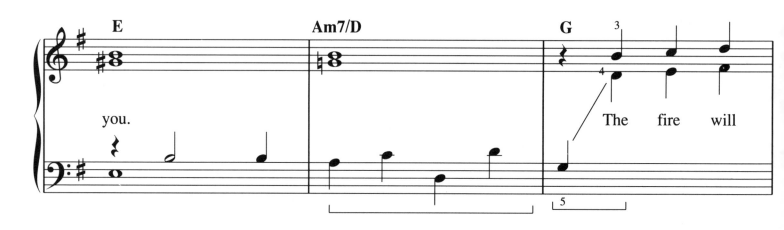

you.   The fire will

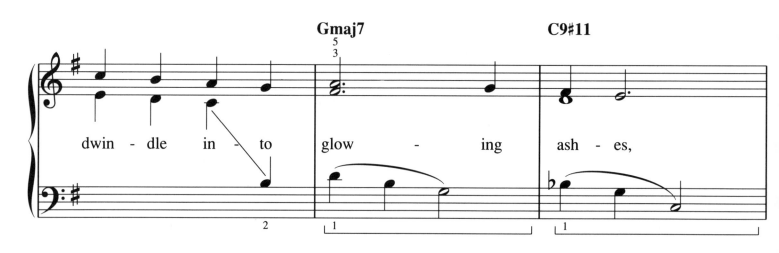

dwin - dle in - to   glow - ing   ash - es,

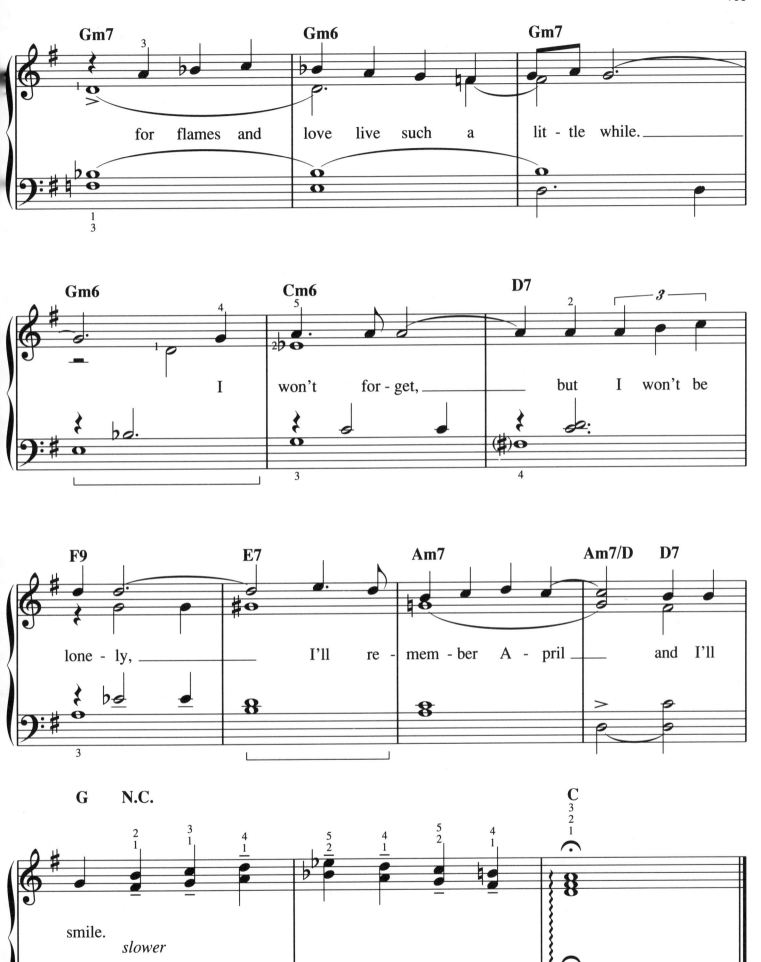

I'VE GOT YOU UNDER MY SKIN

(From "BORN TO DANCE")

Words and Music by
COLE PORTER

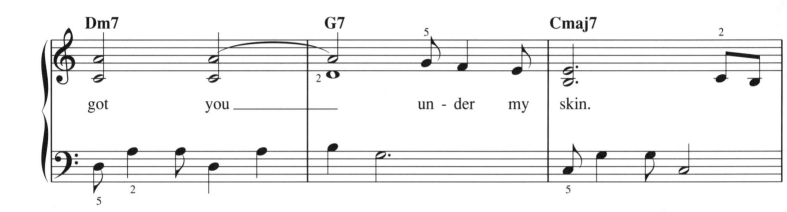

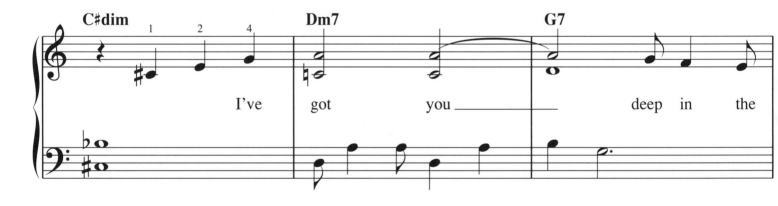

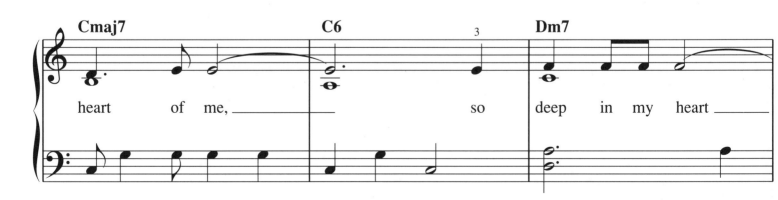

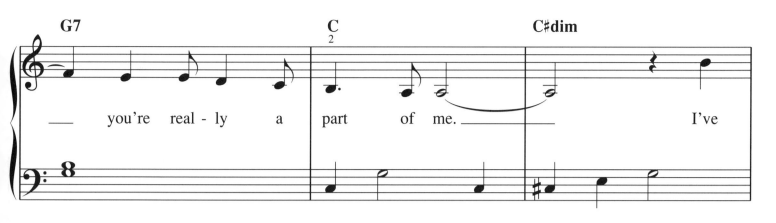

G7   **C**   **C#dim**

___ you're real - ly a part of me. _____ I've

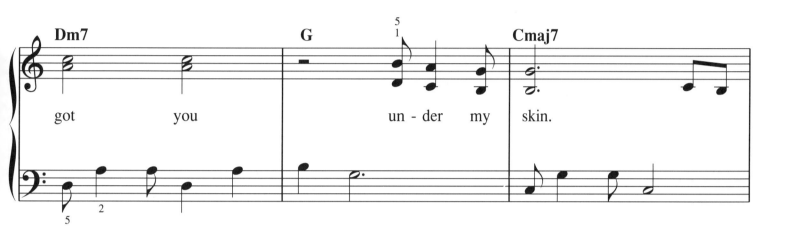

Dm7   **G**   **Cmaj7**

got you un - der my skin.

C6   **Dm7**   **G7**   **Cmaj7**

I tried so _____ not to give in,

C#dim   **Dm7♭5**   **G7♭9**

I said to my - self, "This af - fair nev - er will

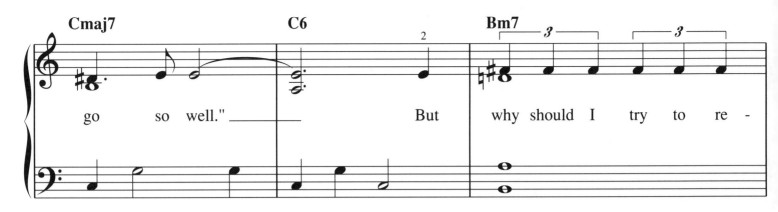

go so well." _____ But why should I try to re -

sist when, dar - ling, I know so well, I've

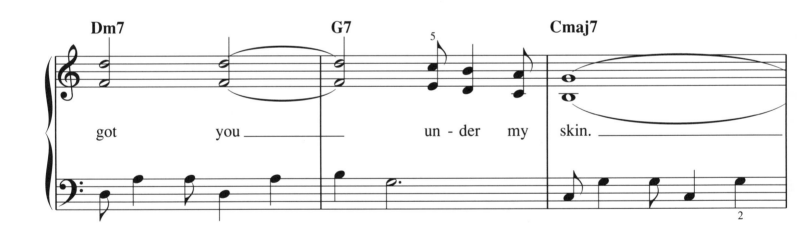

got you _____ un - der my skin. _____

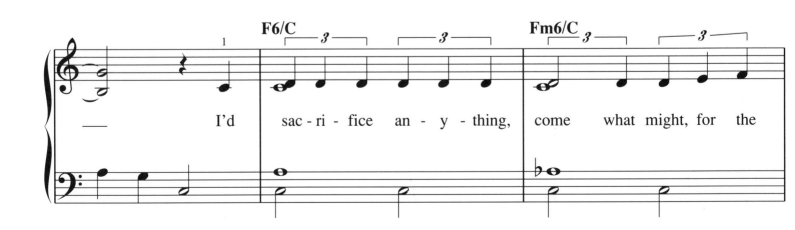

_____ I'd sac - ri - fice an - y - thing, come what might, for the

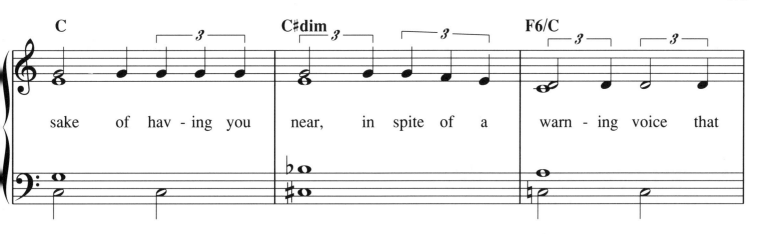

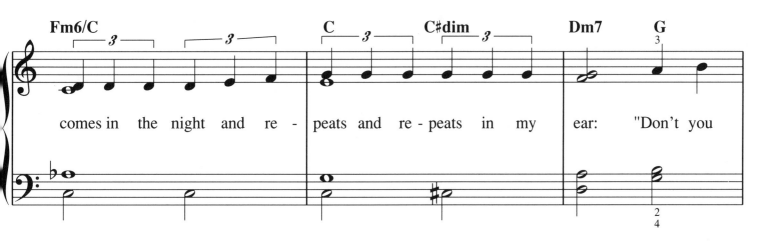

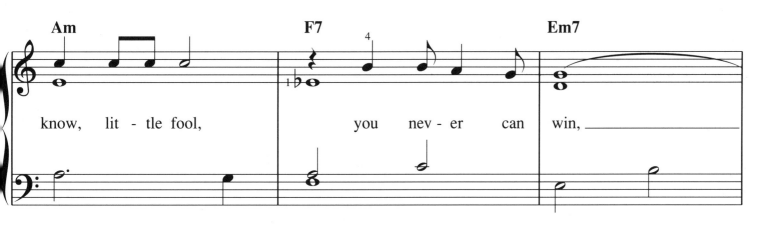

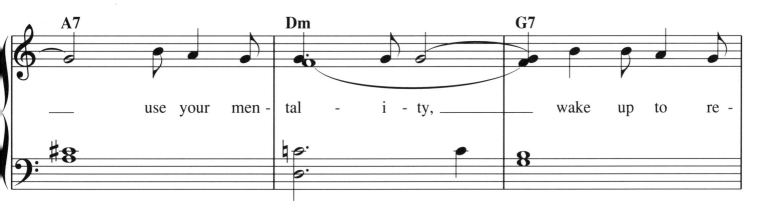

114

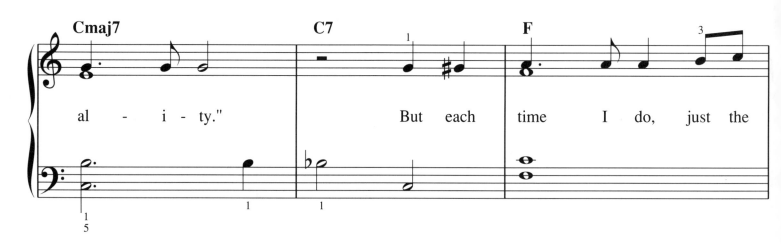

al - i - ty." But each time I do, just the

thought of you makes me stop be - fore I be - gin, 'cause I've

got you_____ un - der my skin._____

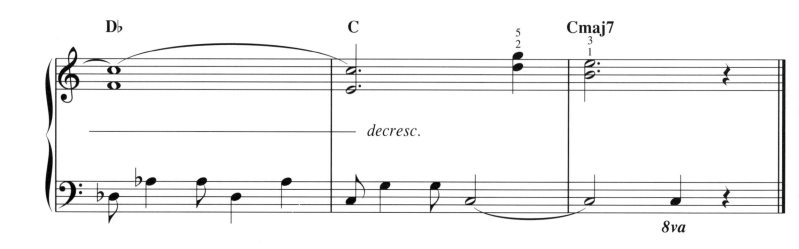

decresc.

8va

IN THE STILL OF THE NIGHT

Words and Music by
COLE PORTER

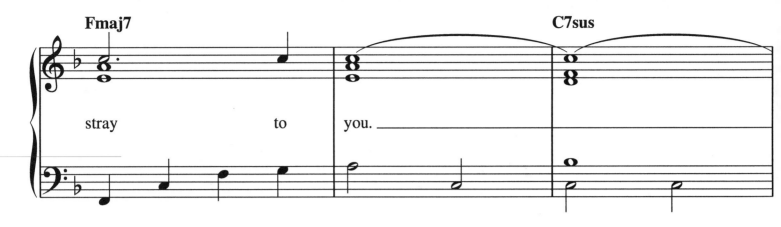

Fmaj7   **C7sus**

stray   to   you. _____

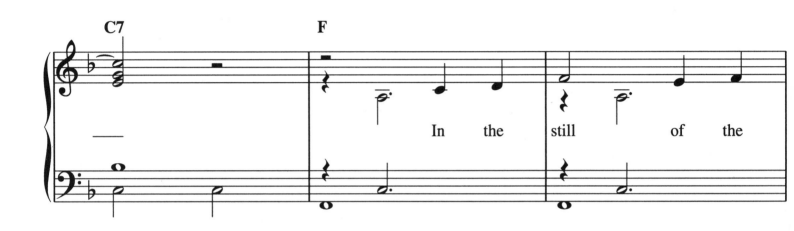

C7   **F**

In   the   still   of   the

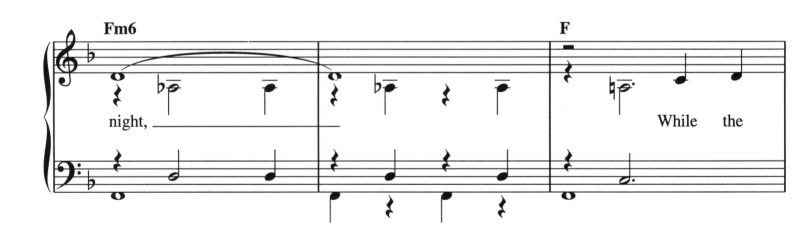

Fm6   **F**

night, _____   While   the

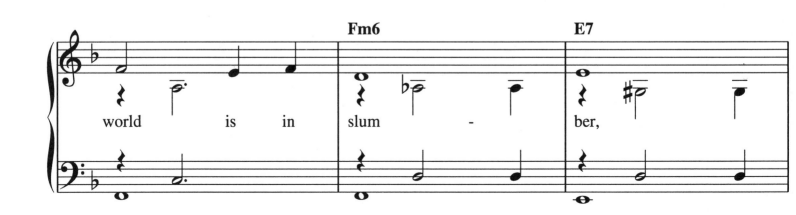

         Fm6   **E7**

world   is   in   slum -   ber,

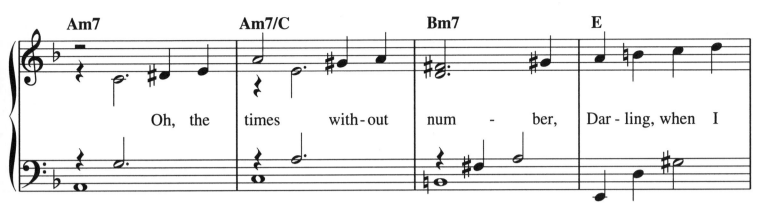

Oh, the times with-out num - ber, Dar - ling, when I

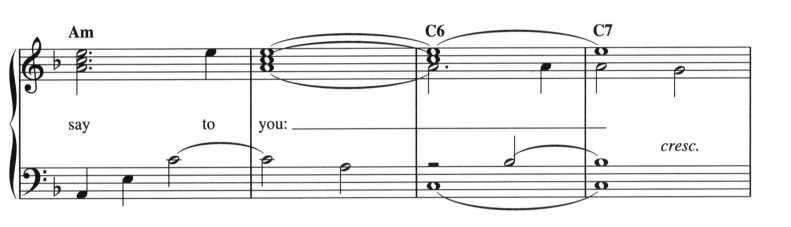

say to you: "Do

you love me

As I love you?

118

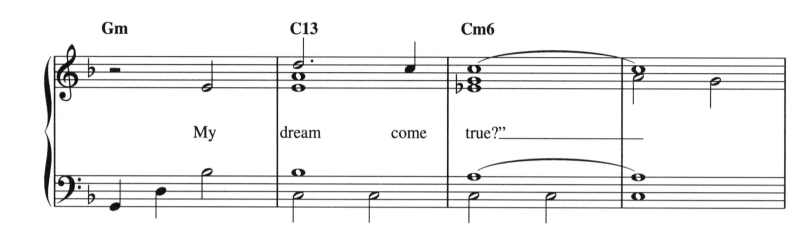

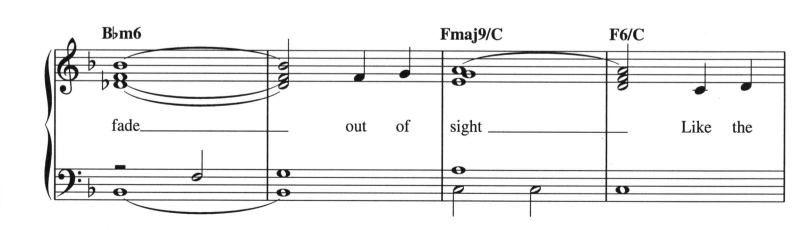

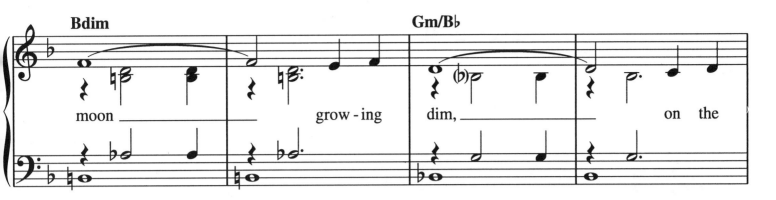

moon _____ grow - ing dim, _____ on the

rim _____ of the hill _____ in the

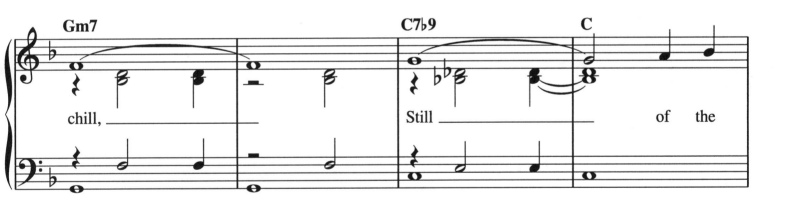

chill, _____ Still _____ of the

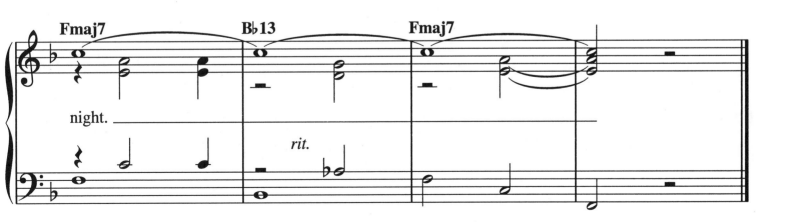

night. _____

rit.

INDIANA
(BACK HOME AGAIN IN INDIANA)

Words by BALLARD MACDONALD
Music by JAMES F. HANLEY

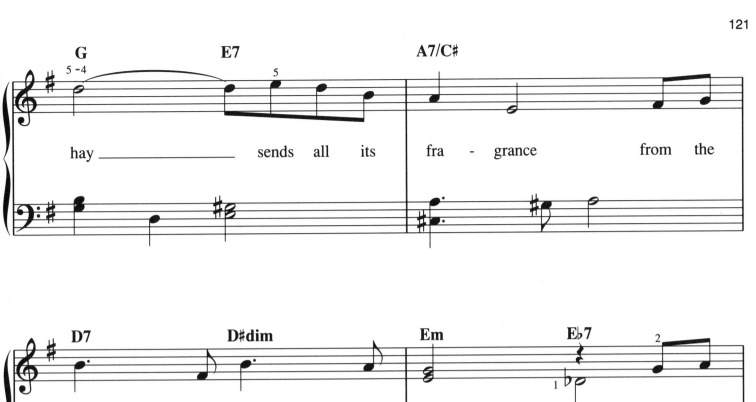

hay _____ sends all its fra - grance from the

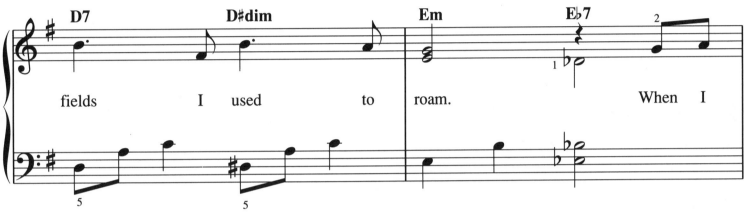

fields I used to roam. When I

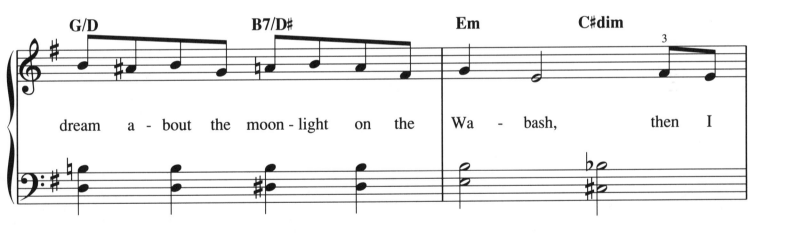

dream a - bout the moon - light on the Wa - bash, then I

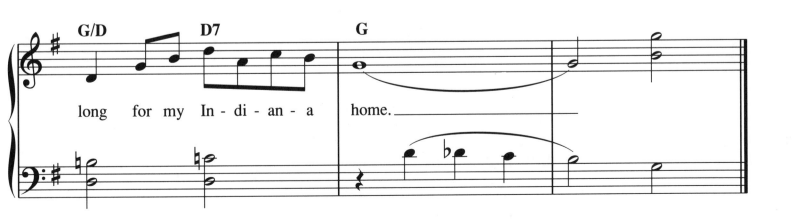

long for my In - di - an - a home. _____

IT'S ALL RIGHT WITH ME

(From "CAN-CAN")

Words and Music by
COLE PORTER

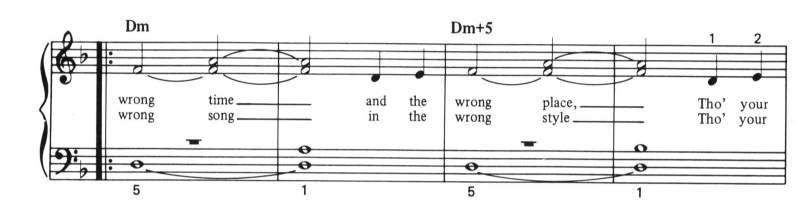

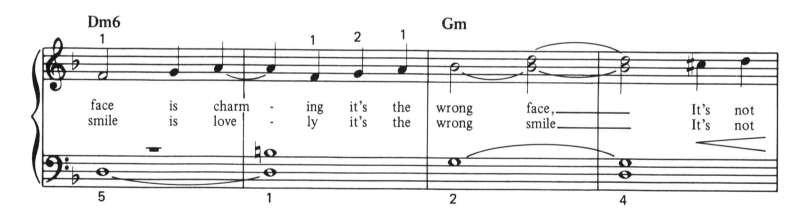

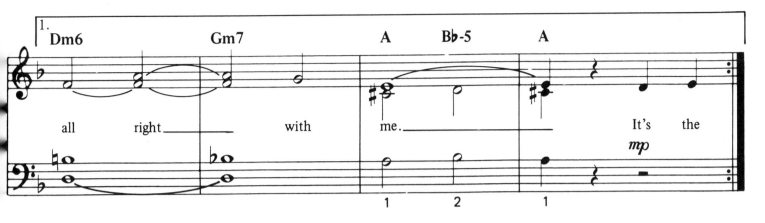

1. Dm6 · · Gm7 · A · Bb-5 · A

all right _____ with me. _____ It's the
mp

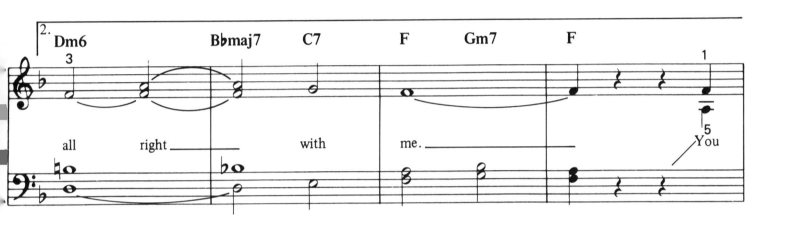

2. Dm6 · Bbmaj7 · C7 · F · Gm7 · F

all right _____ with me. _____ You

F7-9 · Fdim

can't know how hap - py I am that we met, I'm

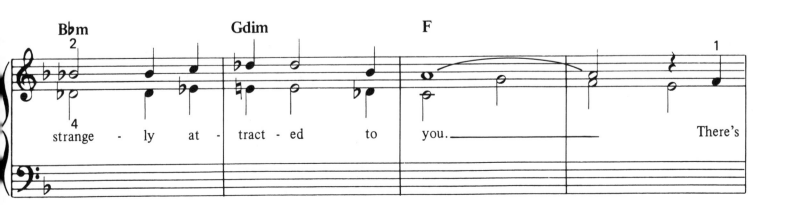

Bbm · Gdim · F

strange - ly at - tract - ed to you. _____ There's

124

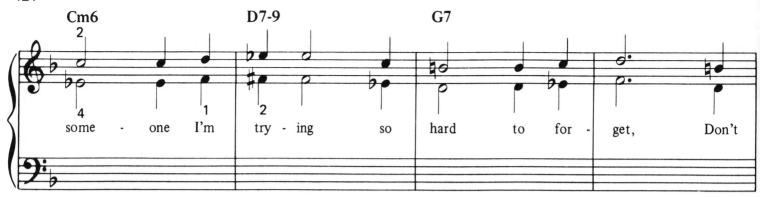

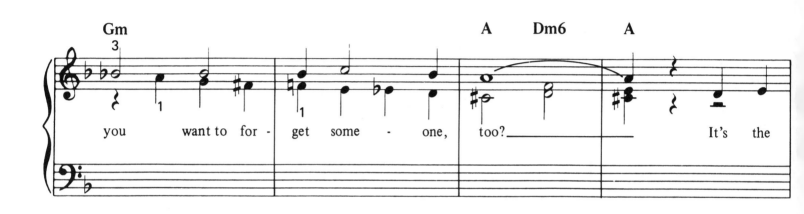

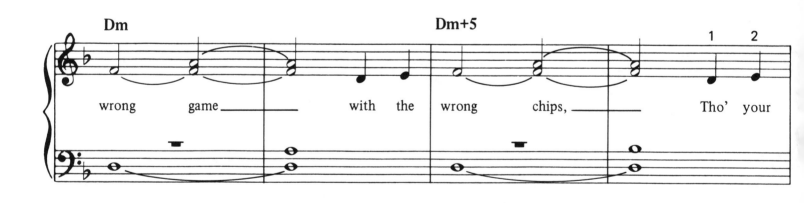

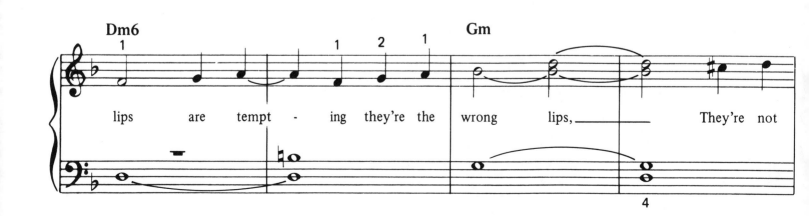

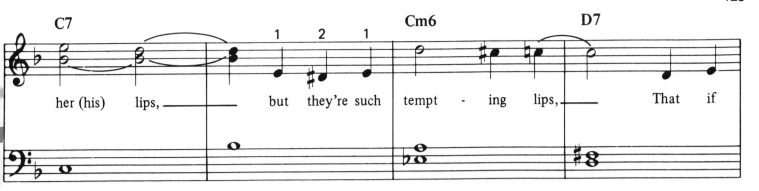

C7

her (his) lips, ———— but they're such

Cm6

tempt - ing lips, ————

D7

That if

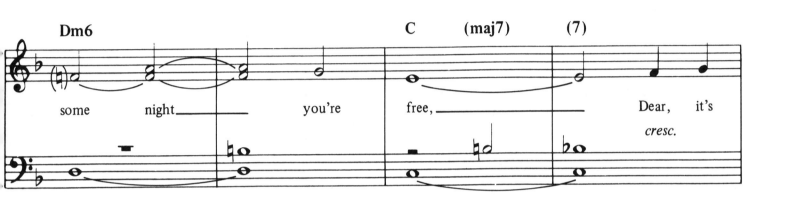

Dm6

some night ———— you're

C   (maj7)   (7)

free, ————————

Dear, it's
cresc.

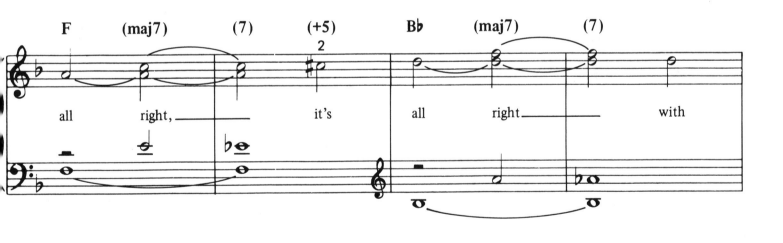

F   (maj7)   (7)   (+5)

all   right, ————   it's

Bb   (maj7)   (7)

all   right ————   with

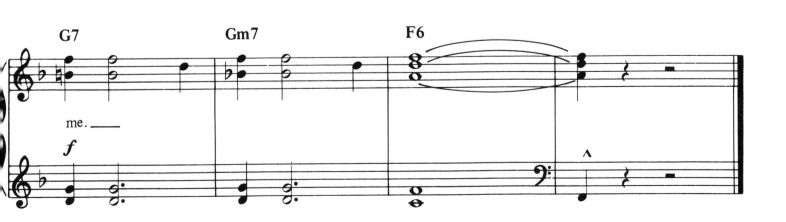

G7

me. ————
f

Gm7

F6

IT DON'T MEAN A THING
(If It Ain't Got That Swing)

Words and Music by DUKE ELLINGTON
and IRVING MILLS

Moderately

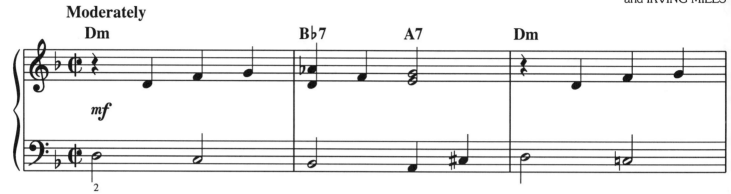

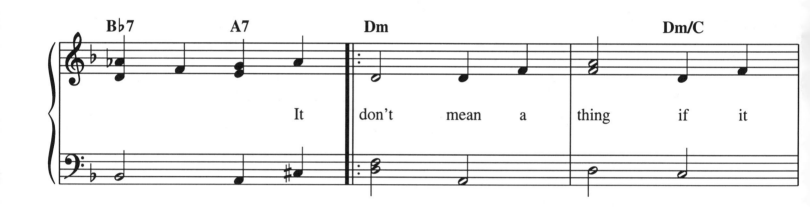

It don't mean a thing if it

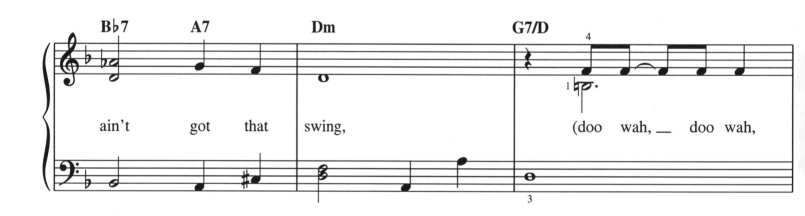

ain't got that swing, (doo wah, ___ doo wah,

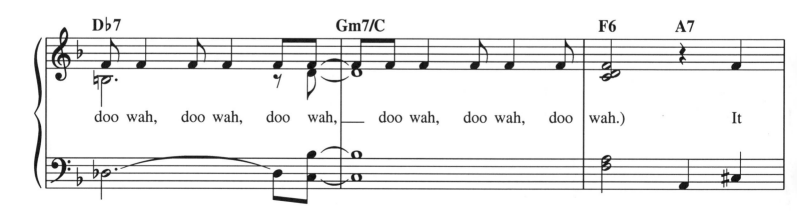

doo wah, doo wah, doo wah, ___ doo wah, doo wah, doo wah.) It

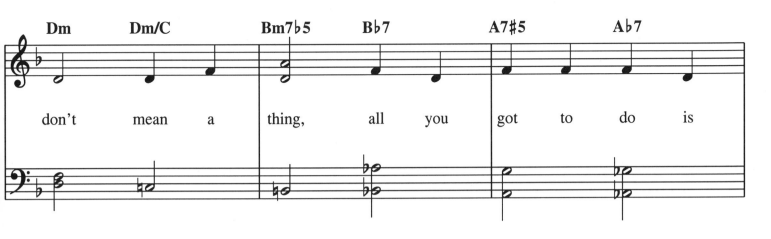

don't mean a thing, all you got to do is

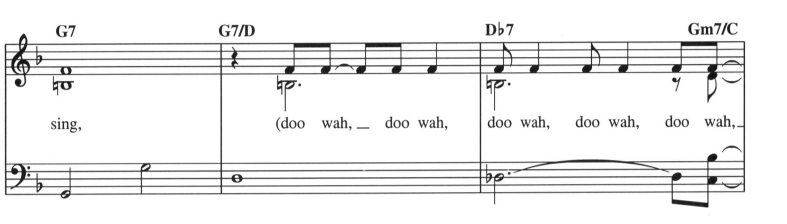

sing, (doo wah, __ doo wah, doo wah, doo wah, doo wah,

__ doo wah, doo wah, doo wah.) It makes no diff - 'rence

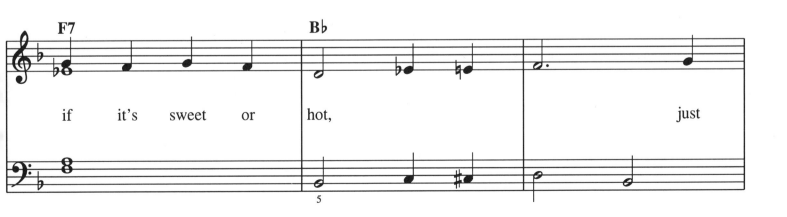

if it's sweet or hot, just

128

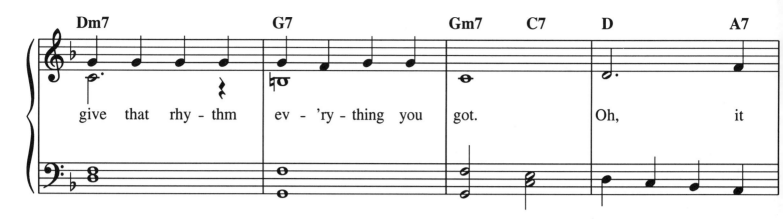

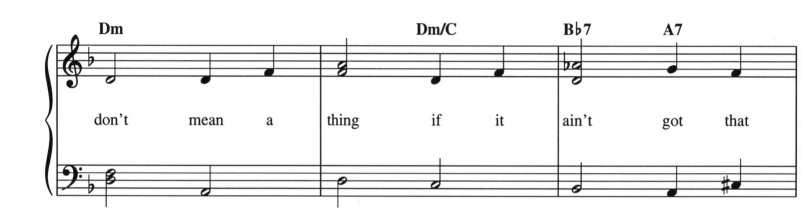

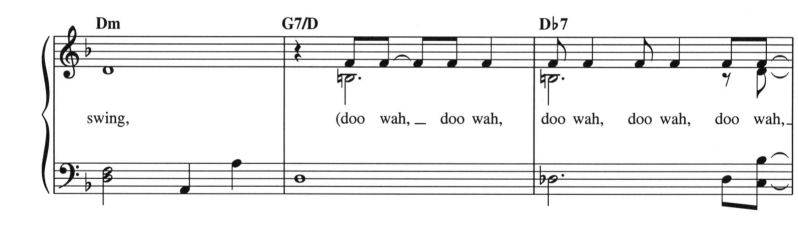

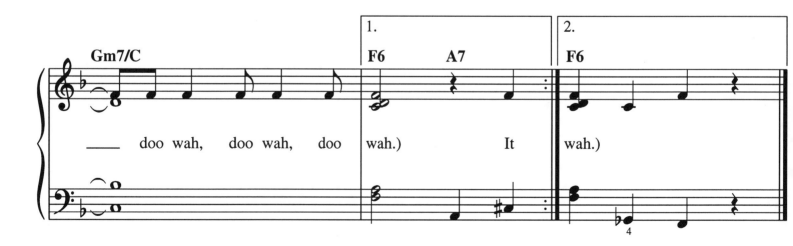

THE LADY IS A TRAMP
(From "BABES IN ARMS")

Words by LORENZ HART
Music by RICHARD RODGERS

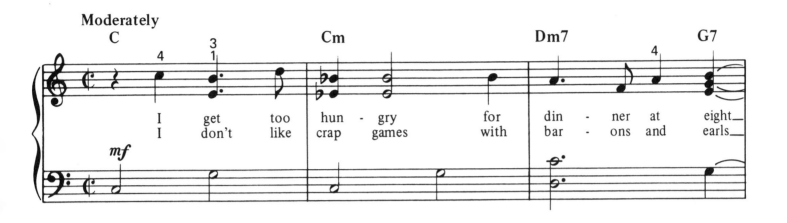

130

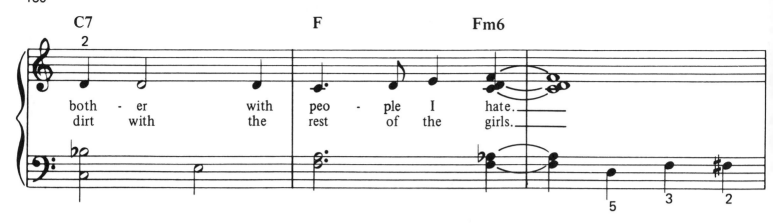

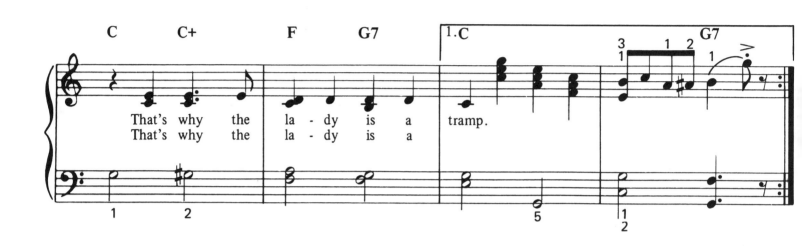

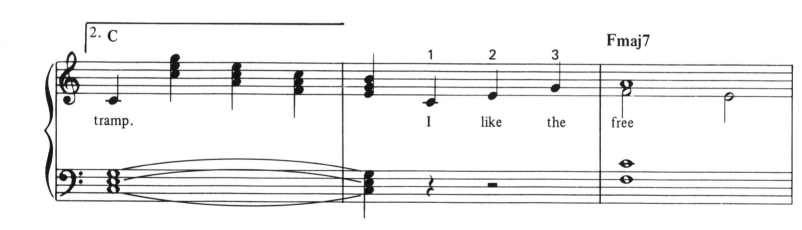

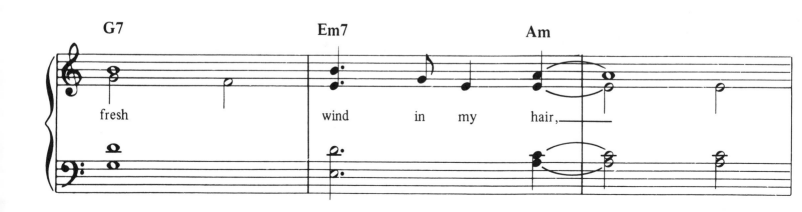

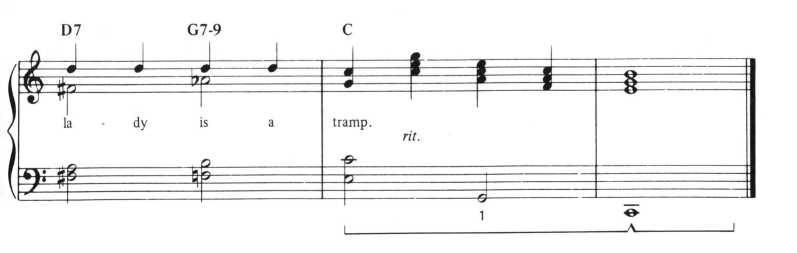

JUST IN TIME
(From "BELLS ARE RINGING")

Words by BETTY COMDEN and ADOLPH GREEN
Music by JULE STYNE

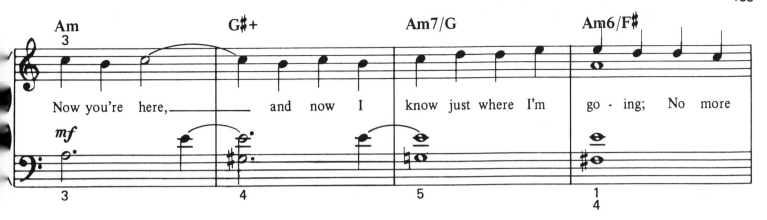

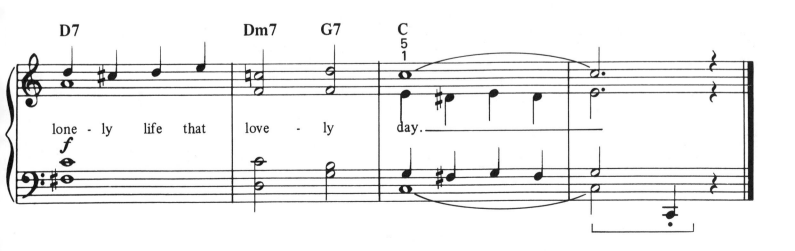

JUST ONE OF THOSE THINGS

Words and Music by
COLE PORTER

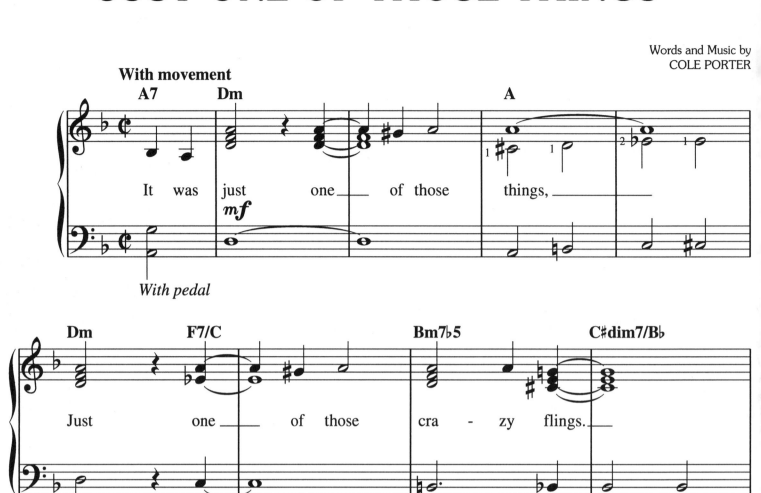

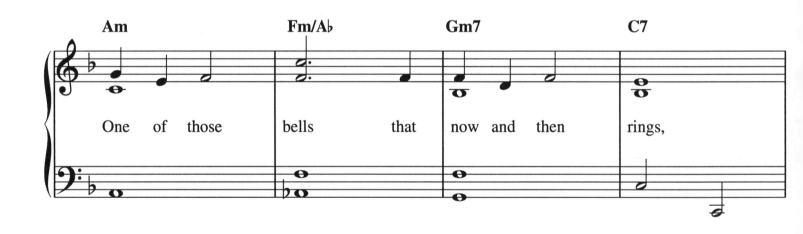

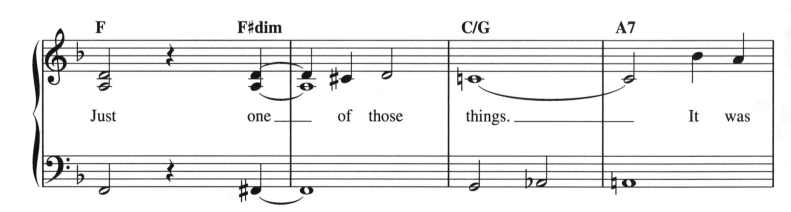

just one ___ of those nights, ___

Just one ___ of those fab - u - lous flights, A

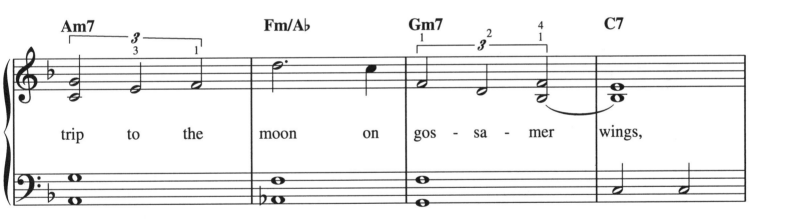

trip to the moon on gos - sa - mer wings,

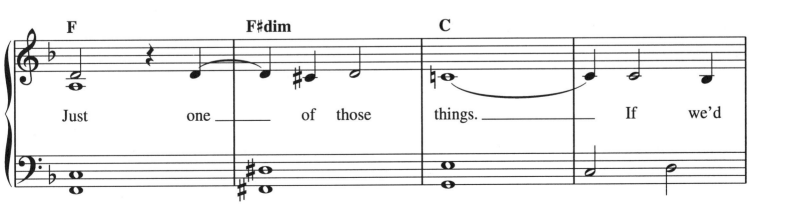

Just one ___ of those things. ___ If we'd

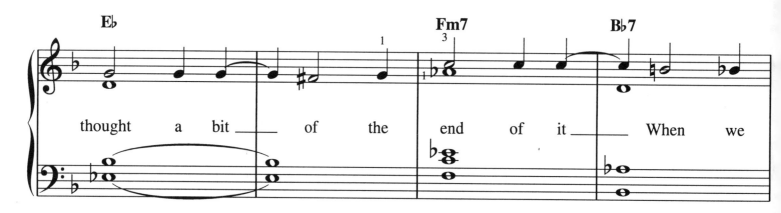

thought   a   bit ____ of   the   end   of   it ____   When   we

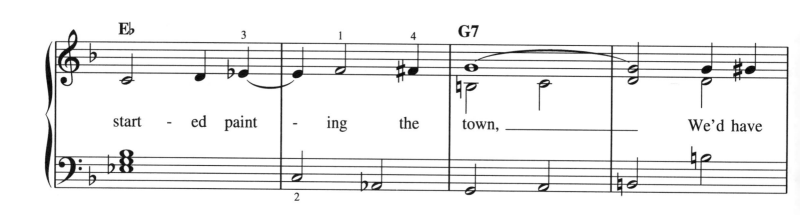

start   -   ed   paint   -   ing   the   town, _____   We'd   have

been   a - ware ____   That   our   love   af - fair ____   Was   too

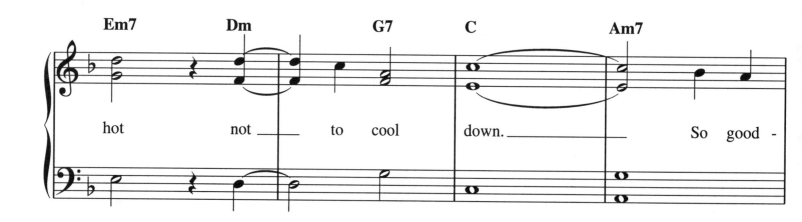

hot   not ____ to   cool   down. _____   So   good -

bye, dear, and A - men,

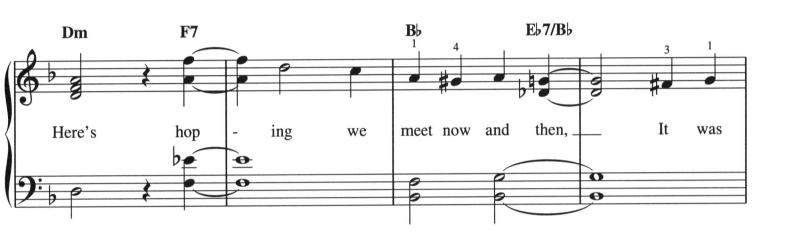

Here's hop - ing we meet now and then, It was

great fun But it was just one of those

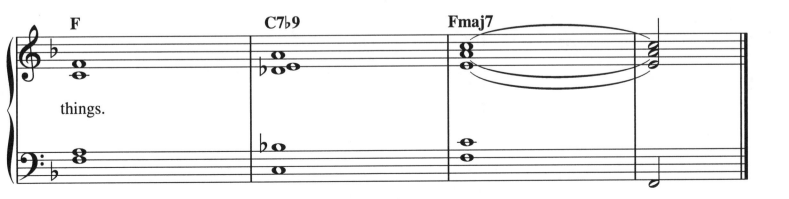

things.

LET THERE BE LOVE

Lyric by IAN GRANT
Music by LIONEL RAND

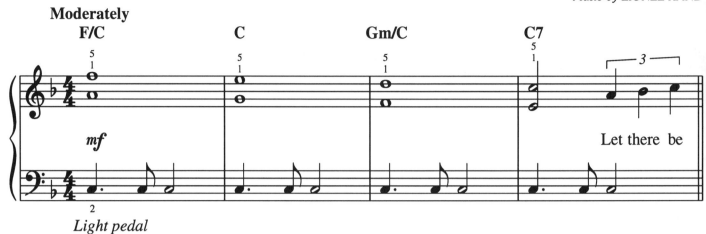

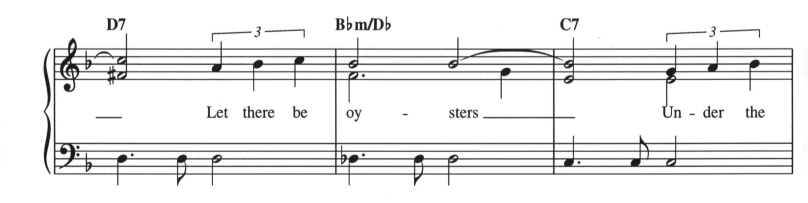

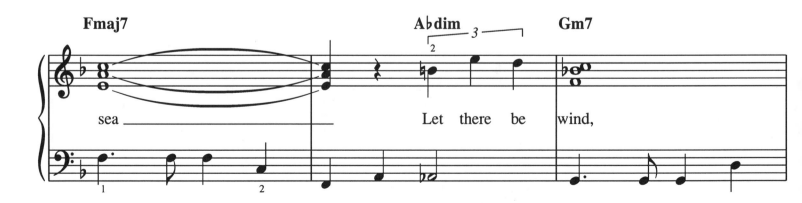

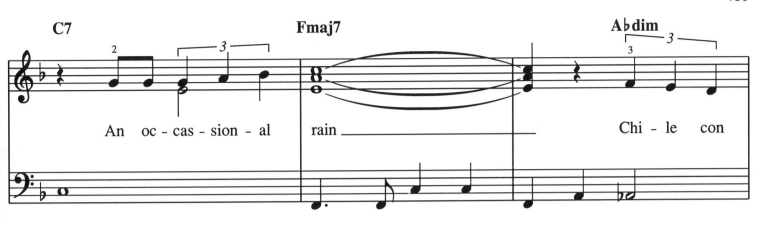

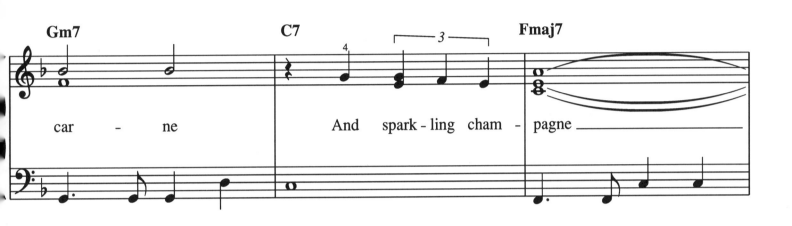

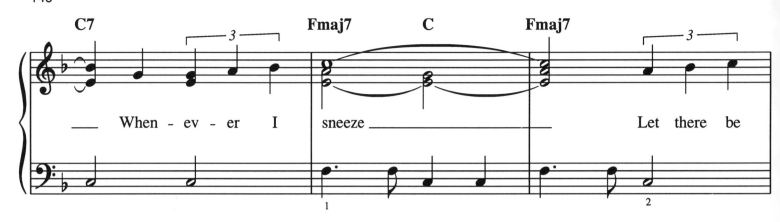

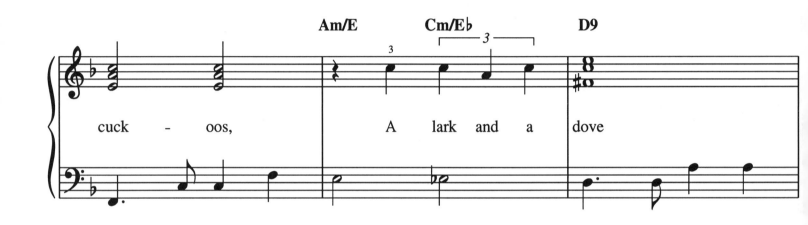

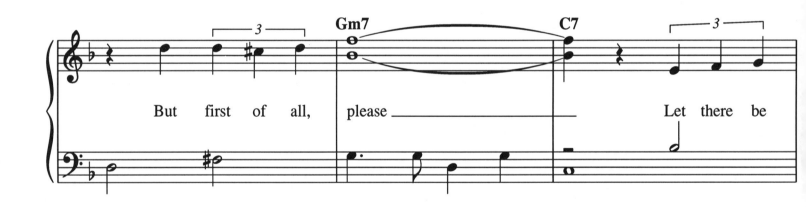

LIMEHOUSE BLUES
(From "ZIEGFELD FOLLIES")

Words by DOUGLAS FURBER
Music by PHILIP BRAHAM

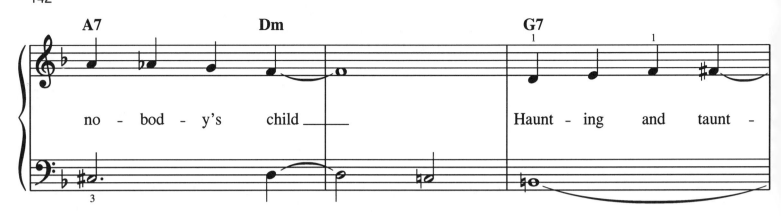

no - bod - y's child ___ Haunt - ing and taunt -

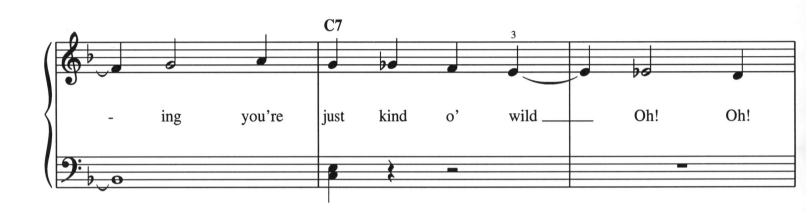

- ing you're just kind o' wild ___ Oh! Oh!

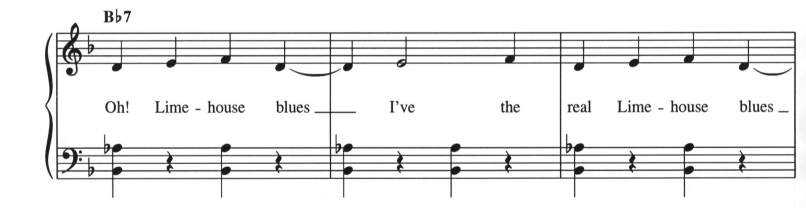

Oh! Lime - house blues ___ I've the real Lime - house blues ___

___ Can't seem to shake ___ off those

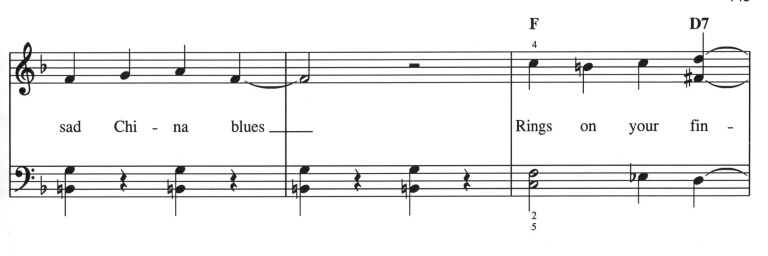

sad Chi - na blues ____ Rings on your fin -

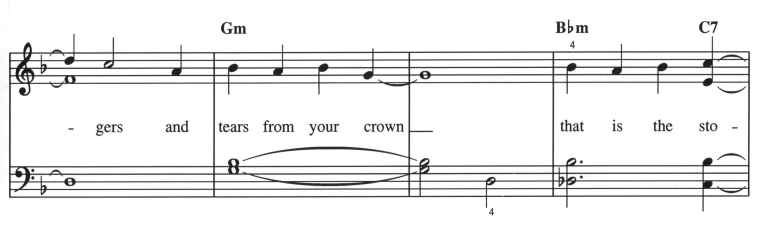

- gers and tears from your crown ____ that is the sto -

1.

- ry of old Chi - na town. ____

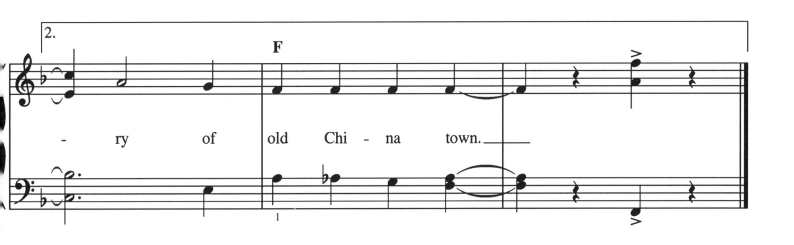

2.

- ry of old Chi - na town. ____

LITTLE GIRL BLUE

Words by LORENZ HART
Music by RICHARD RODGERS

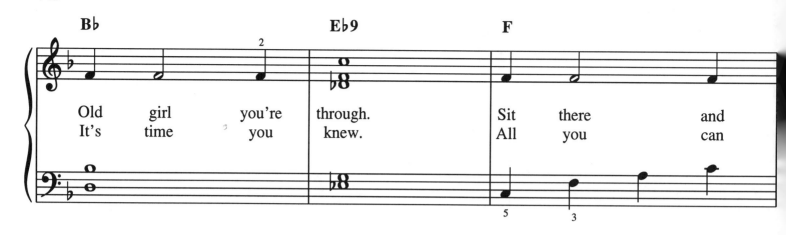

Old girl you're through. Sit there and
It's time you knew. All you can

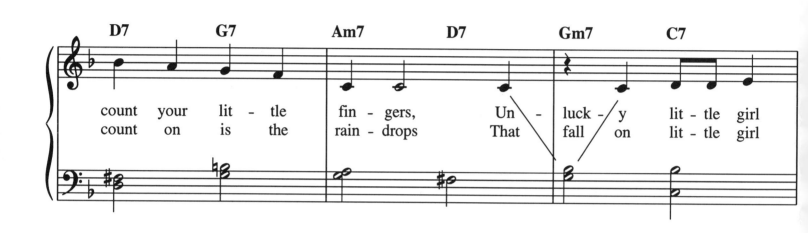

count your lit - tle fin - gers, Un - luck - y lit - tle girl
count on is the rain - drops That fall on lit - tle girl

1.
blue.

2.
blue.

No use, old girl, you may as well sur -

ren - der. Your hope is get - ting slen - der, Why

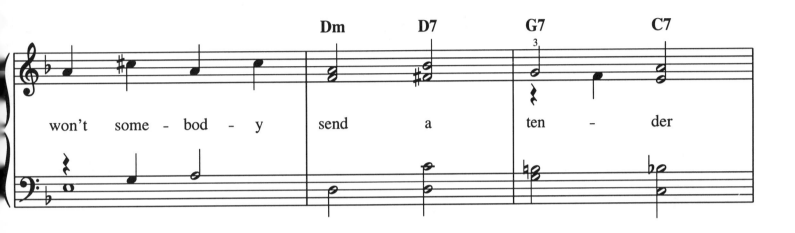

won't some - bod - y send a ten - der

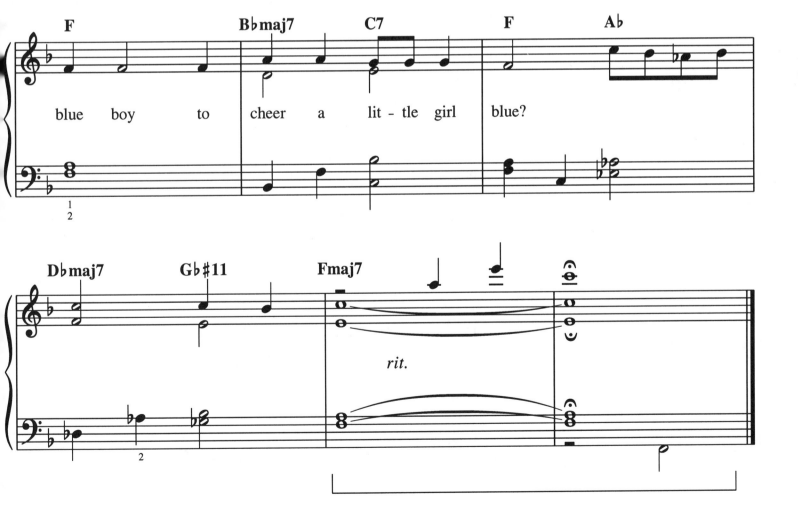

blue boy to cheer a lit - tle girl blue?

rit.

LONG AGO (AND FAR AWAY)
(From "COVER GIRL")

Words by IRA GERSHWIN
Music by JEROME KERN

Moderately slow

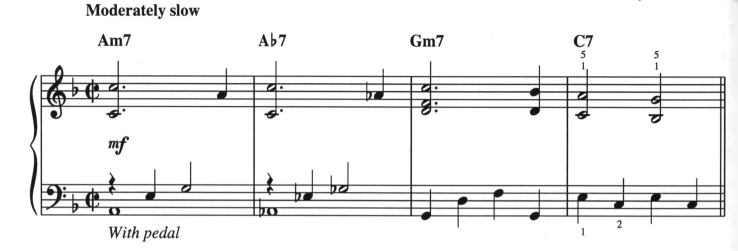

With pedal

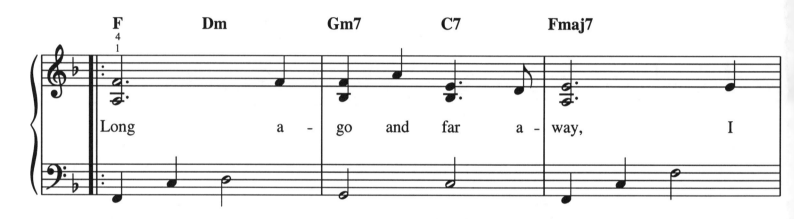

Long   a - go and far a - way,   I

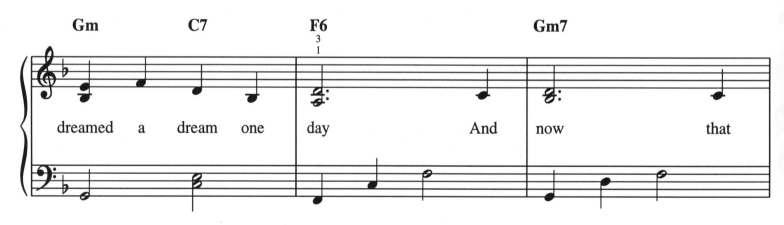

dreamed a dream one   day   And   now   that

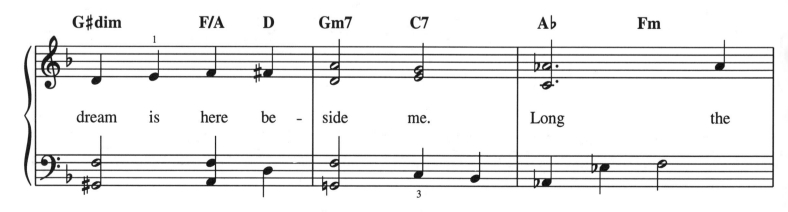

dream is here be - side me.   Long   the

150

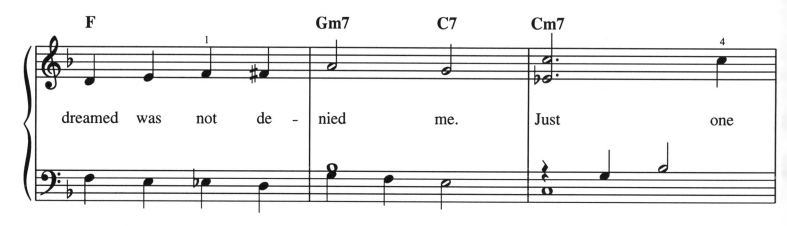

dreamed was not de - nied me. Just one

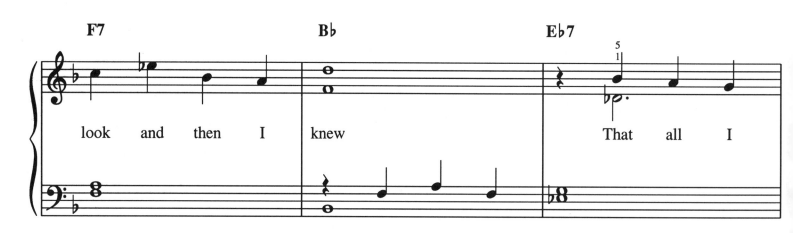

look and then I knew That all I

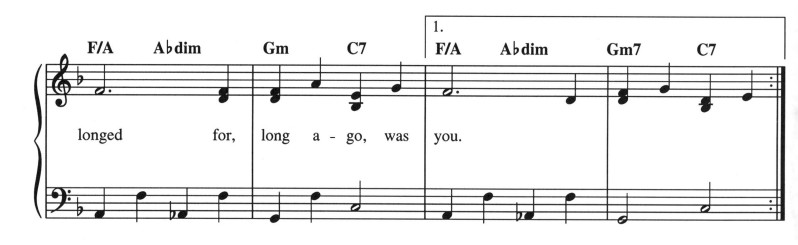

longed for, long a - go, was you.

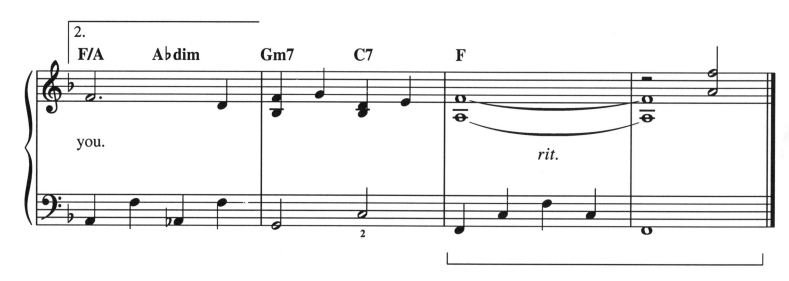

you. rit.

LOVE FOR SALE
(From "THE NEW YORKERS")

Words and Music by
COLE PORTER

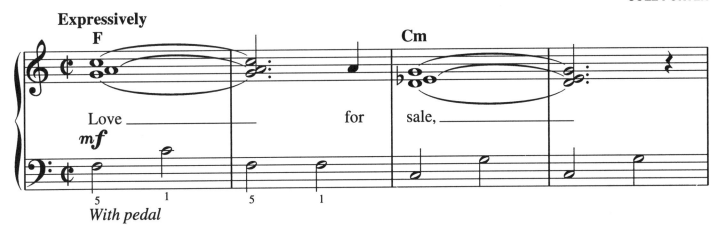

Love _____ for sale, _____ Ap - pe - tiz - ing young love for sale. _____

Love that's fresh and still un - spoiled, Love that's on - ly

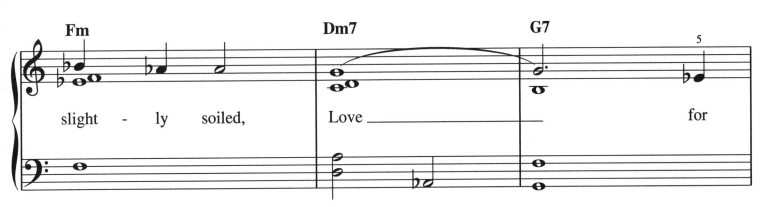

slight - ly soiled, Love _____ for

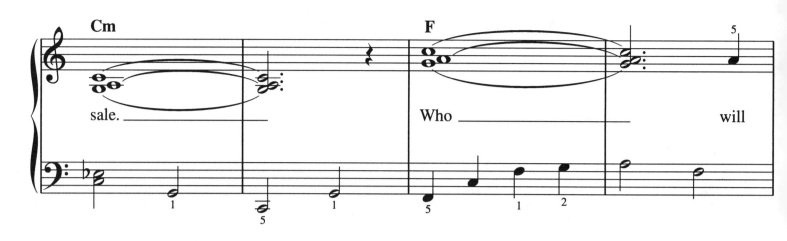

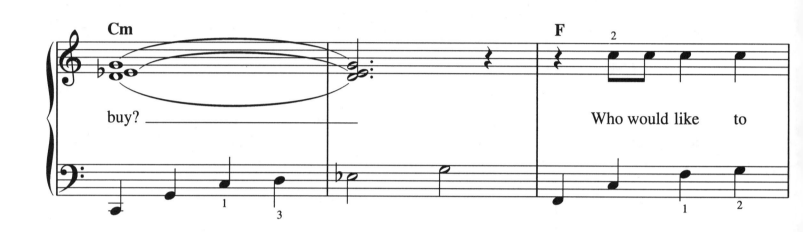

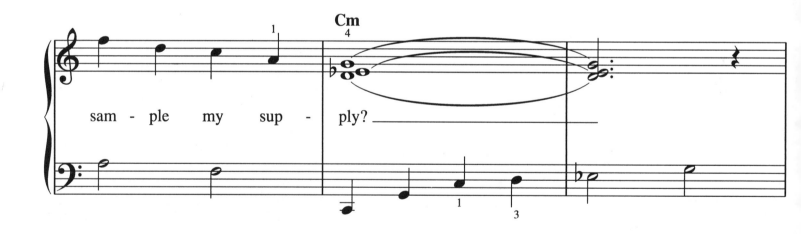

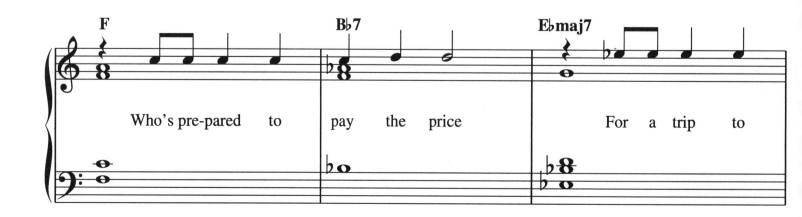

153

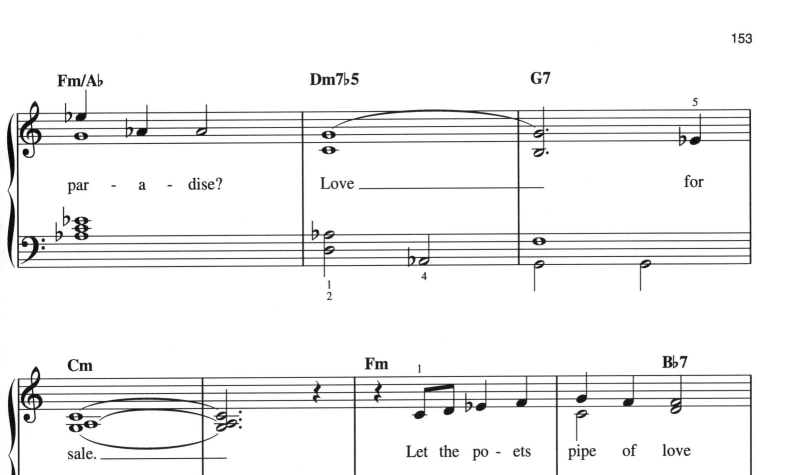

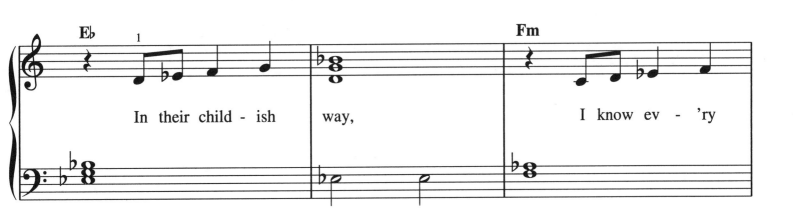

If you want the thrill of love, I've been thru the

mill of love; Old love, new love,

Ev-'ry love but true love. Love _____ for

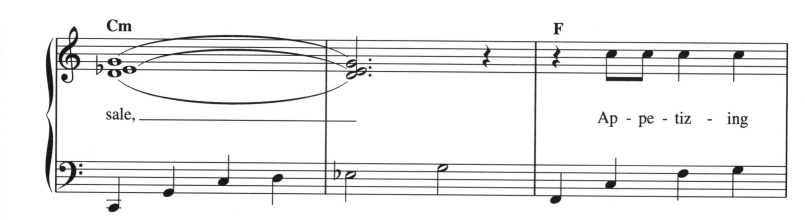

sale, _____ Ap - pe - tiz - ing

young love   for   sale. _____   If you want to

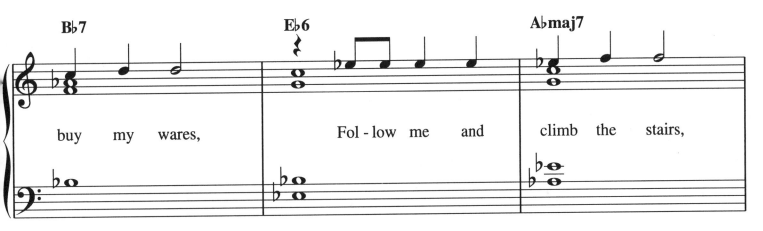

buy   my   wares,   Fol - low me   and   climb   the   stairs,

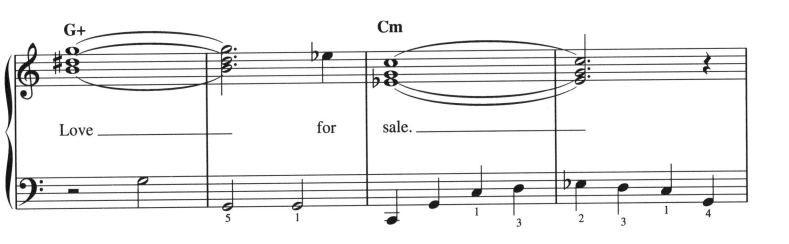

Love _____   for   sale. _____

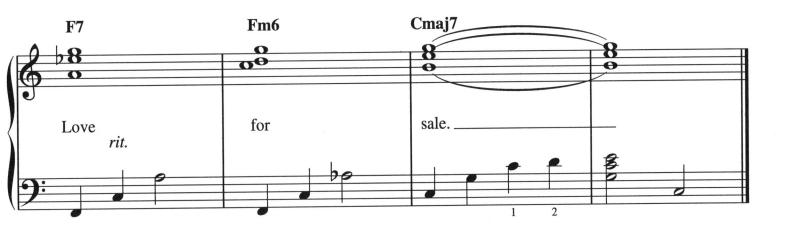

Love   for   sale. _____

LOVER, COME BACK TO ME
(From "THE NEW MOON")

Lyrics by OSCAR HAMMERSTEIN II
Music by SIGMUND ROMBERG

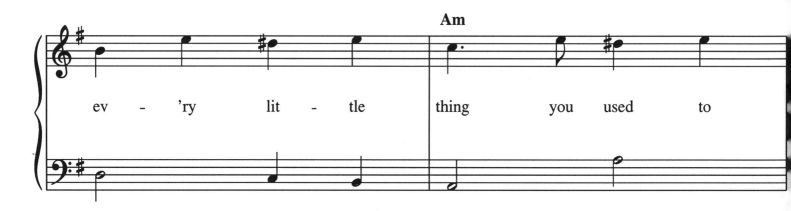

ev - 'ry lit - tle thing you used to

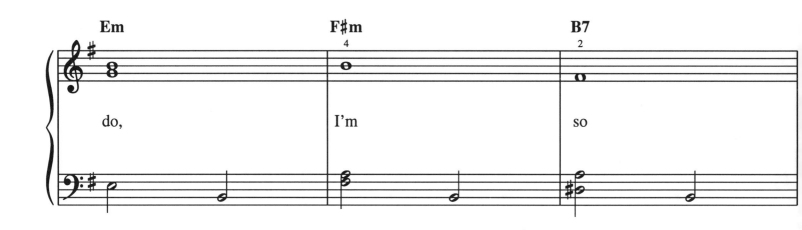

do, I'm so

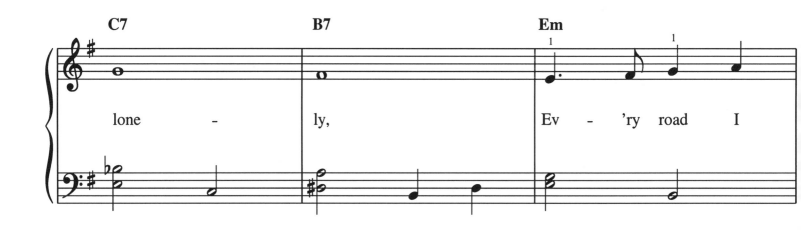

lone - ly, Ev - 'ry road I

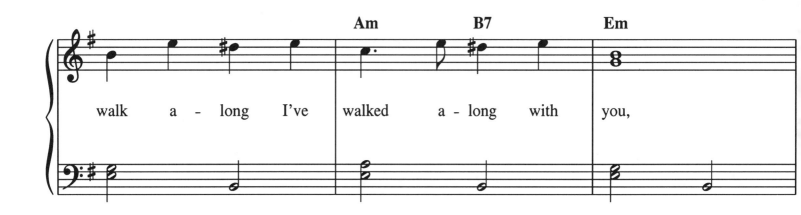

walk a - long I've walked a - long with you,

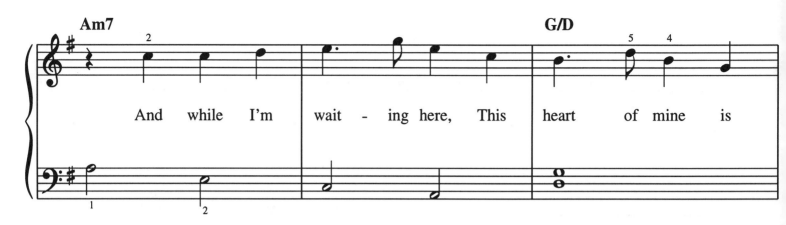

And while I'm wait - ing here, This heart of mine is

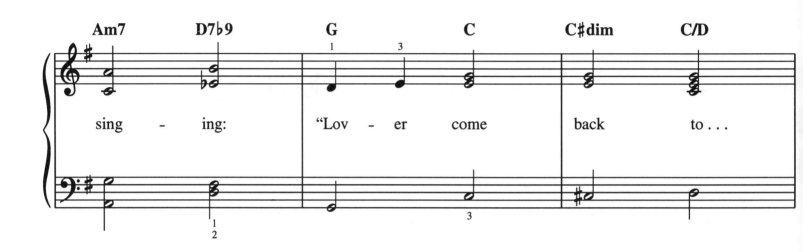

sing - ing: "Lov - er come back to . . .

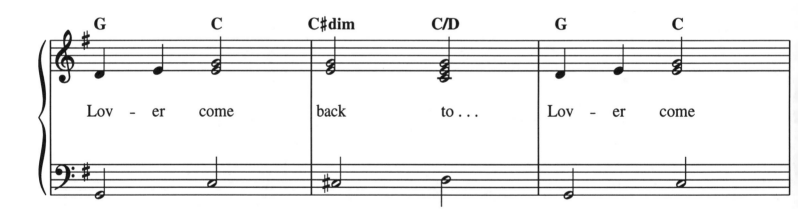

Lov - er come back to . . . Lov - er come

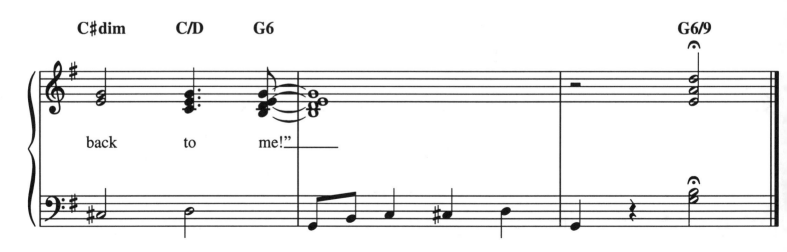

back to me!"

MOOD INDIGO

Words and Music by DUKE ELLINGTON,
IRVING MILLS and ALBANY BIGARD

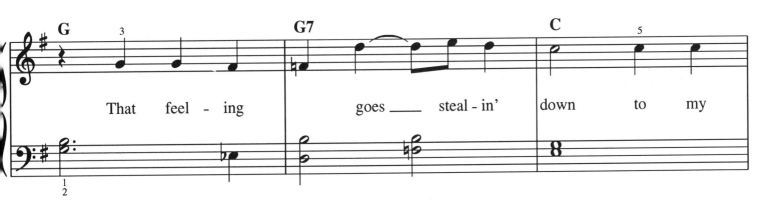

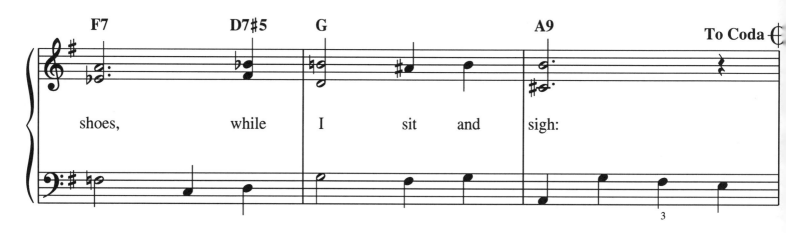

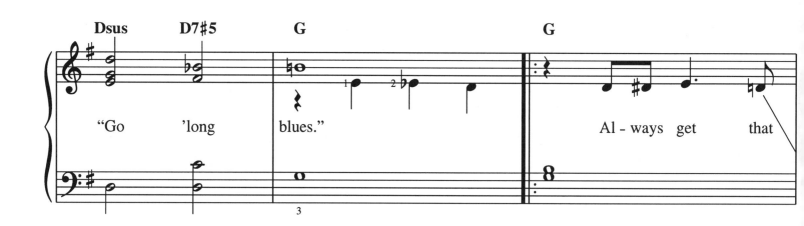

163

LULLABY OF THE LEAVES

Words by JOE YOUNG
Music by BERNICE PETKERE

I'm breez-ing a-long, a - long with the breeze, I'm

hear-ing a song, a song thru the trees, ooh ooh ooh ooh ooh ooh

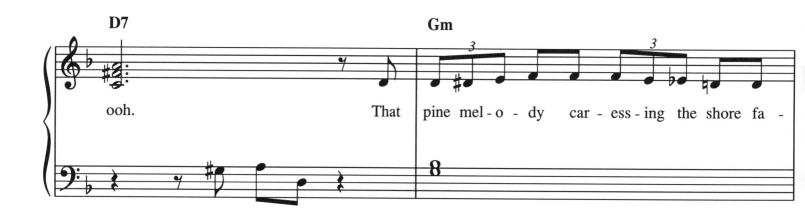

ooh. That pine mel-o-dy car-ess-ing the shore fa -

mil - iar to me, I've heard it be-fore, ooh ooh ooh ooh.

MANHATTAN
(From "GARRICK GAIETIES")

Lyric by LORENZ HART
Music by RICHARD RODGERS

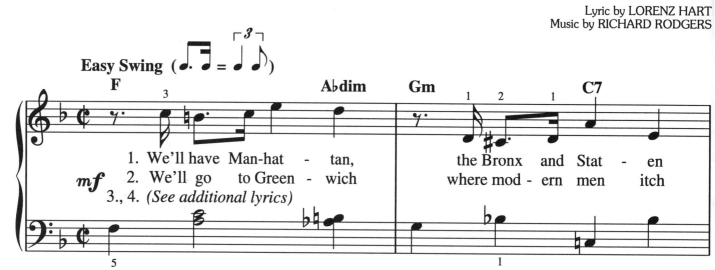

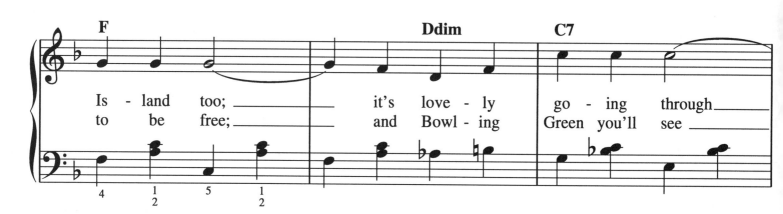

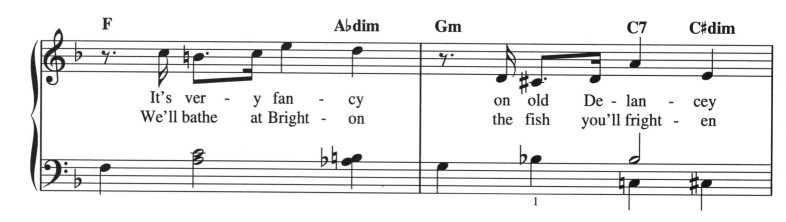

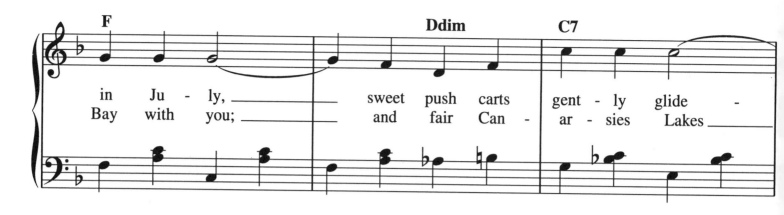

in Ju - ly, _____ sweet push carts gent - ly glide -
Bay with you; _____ and fair Can - ar - sies Lakes _____

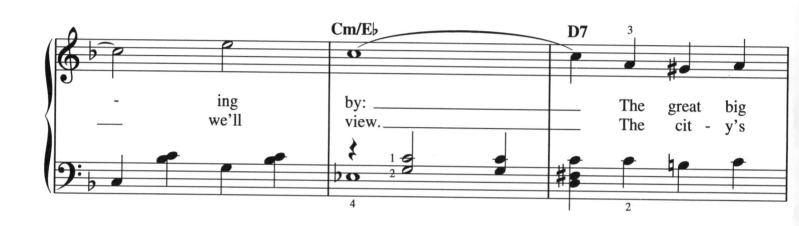

- ing by: _____ The great big
we'll view. _____ The cit - y's

cit - y's a won - d'rous toy just made for a girl and
bus - tle can - not des - troy the dreams of a girl and

boy. We'll turn Man - hat - tan
boy. We'll turn Man - hat - tan

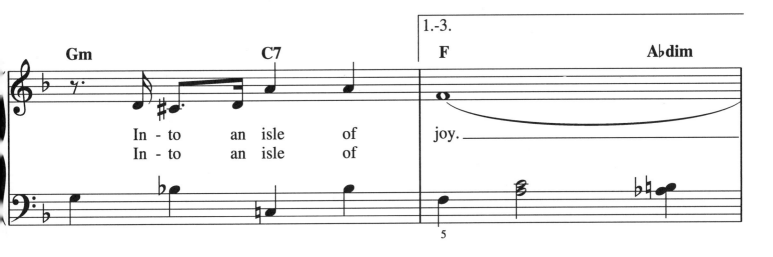

Gm　　　　C7　　　　　1.-3. F　　　　　Abdim

In - to　an isle　of　joy.
In - to　an isle　of

5

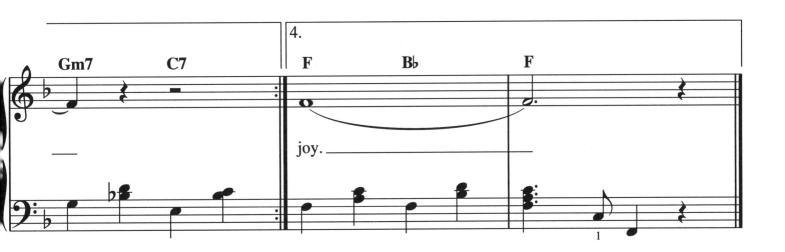

Gm7　　C7　　　4. F　　　Bb　　　F

joy.

1

Additional Lyrics

3. We'll go to Yonkers where true love conquers in the wilds;
   And starve together, dear, in Childs'.
   We'll go to Coney and eat bologny on a roll;
   In Central Park we'll stroll, where our first kiss we stole, soul to soul.
   And for some high fare, we'll go to "My Fair Lady," say,
   We'll hope to see it close some day.
   The city's clamor can never spoil
   The dreams of a boy and goil.
   We'll turn Manhattan into an isle of joy.

4. We'll have Manhattan, the Bronx and Staten Island, too;
   We'll try to cross Fifth Avenue.
   As black as onyx we'll find the Bronix Park Express;
   Our Flatbush flat, I guess, will be a big success, more or less.
   A short vacation on Inspiration Point we'll spend,
   And in the station house we'll end.
   But civic virtue cannot destroy
   The dreams of a girl and boy.
   We'll turn Manhattan into an isle of joy.

MEDITATION
(MEDITACÁO)

English Words by NORMAN GIMBEL
Original Words by NEWTON MENDONCA
Music by ANTONIO CARLOS JOBIM

174

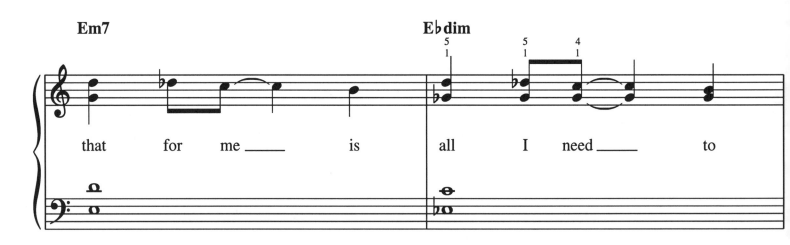

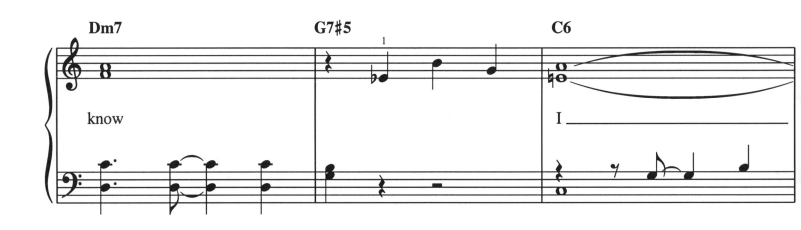

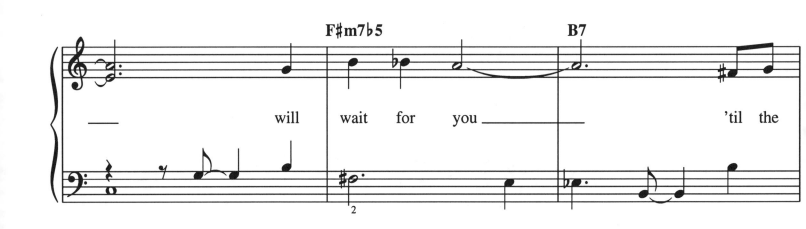

MERCY, MERCY, MERCY

Composed by JOSEF ZAWINUL

MIDNIGHT SUN

Words and Music by LIONEL HAMPTON,
SONNY BURKE, and JOHNNY MERCER

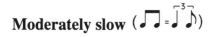

With pedal

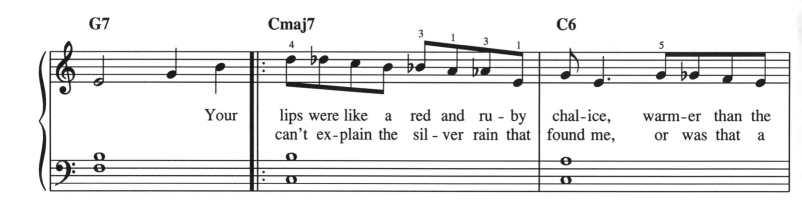

Your | lips were like a red and ru-by | chal-ice, warm-er than the
can't ex-plain the sil-ver rain that | found me, or was that a

sum-mer night,_____ | The | clouds were like an a-la-bas-ter
moon-lit veil?_____ | The | mu-sic of the u-ni-verse a-

pal-ace ris-ing to a | snow-y height._____ | Each
round me, or was that a | night-in-gale?_____ | And

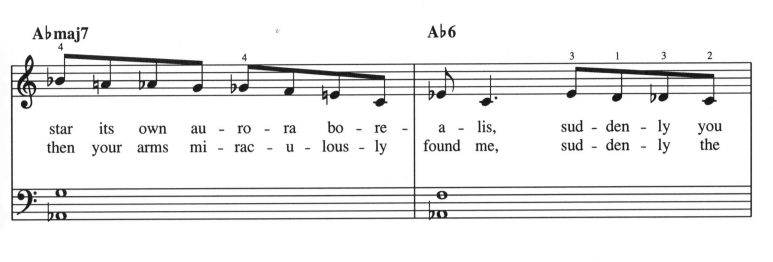

star its own au - ro - ra bo - re - a - lis, sud - den - ly you
then your arms mi - rac - u - lous - ly found me, sud - den - ly the

held me tight, ___ I could see the mid - night sun. ___
sky turned pale, ___ I could see the

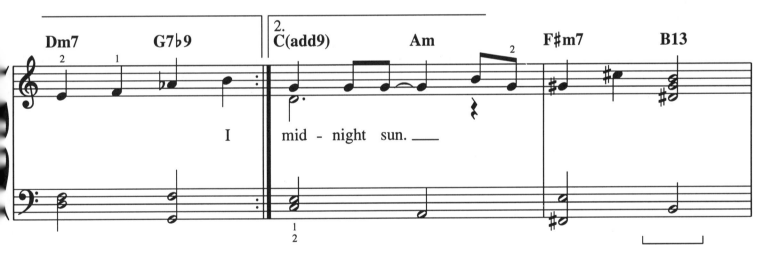

I mid - night sun. ___

Was there such a night, it's a thrill I still don't quite be -

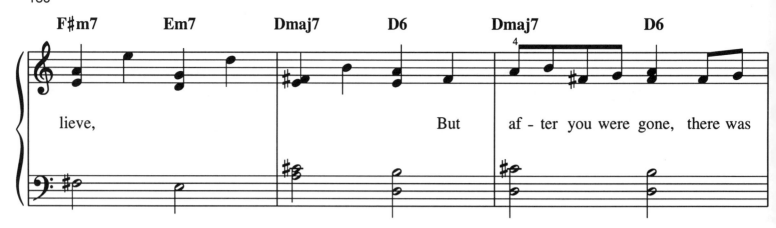

lieve, But af - ter you were gone, there was

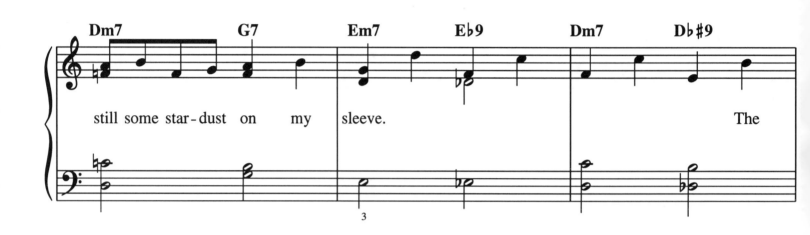

still some star - dust on my sleeve. The

flame of it may dwin - dle to an em - ber, and the stars for -

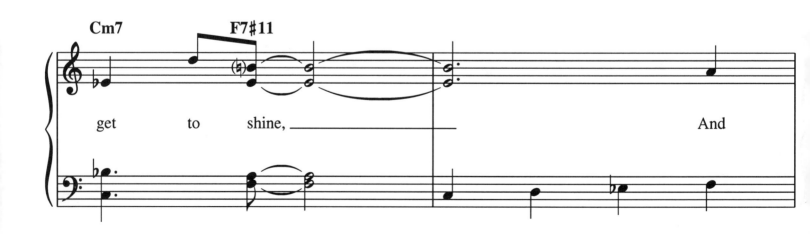

get to shine, _____ And

we may see the mead-ow in De- cem- ber, ic - y white and

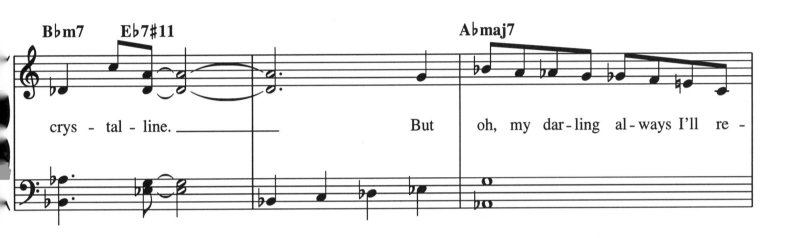

crys - tal - line._____ But oh, my dar-ling al-ways I'll re -

mem-ber, when your lips were close to mine, _____ And { I / we } saw the

mid - night sun. __

MISTY

Words by JOHNNY BURKE
Music by ERROLL GARNER

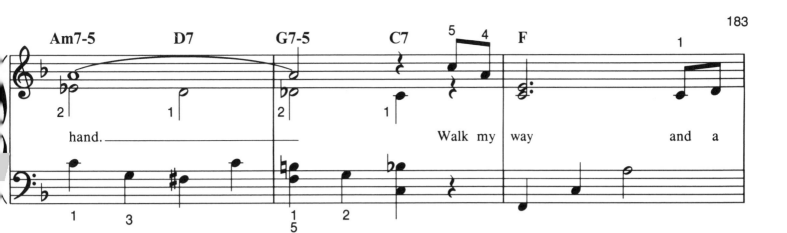

184

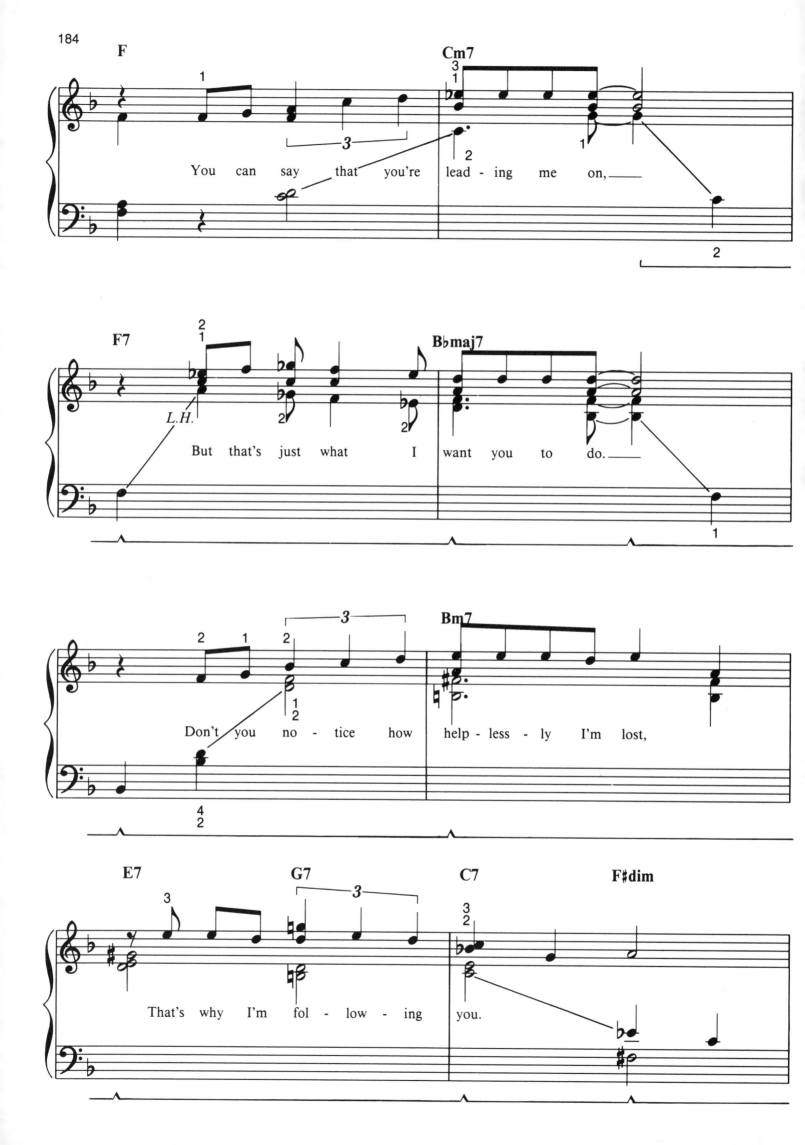

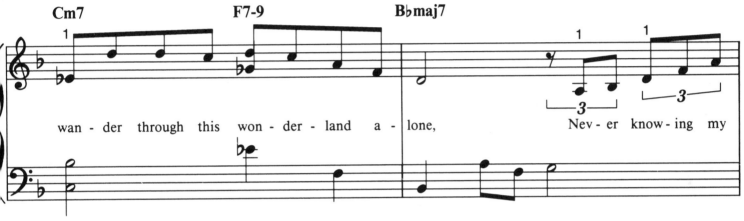

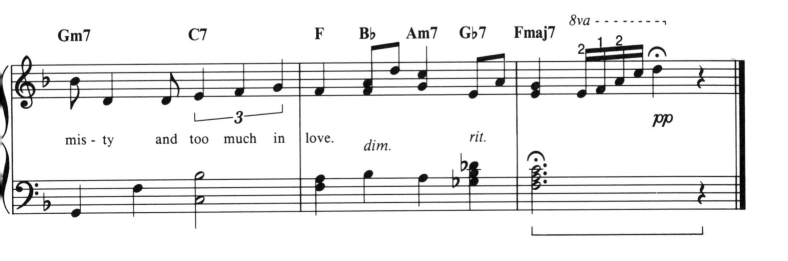

MOONLIGHT IN VERMONT

Words and Music by JOHN BLACKBURN
and KARL SUESSDORF

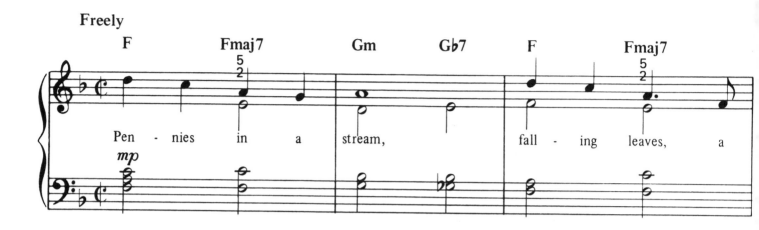

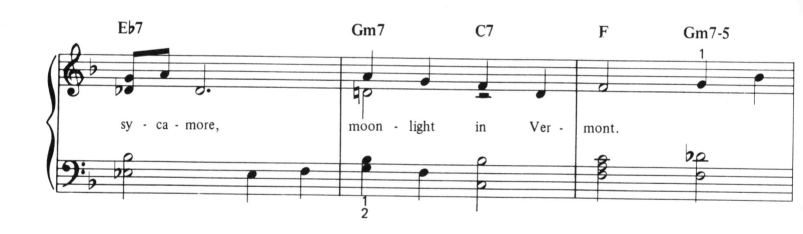

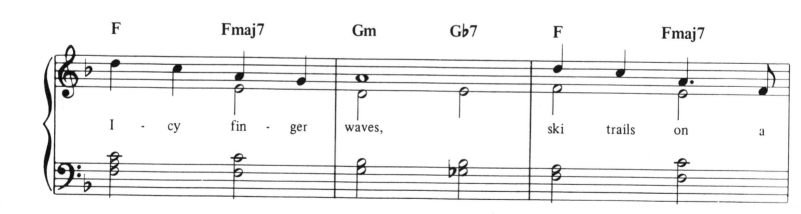

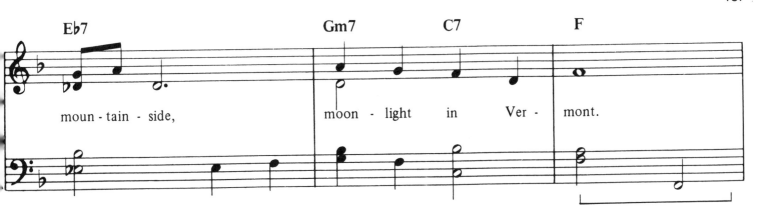

moun - tain - side,   moon - light in Ver - mont.

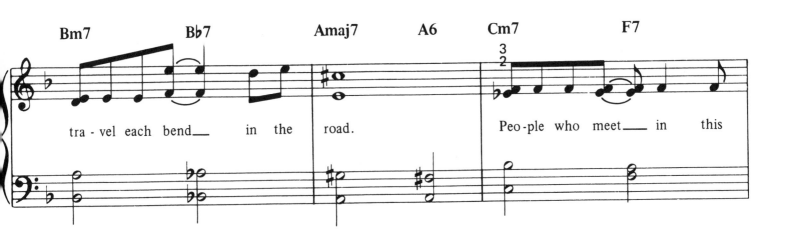

Tel - e - graph ca - bles, they sing down the high - way, and

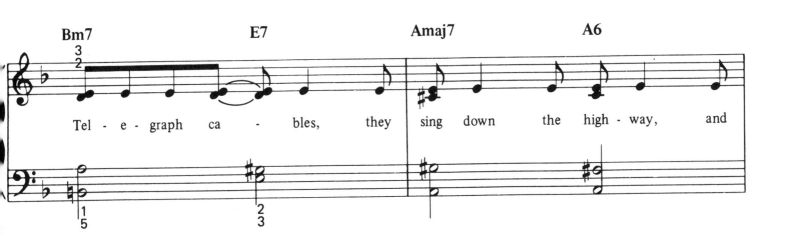

tra - vel each bend___ in the road.   Peo - ple who meet___ in this

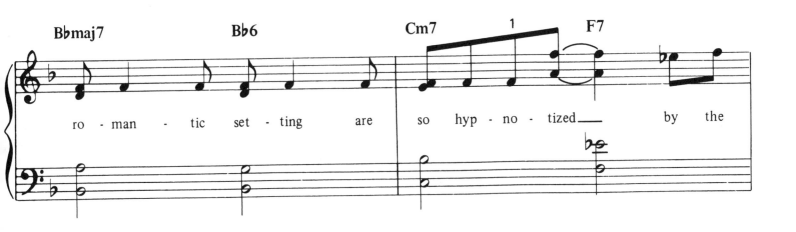

ro - man - tic set - ting are so hyp - no - tized___ by the

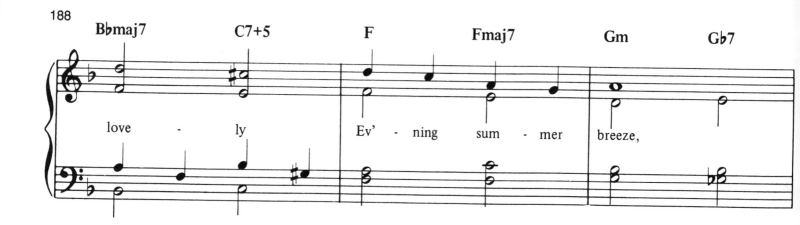

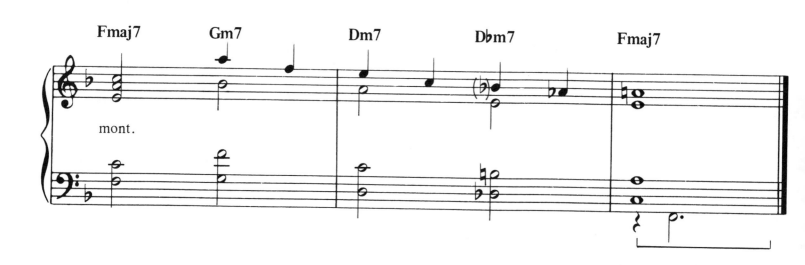

MORE THAN YOU KNOW

Words by WILLIAM ROSE and EDWARD ELISCU
Music by VINCENT YOUMANS

right,   wheth - er you're   wrong,   {Man}
                                         {Girl} o'   my   heart I'll   string a -

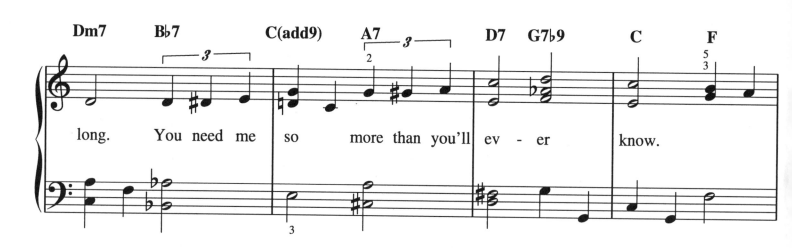

long.   You need me   so   more than you'll ev - er   know.

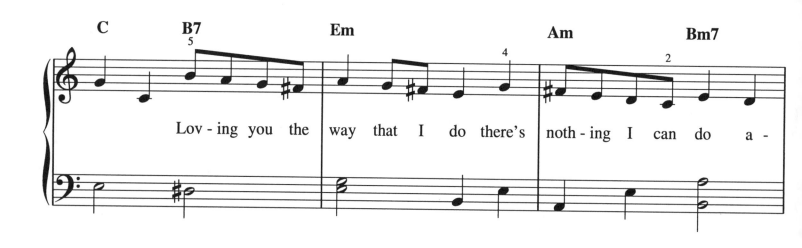

Lov - ing you the   way that I do there's   noth - ing I can do a -

bout   it. _____   Lov - ing may be   all   you can give but

MY FUNNY VALENTINE
(From "BABES IN ARMS")

Words by LORENZ HART
Music by RICHARD RODGERS

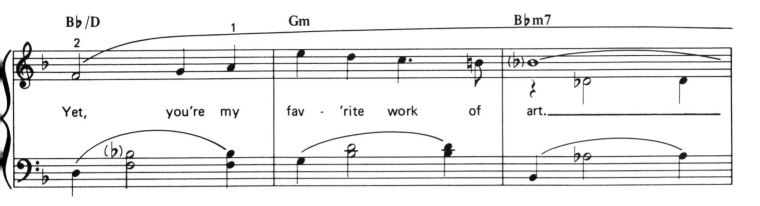

Yet, you're my fav - 'rite work of art._____

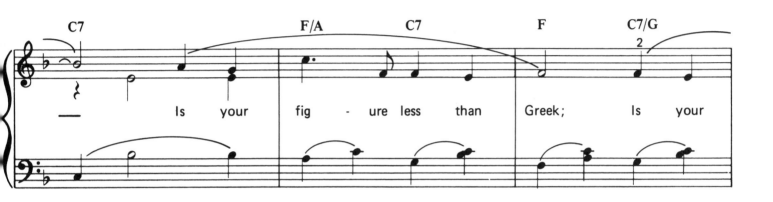

___ Is your fig - ure less than Greek; Is your

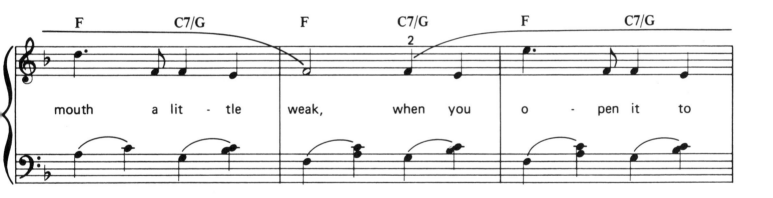

mouth a lit - tle weak, when you o - pen it to

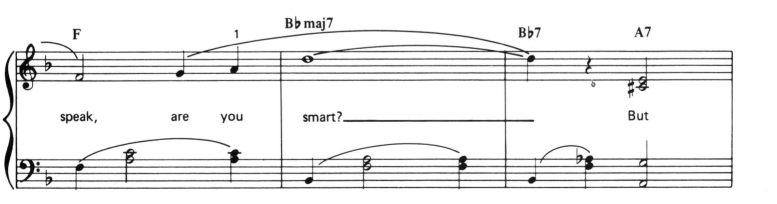

speak, are you smart?_____ But

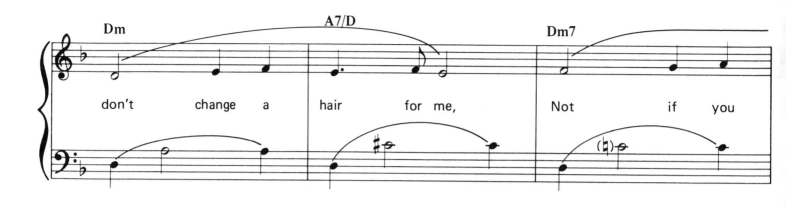

don't change a hair for me, Not if you

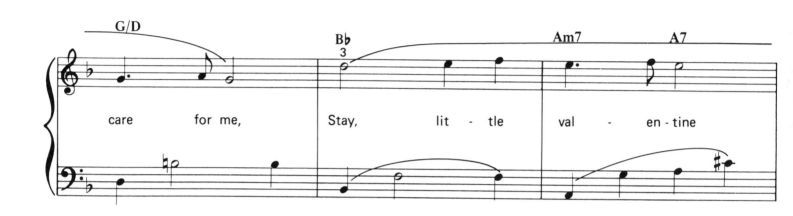

care for me, Stay, lit - tle val - en - tine

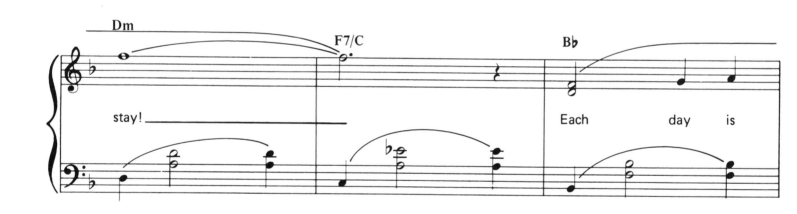

stay! _____ Each day is

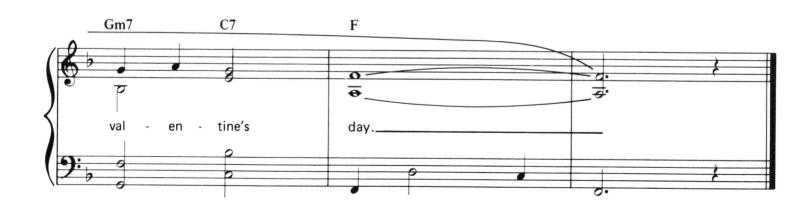

val - en - tine's day. _____

MY ROMANCE
(From "JUMBO")

Words by LORENZ HART
Music by RICHARD RODGERS

MY SHIP
(From The Musical Production "LADY IN THE DARK")

Words by IRA GERSHWIN
Music by KURT WEILL

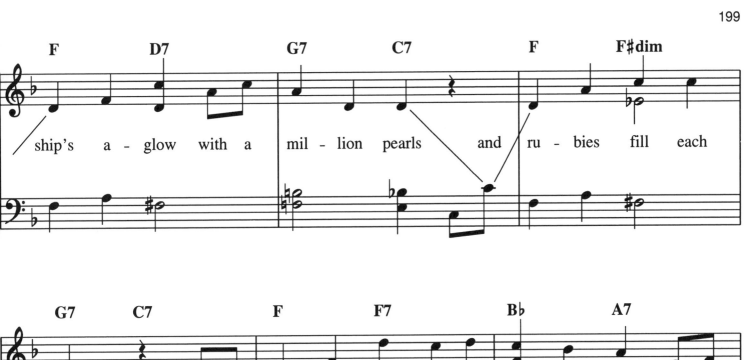

ship's a-glow with a mil-lion pearls and ru-bies fill each

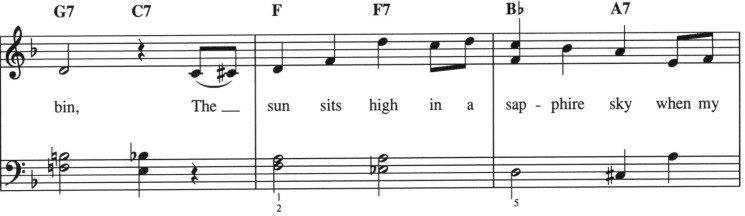

bin, The __ sun sits high in a sap-phire sky when my

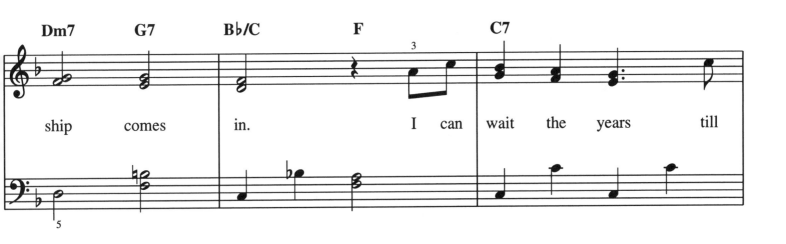

ship comes in. I can wait the years till

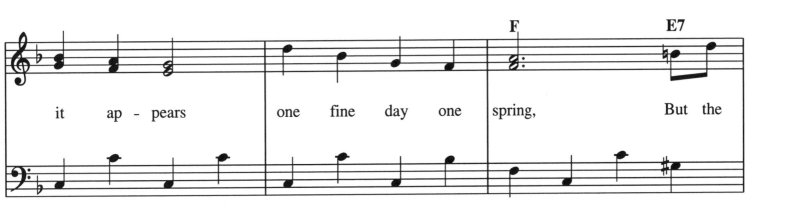

it ap-pears one fine day one spring, But the

pearls and such they won't mean much if there's

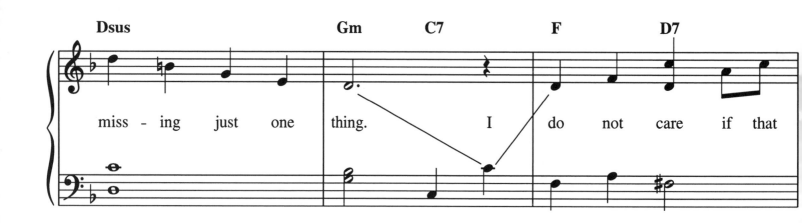

miss - ing just one thing. I do not care if that

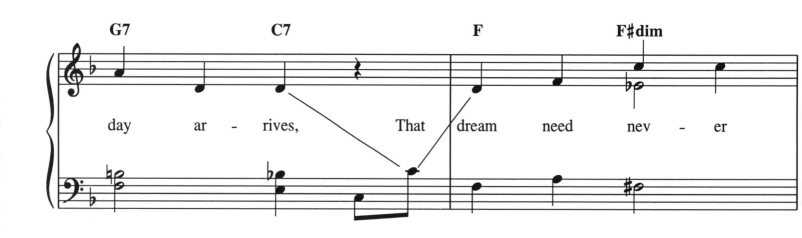

day ar - rives, That dream need nev - er

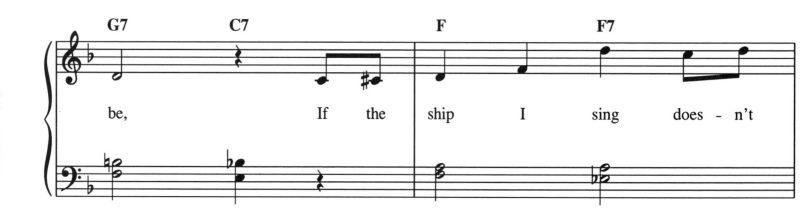

be, If the ship I sing does - n't

NICE WORK IF YOU CAN GET IT

(From "A DAMSEL IN DISTRESS")

Music and Lyrics by GEORGE GERSHWIN
and IRA GERSHWIN

Moderately

Light pedal

Hold - ing hands at

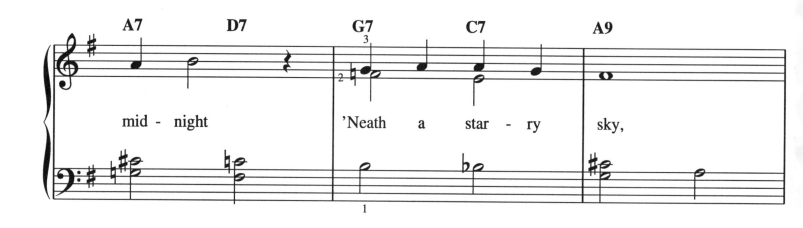

mid - night   'Neath a star - ry   sky,

Nice   work if you can get it,   And you can   get it   if   you try.

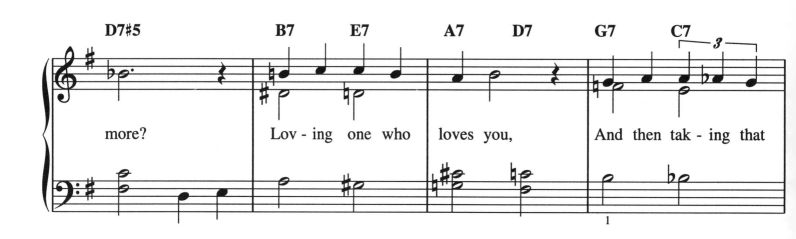

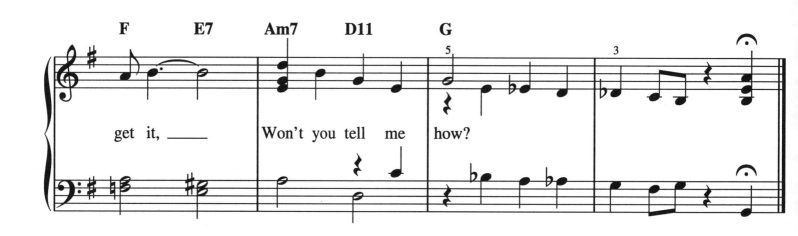

NIGHT AND DAY
(From "THE GAY DIVORCÉ")

Words and Music by
COLE PORTER

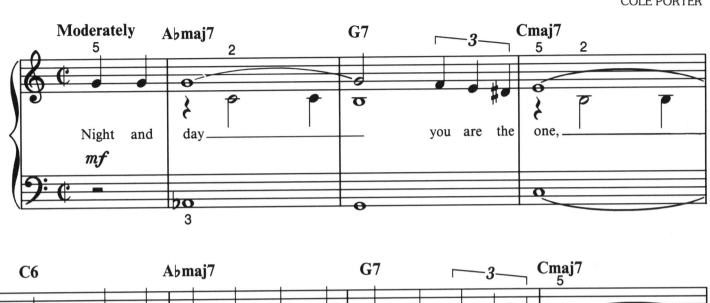

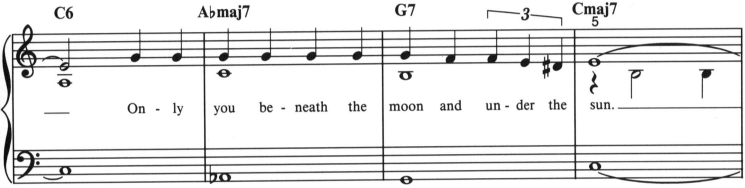

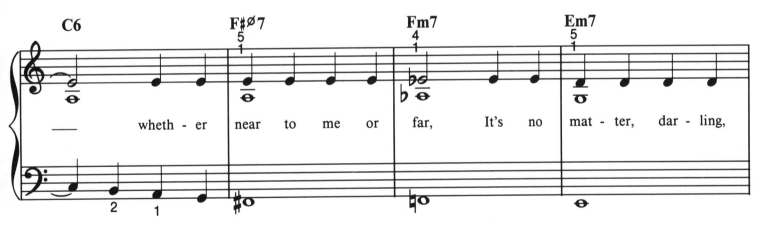

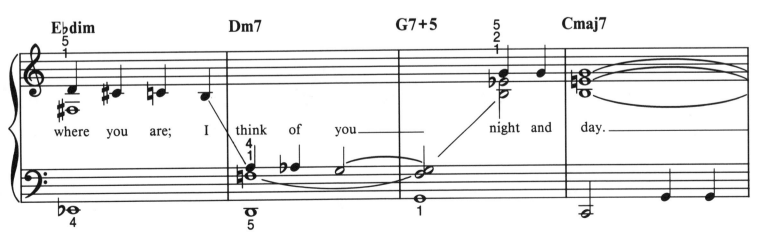

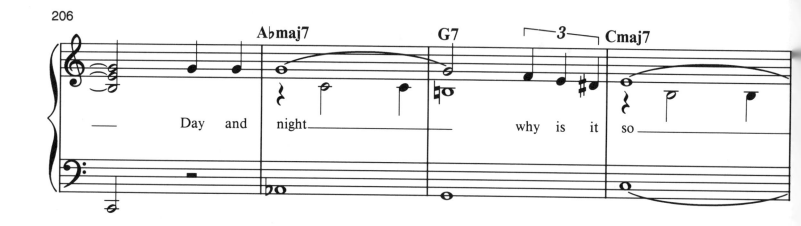

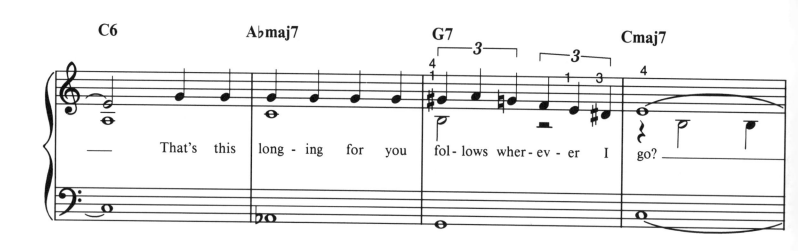

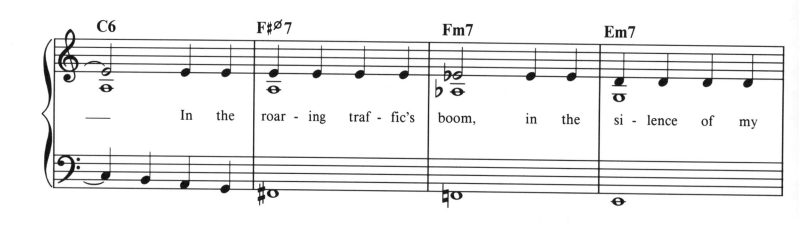

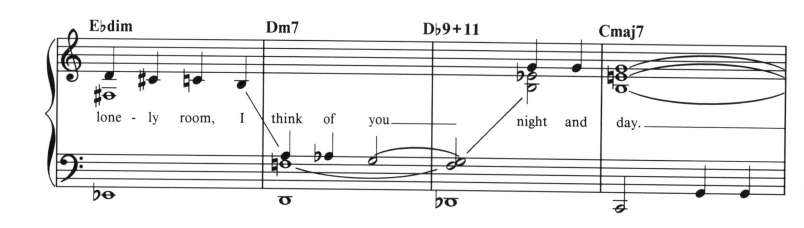

207

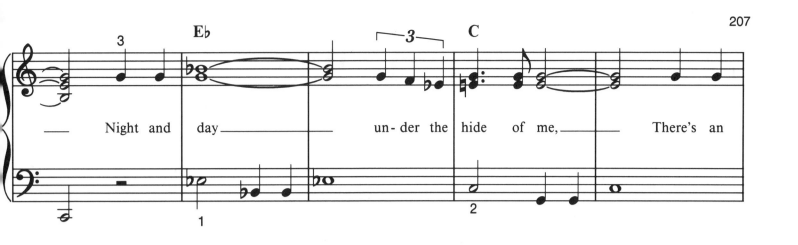

Night and day under the hide of me, There's an

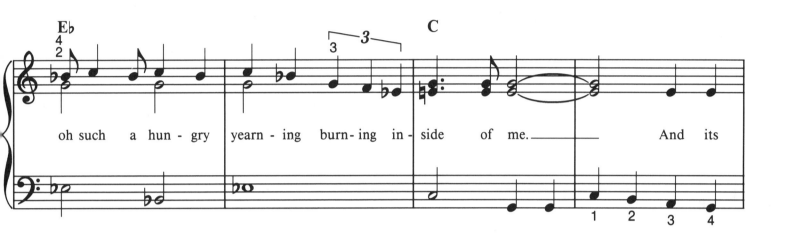

oh such a hun-gry yearn-ing burn-ing in-side of me. And its

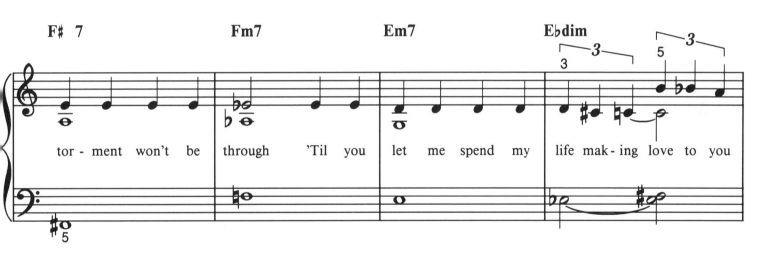

tor-ment won't be through 'Til you let me spend my life mak-ing love to you

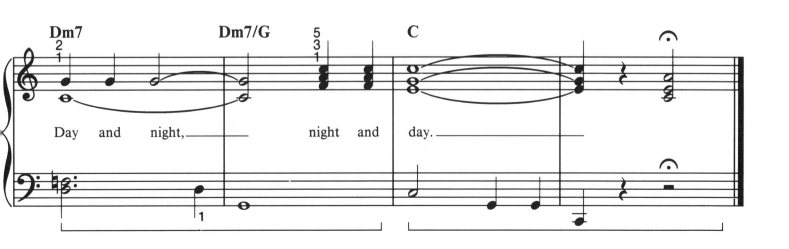

Day and night, night and day.

OL' MAN RIVER
(From "SHOW BOAT")

Words by OSCAR HAMMERSTEIN II
Music by JEROME KERN

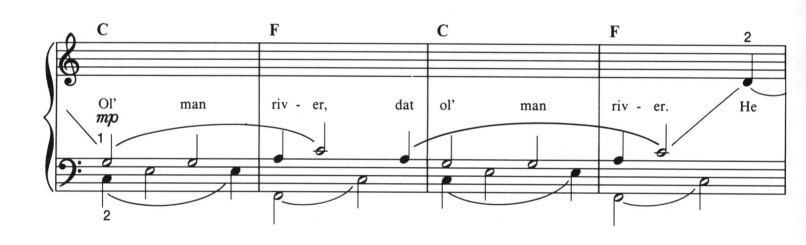

Ol' man riv-er, dat ol' man riv-er. He

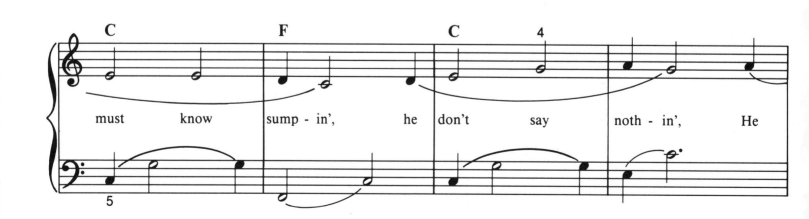

must know sump-in', he don't say noth-in', He

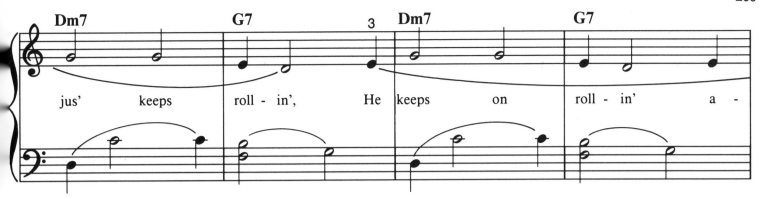

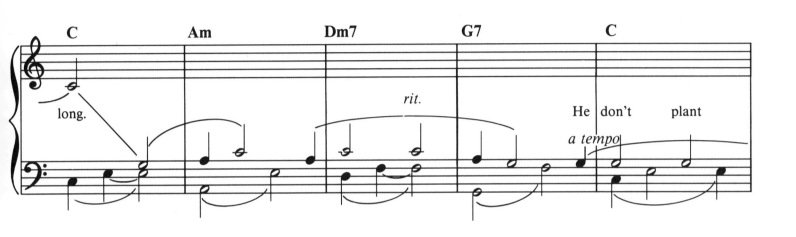

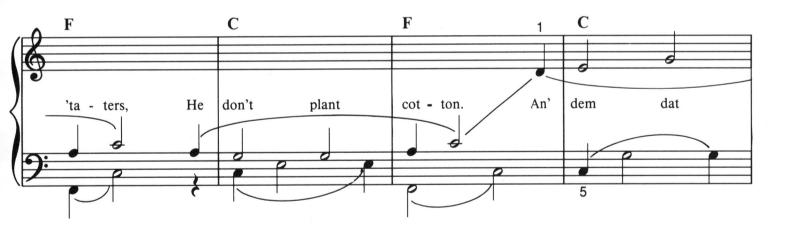

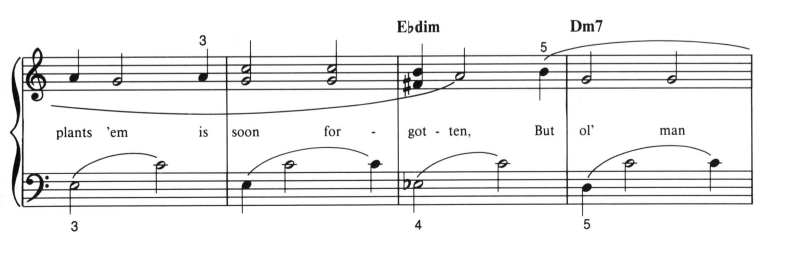

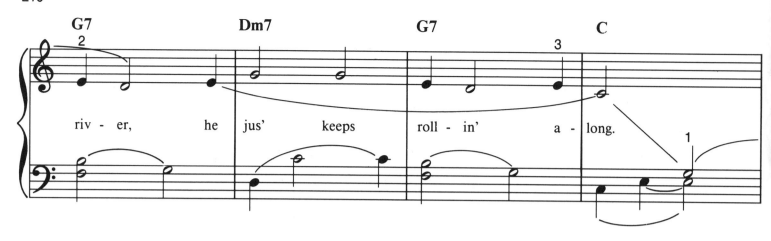

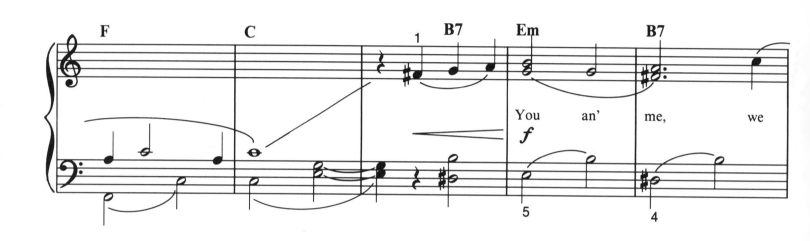

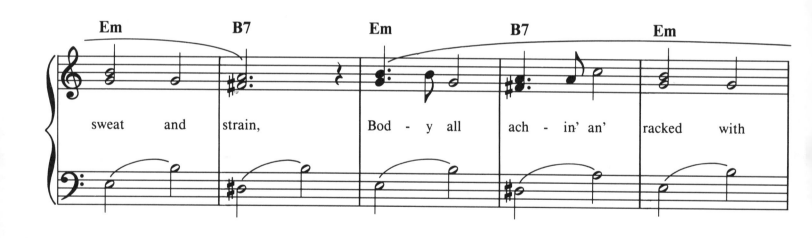

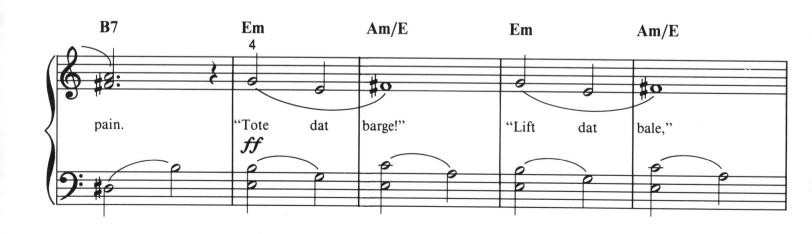

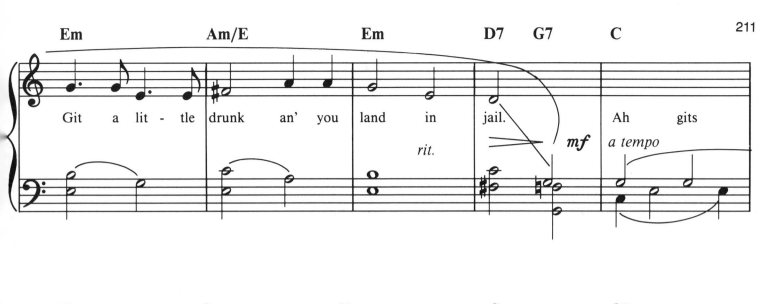

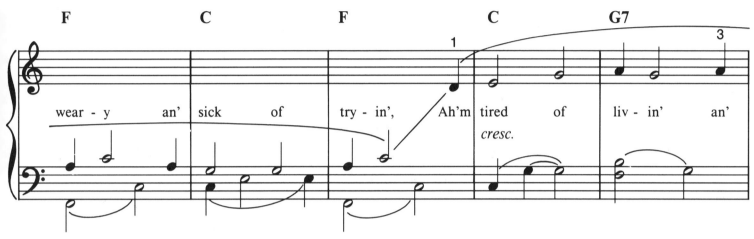

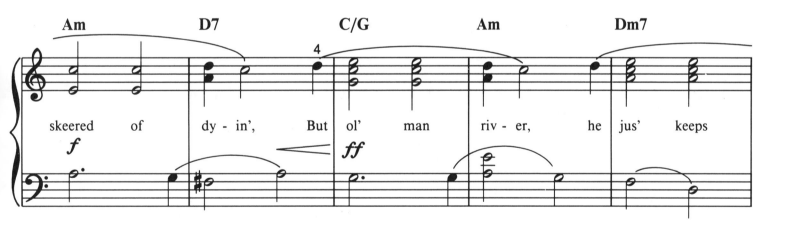

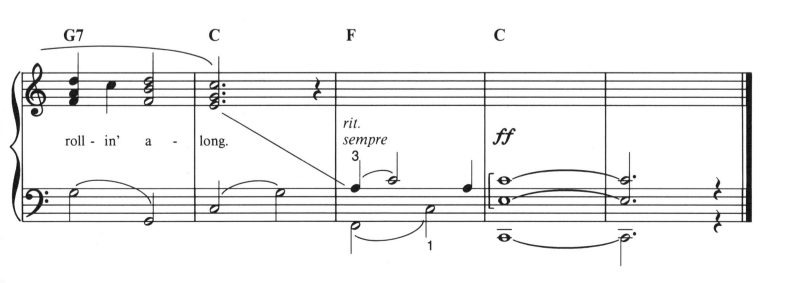

OLD DEVIL MOON
(From "FINIAN'S RAINBOW")

Words by E.Y. HARBURG
Music by BURTON LANE

Moderately

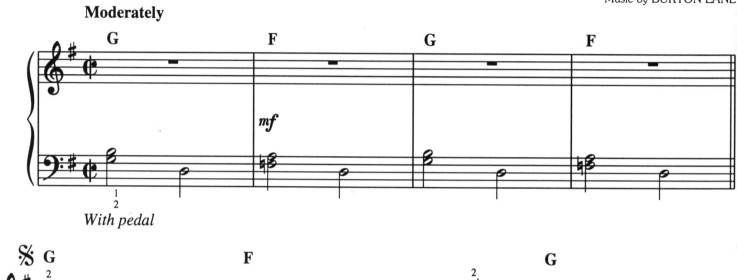

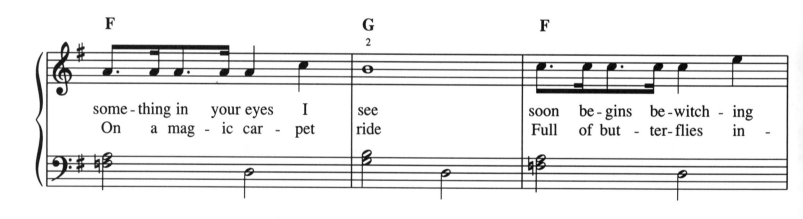

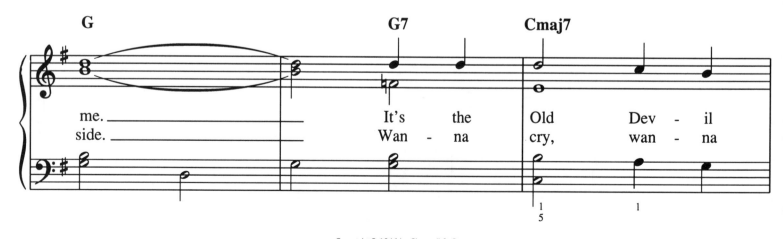

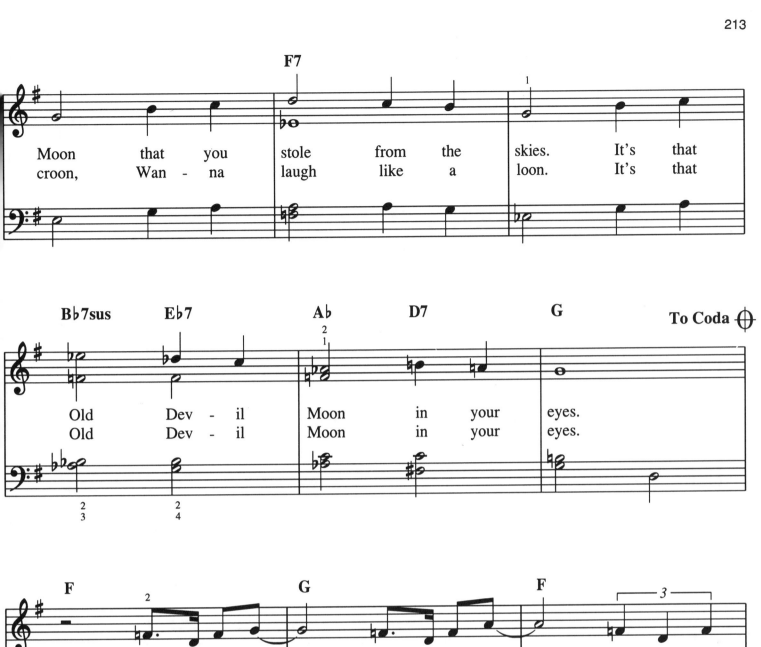

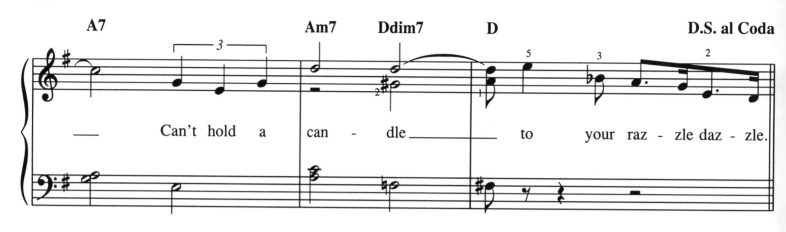

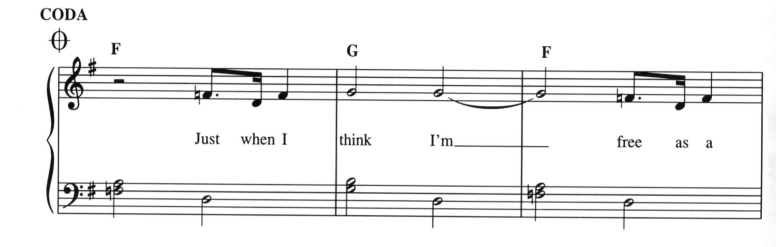

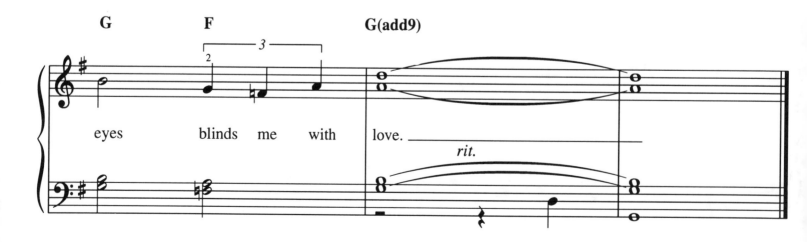

ONE MINT JULEP

Words and Music by
RUDOLPH TOOMBS

Slow Rock

ONE NOTE SAMBA
(Samba De Uma Nota So)

Original Lyrics by NEWTON MENDONCA
English Lyrics by ANTONIO CARLOS JOBIM
Music by ANTONIO CARLOS JOBIM

one we've just ___ been through   through   As I'm bound to be ___ the

un - a - void - a - ble   con - se quence _ of   you.

There's so man - y peo - ple who can   talk and talk and talk and just say

no - thing, ___ or near - ly   no - thing. ___

E♭m7 ... A♭7

I have used up all the scale I know and at the end I've come to

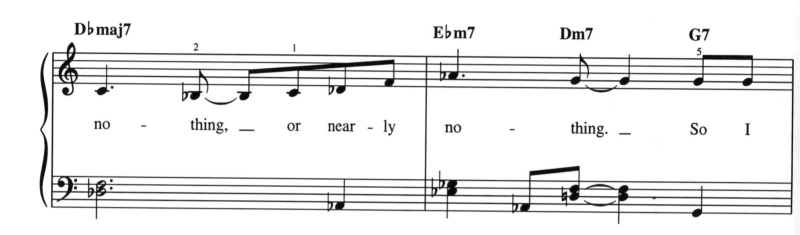

D♭maj7 ... E♭m7 ... Dm7 ... G7

no - thing, __ or near - ly no - thing. __ So I

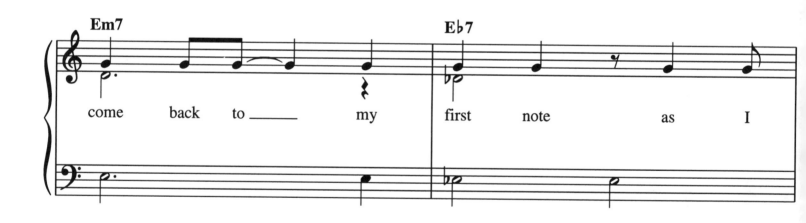

Em7 ... E♭7

come back to _____ my first note as I

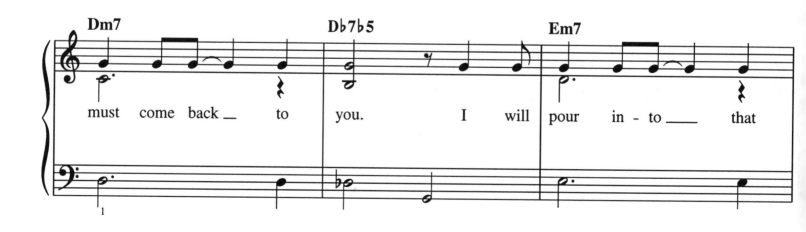

Dm7 ... D♭7♭5 ... Em7

must come back __ to you. I will pour in - to _____ that

POLKA DOTS AND MOONBEAMS

Words by JOHNNY BURKE
Music by JIMMY VAN HEUSEN

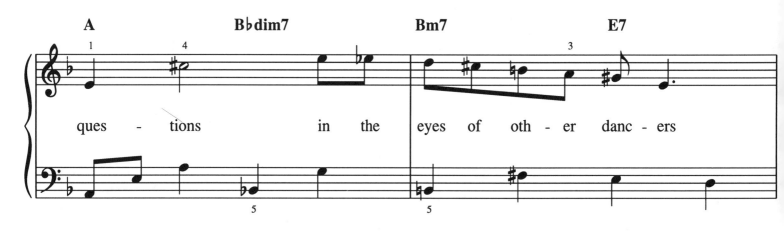

A   **B♭dim7**   **Bm7**   **E7**

ques - tions   in the   eyes of oth - er danc - ers

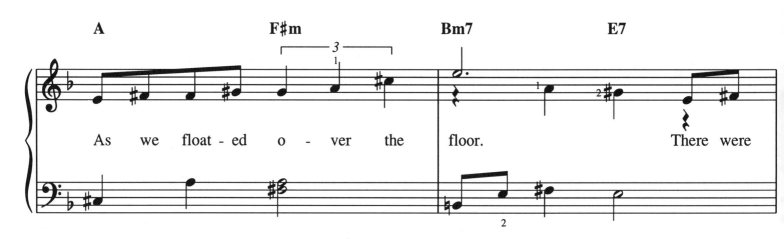

A   **F♯m**   **Bm7**   **E7**

As we float - ed o - ver the   floor.   There were

A   **B♭dim7**   **Bm7**   **E7**

ques - tions   but my   heart knew all the an - swers,

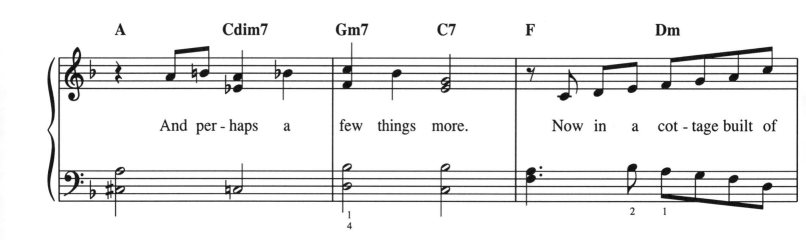

A   **Cdim7**   **Gm7**   **C7**   **F**   **Dm**

And per - haps a   few things more.   Now in a cot - tage built of

QUIET NIGHTS OF QUIET STARS
(Corcovado)

English Words by GENE LEES
Original Words and Music by ANTONIO CARLOS JOBIM

Moderately slow

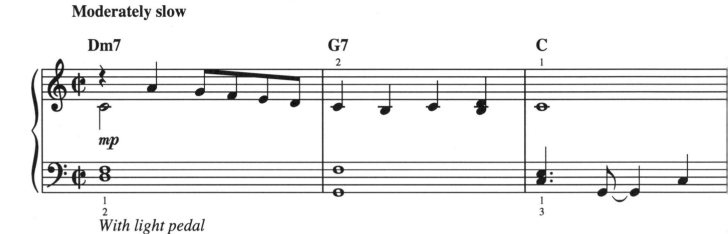
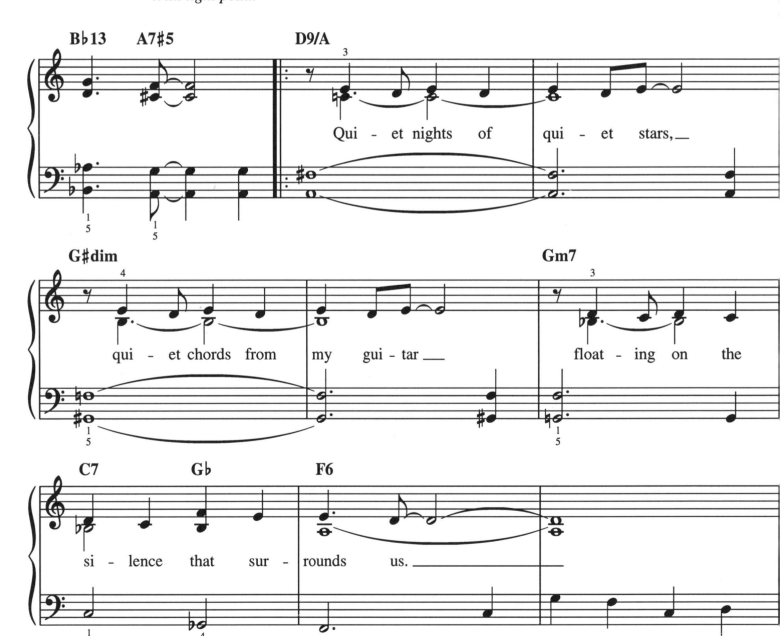

With light pedal

Qui - et nights of qui - et stars,__

qui - et chords from my gui - tar __ float - ing on the

si - lence that sur - rounds us. ___

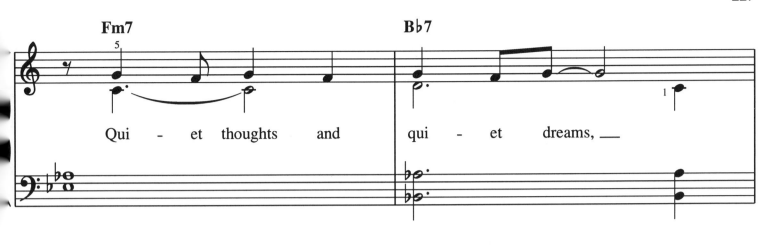

Qui - et thoughts and qui - et dreams, __

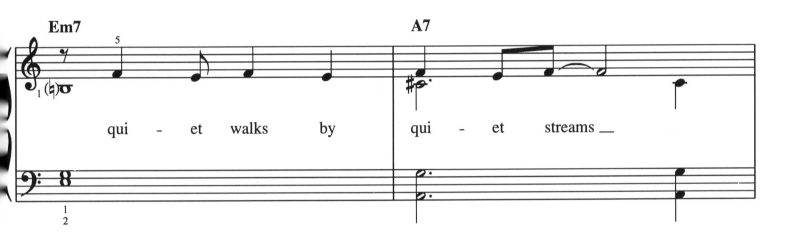

qui - et walks by qui - et streams __

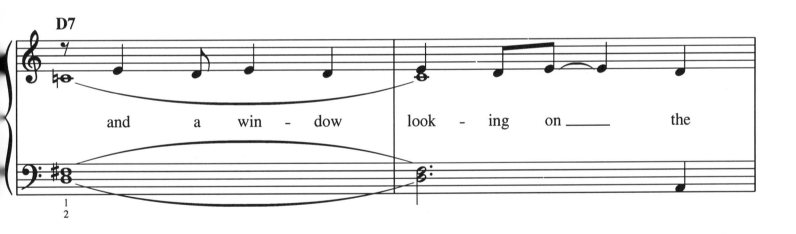

and a win - dow look - ing on ____ the

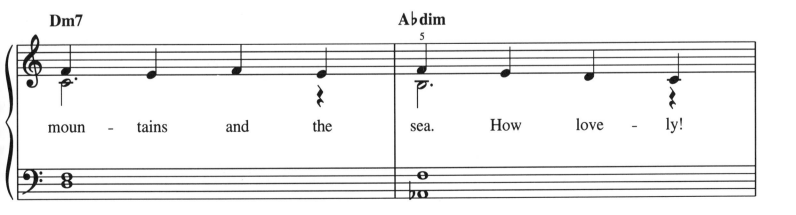

moun - tains and the sea. How love - ly!

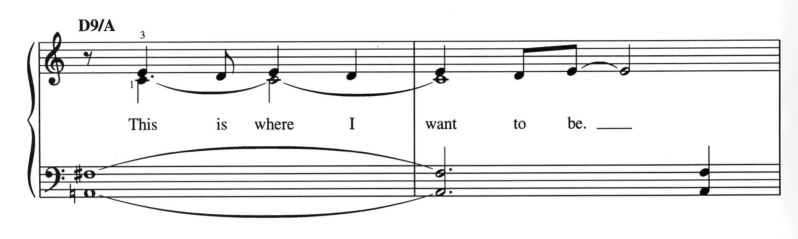

This is where I want to be. ____

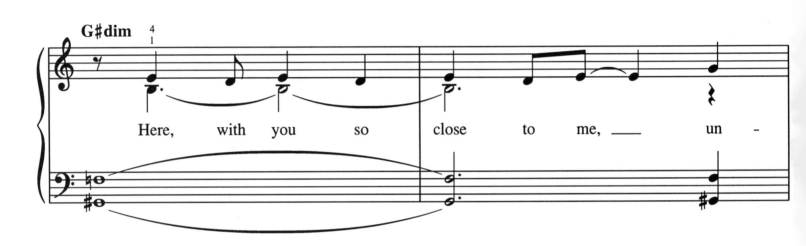

Here, with you so close to me, ____ un -

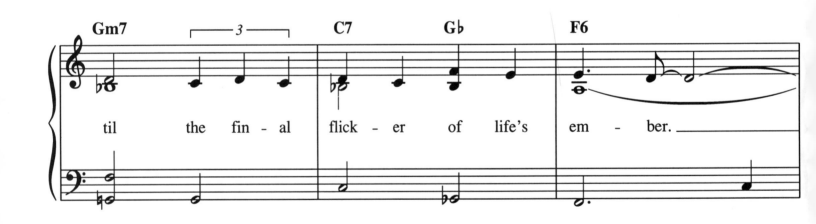

til the fin - al flick - er of life's em - ber. ____

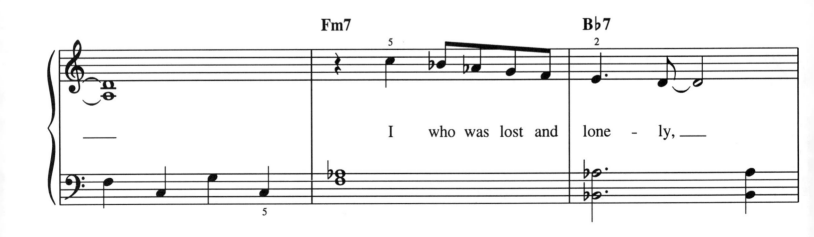

____ I who was lost and lone - ly, ____

SATIN DOLL

Words by JOHNNY MERCER
Music by BILLY STRAYHORN and DUKE ELLINGTON

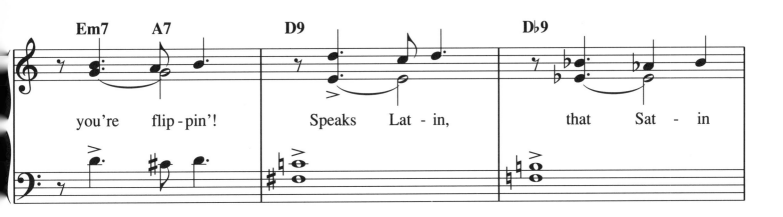

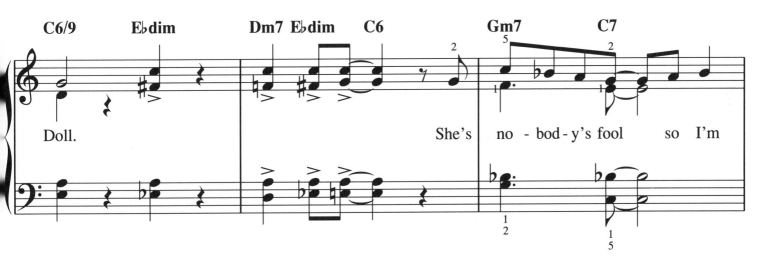

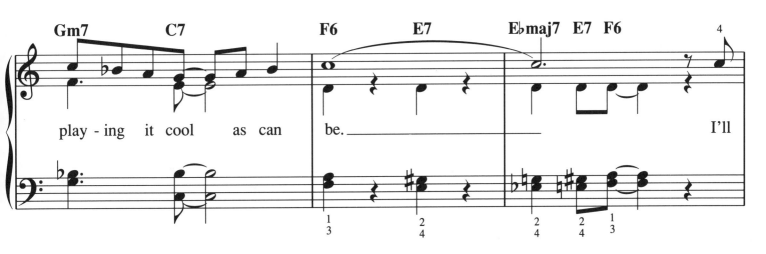

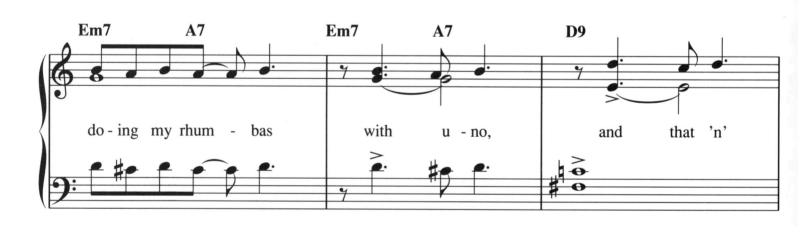

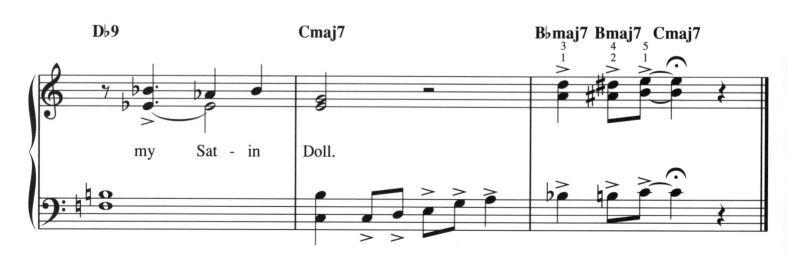

SKYLARK

Words by JOHNNY MERCER
Music by HOAGY CARMICHAEL

235

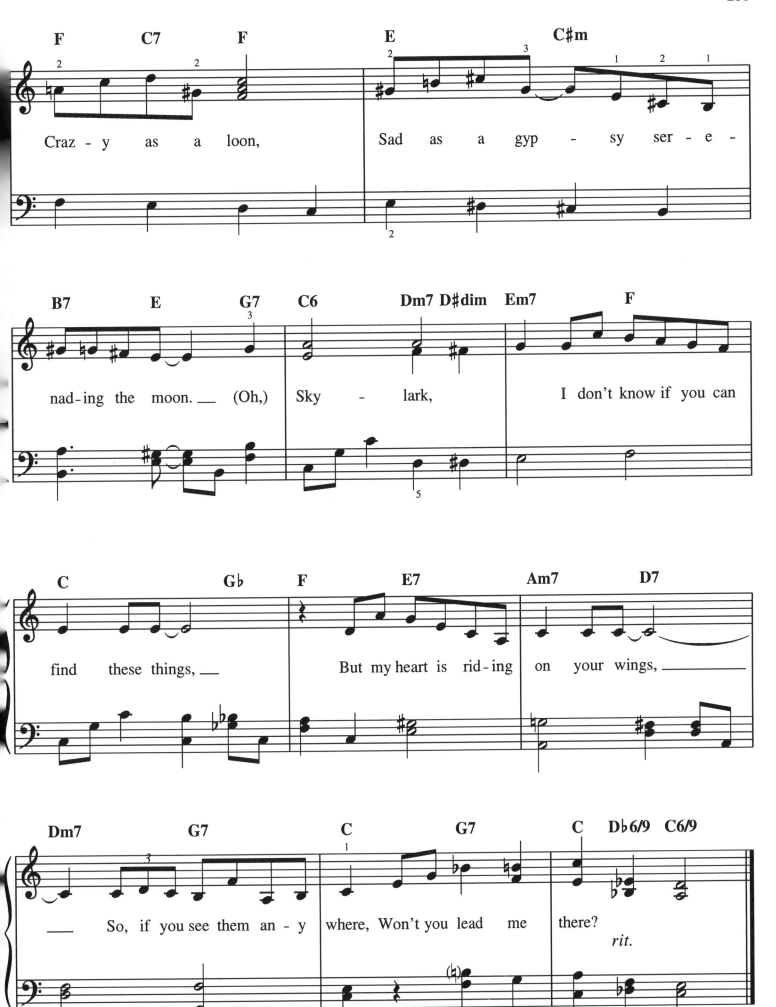

SLIGHTLY OUT OF TUNE
(Desafinado)

English Lyric by JON HENDRICKS and JESSIE CAVANAUGH
Original Text by NEWTON MENDONCA
Music by ANTONIO CARLOS JOBIM

Moderately

238

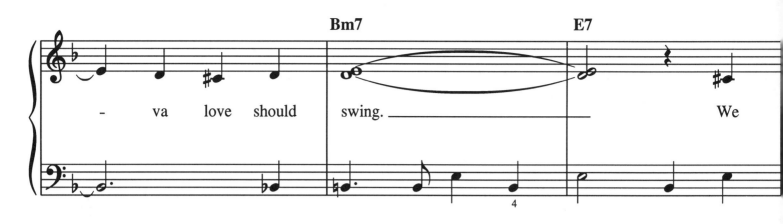

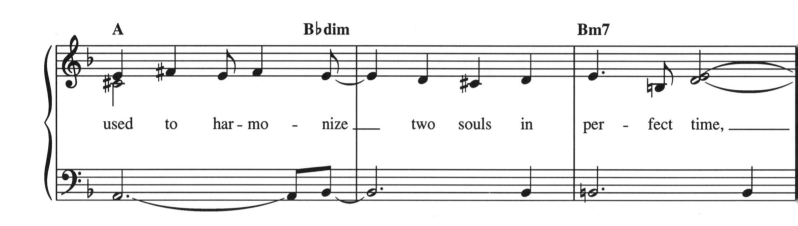

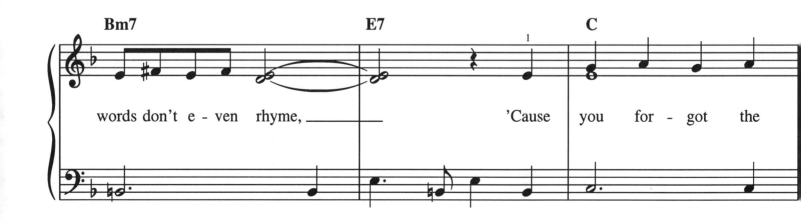

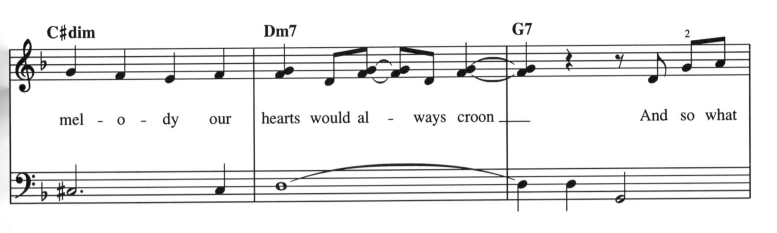

mel - o - dy our hearts would al - ways croon____ And so what

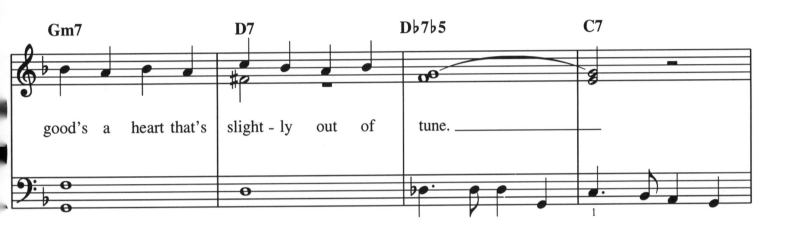

good's a heart that's slight-ly out of tune.____

Tune your heart to mine the way it used to be,____

____ Join with me in har - mo - ny and

sing   a   song   of   lov - ing.   We're   bound   to   get   in   tune   a - gain   be -

fore   too   long.   There'll   be   no   de - sa - fi - na - do

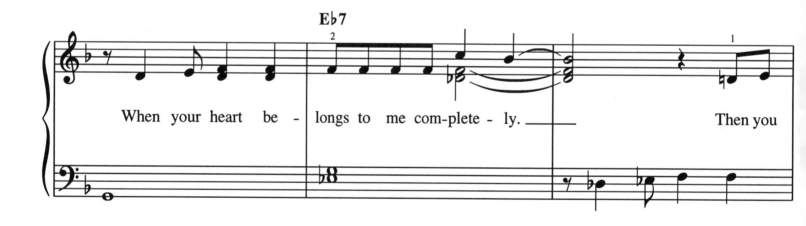

When   your   heart   be - longs   to   me   com-plete - ly. _____   Then   you

won't be slight-ly out of   tune,   You'll sing a - long   with   me.

SMOKE GETS IN YOUR EYES
(From "ROBERTA")

Words by OTTO HARBACH
Music by JEROME KERN

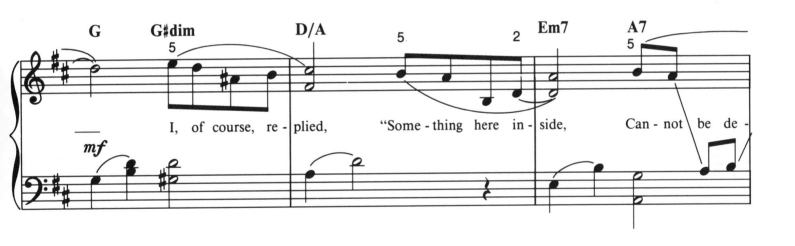

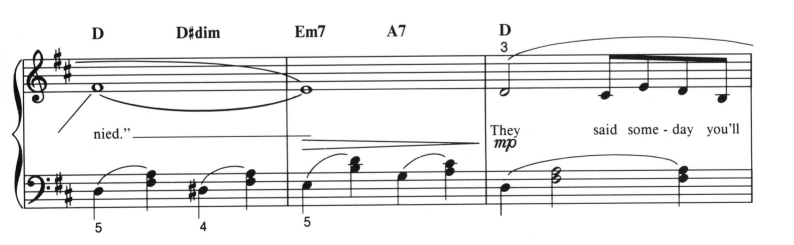

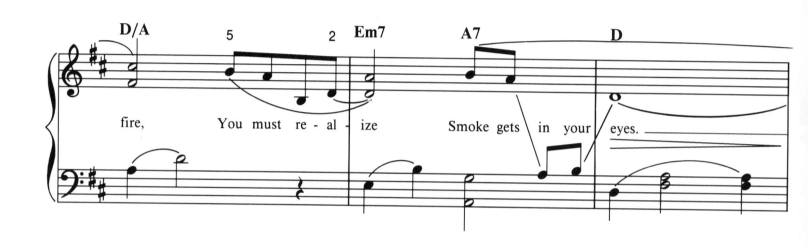

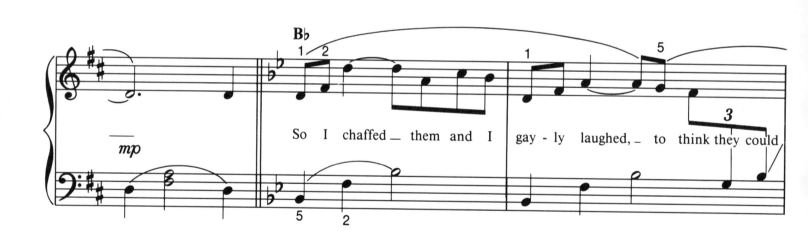

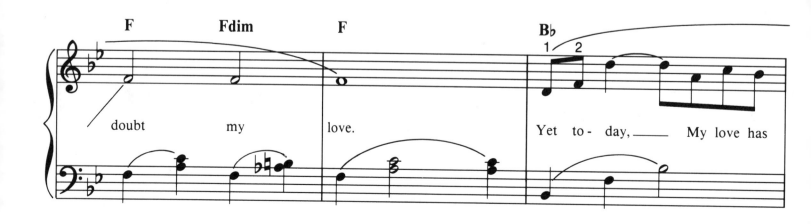

243

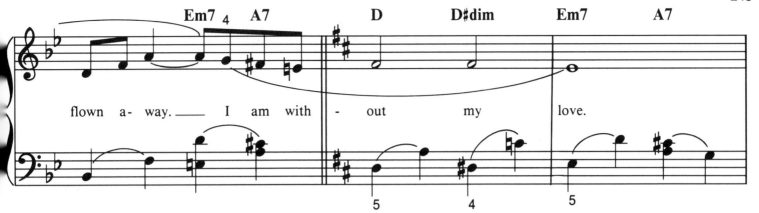

flown a- way. ___ I am with - out my love.

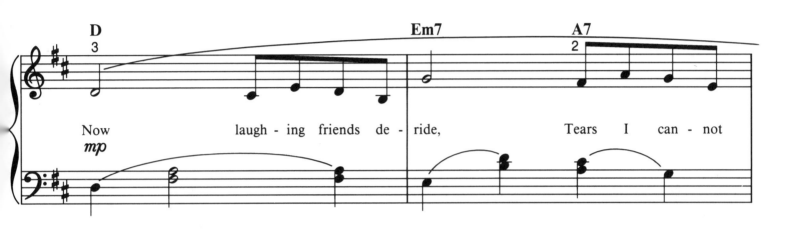

Now laugh - ing friends de - ride, Tears I can - not
mp

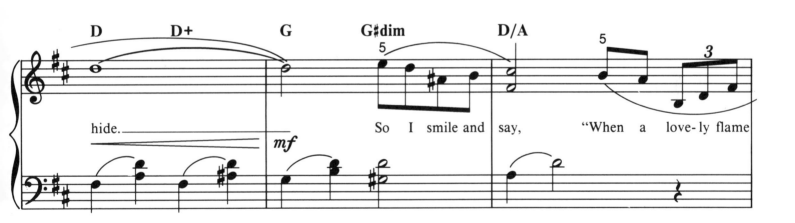

hide. ___ So I smile and say, "When a love- ly flame
mf

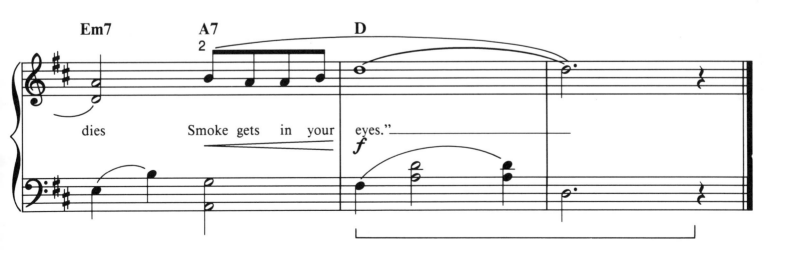

dies Smoke gets in your eyes." ___
f

SOMEDAY MY PRINCE WILL COME

(From "SNOW WHITE AND THE SEVEN DWARFS)

Words by LARRY MOREY
Music by FRANK CHURCHILL

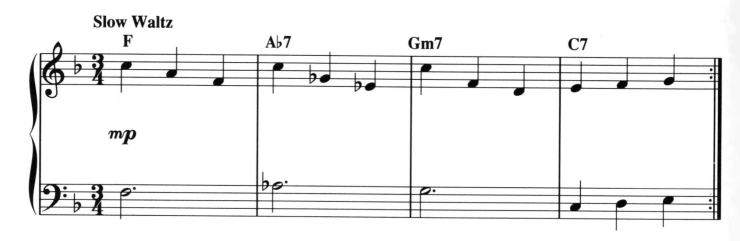

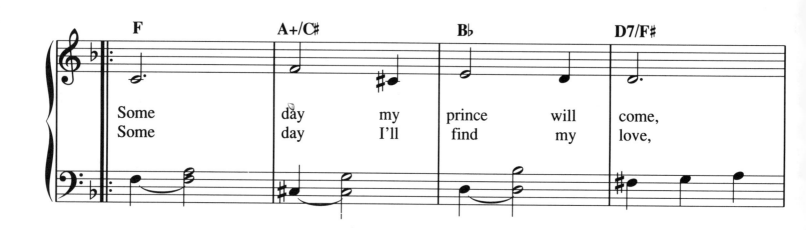

Some day my prince will come,
Some day I'll find my love,

Some day I'll find my love and how
Some one to call my own, and I'll

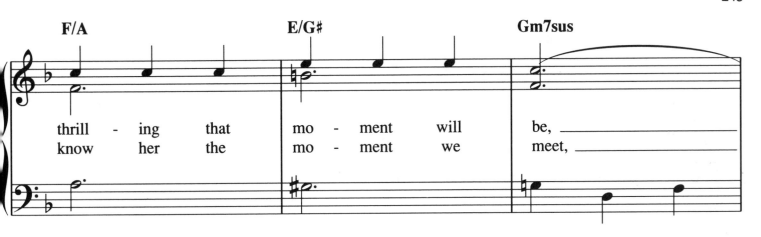

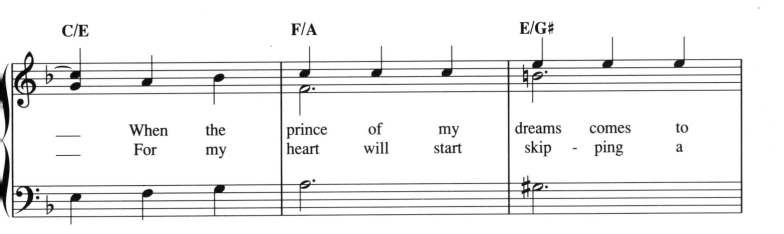

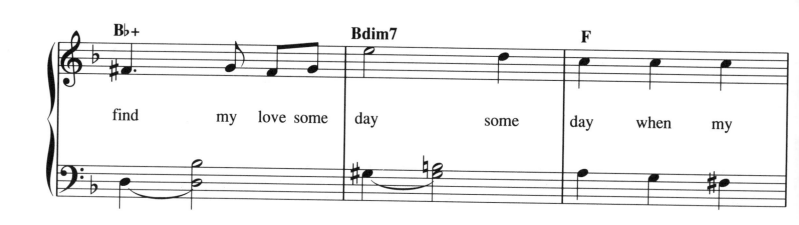

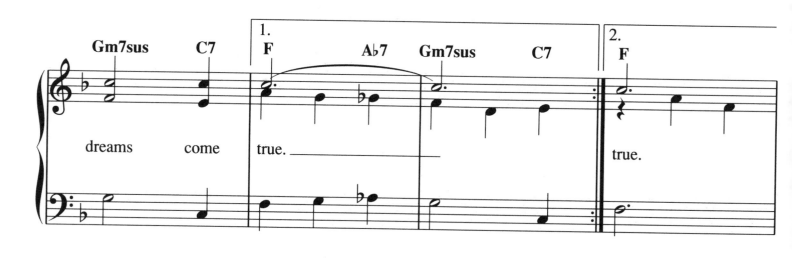

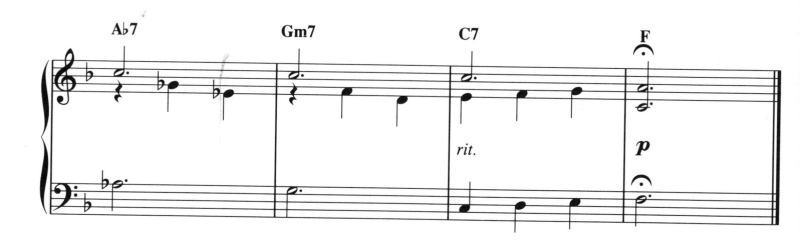

SPEAK LOW
(From The Musical Production "ONE TOUCH OF VENUS")

Words by OGDEN NASH
Music by KURT WEILL

248

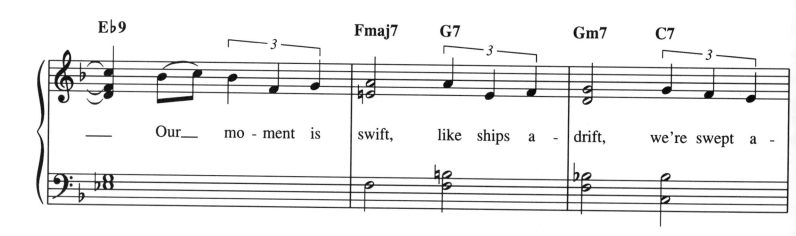

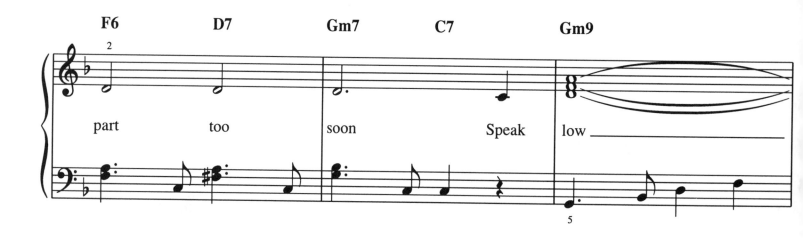

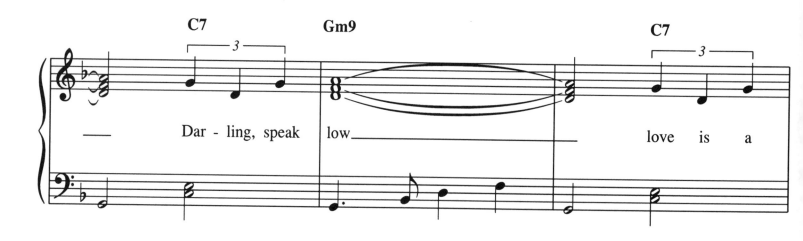

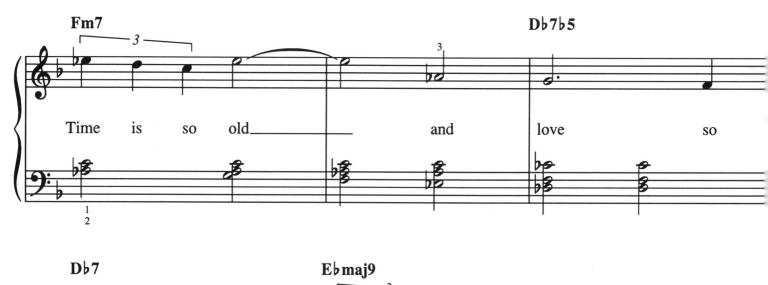

Time is so old___ and love so

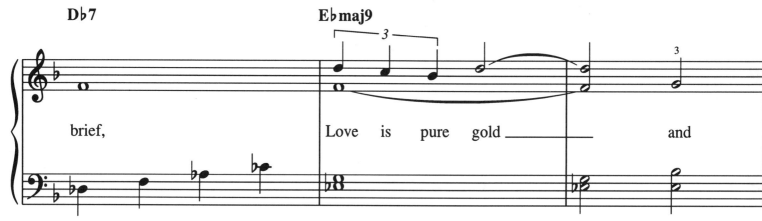

brief, Love is pure gold___ and

time a thief. We're late___

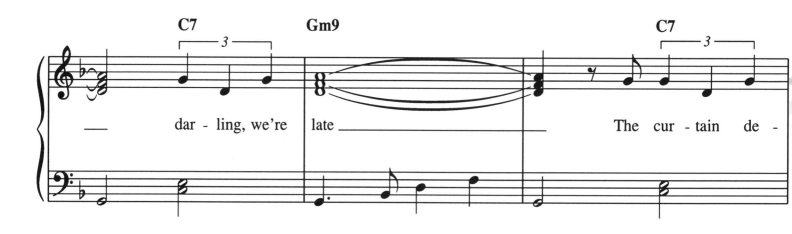

___ dar - ling, we're late___ The cur - tain de -

SPRING CAN REALLY HANG YOU UP THE MOST

Lyrics by FRAN LANDESMAN
Music by TOMMY WOLF

Slowly

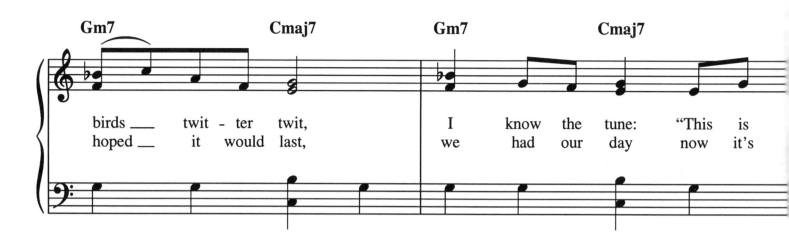

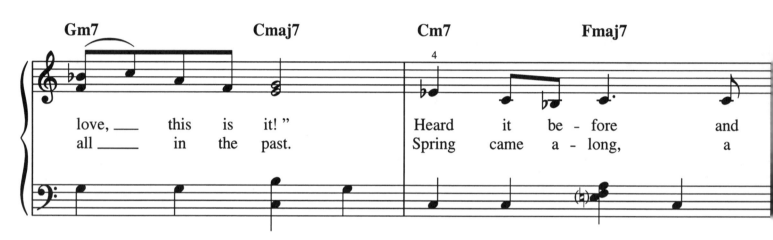

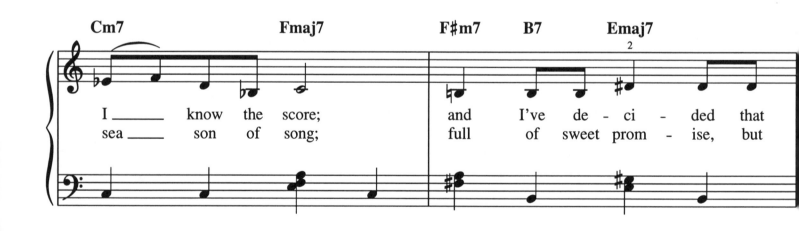

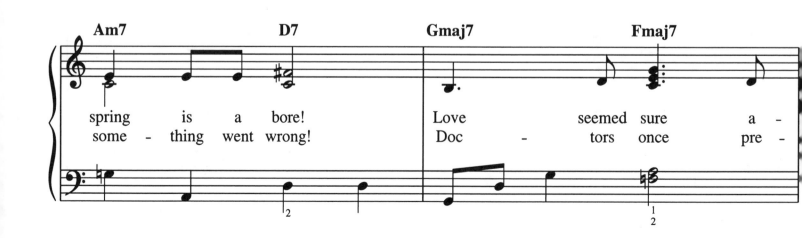

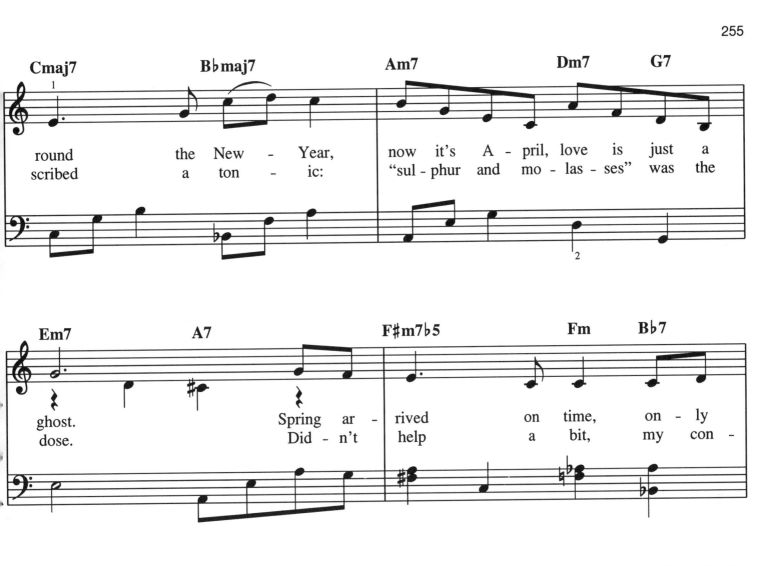

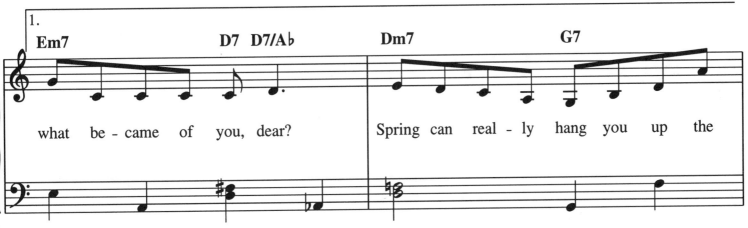

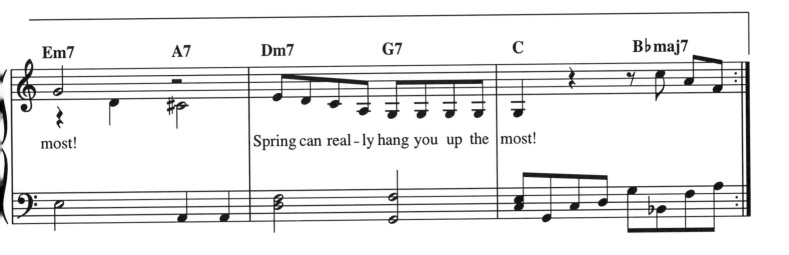

STOMPIN' AT THE SAVOY

Words and Music by BENNY GOODMAN, ANDY RAZAF,
CHICK WEBB and EDGAR SAMPSON

258

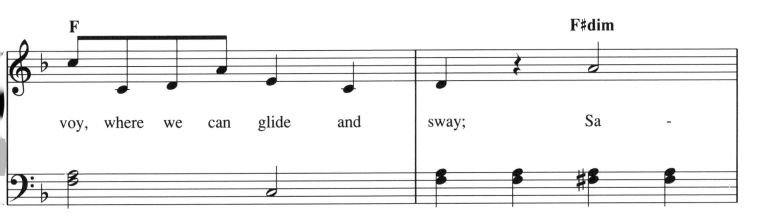

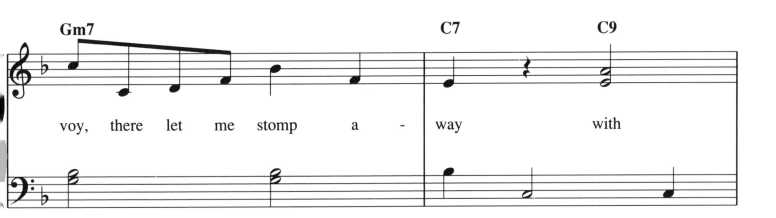

STORMY WEATHER
(KEEPS RAININ' ALL THE TIME)

Lyric by TED KOEHLER
Music by HAROLD ARLEN

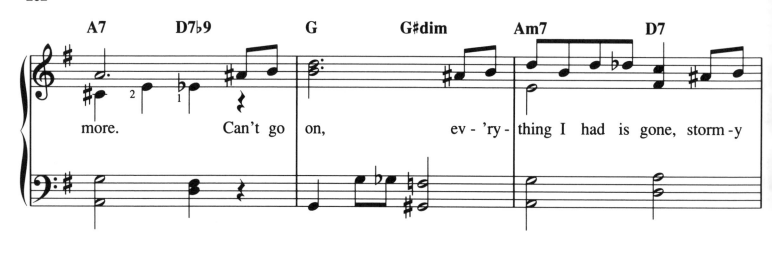

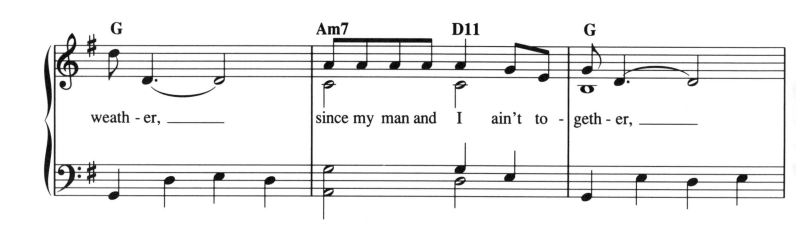

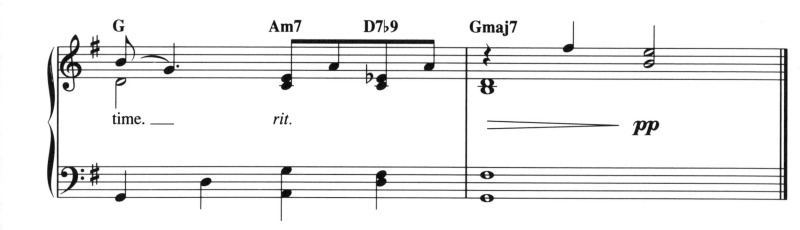

SUMMER SAMBA
(SO NICE)

Original Words and Music by MARCOS VALLE and PAULO SERGIO VALLE
English Words by NORMAN GIMBEL

MCA music publishing

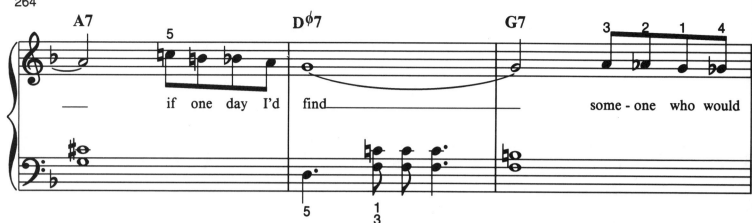

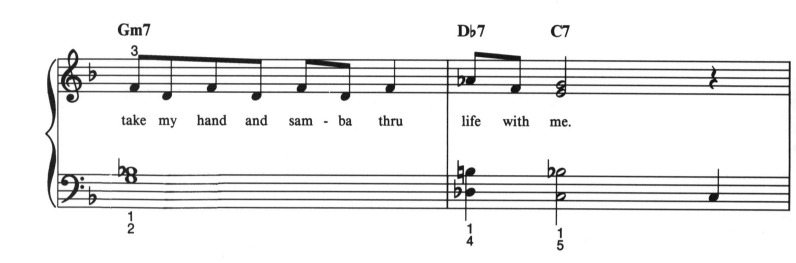

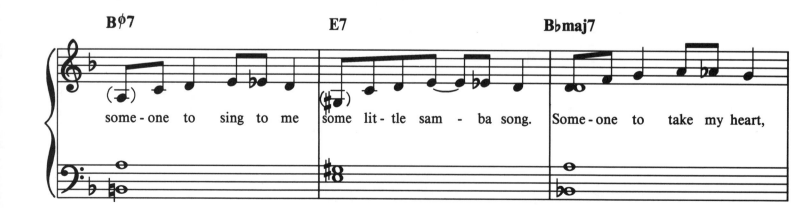

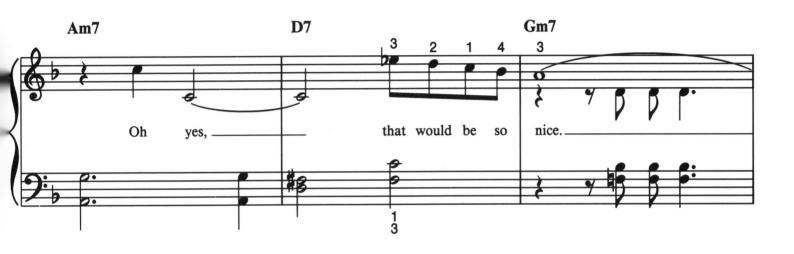

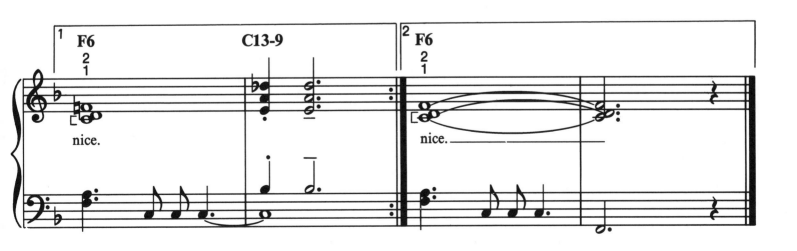

A SUNDAY KIND OF LOVE

Words and Music by BARBARA BELLE,
LOUIS PRIMA, ANITA LEONARD and STAN RHODES

MCA music publishing

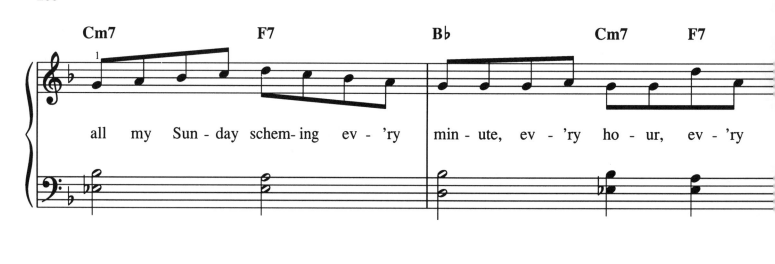

all my Sun - day schem - ing ev - 'ry min - ute, ev - 'ry ho - ur, ev - 'ry

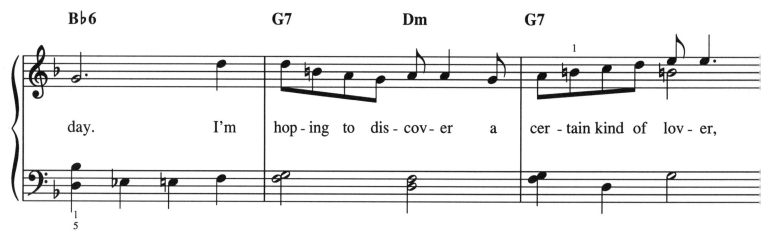

day.   I'm hop - ing to dis - cov - er   a cer - tain kind of lov - er,

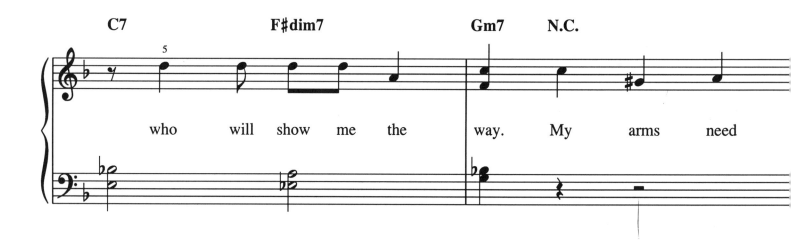

who will show me the way.   My arms need

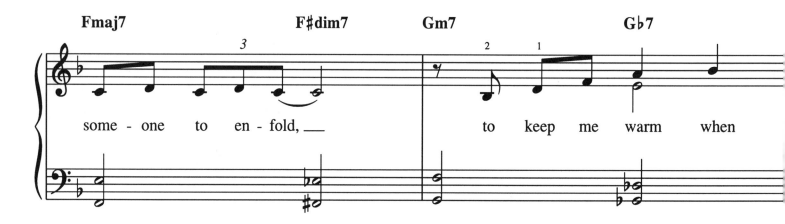

some - one to en - fold, ___   to keep me warm when

269

SWEET GEORGIA BROWN

Words and Music by BEN BERNIE
MACEO PINKARD and KENNETH CASE

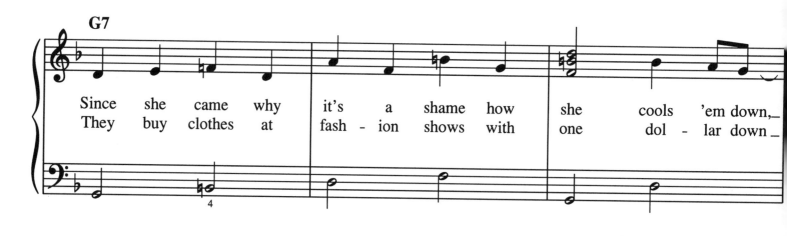

Since she came why it's a shame how she cools 'em down,—
They buy clothes at fash - ion shows with one dol - lar down—

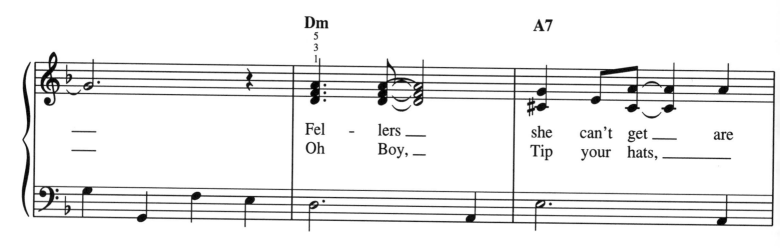

— Fel - lers — she can't get — are
— Oh Boy, — Tip your hats, —

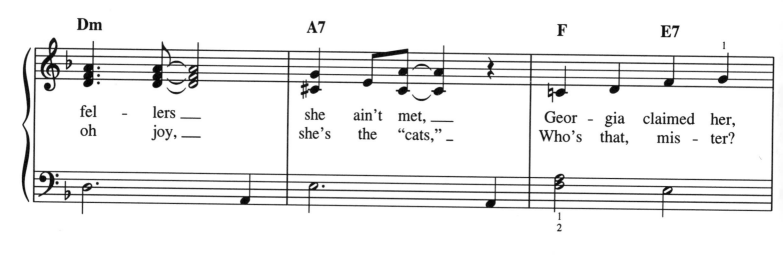

fel - lers — she ain't met, — Geor - gia claimed her,
oh joy, — she's the "cats," — Who's that, mis - ter?

Geor - gia named her sweet Geor - gia Brown.
'Tain't her sis - ter sweet Geor - gia Brown.

THAT'S LIFE

Words and Music by DEAN KAY
and KELLY GORDON

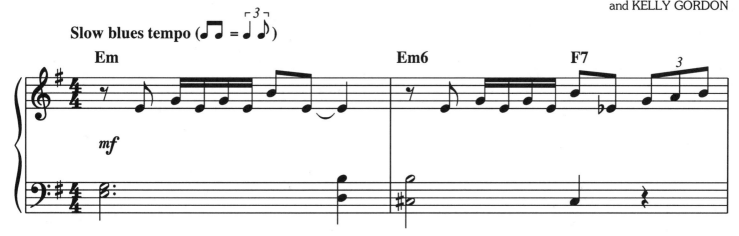

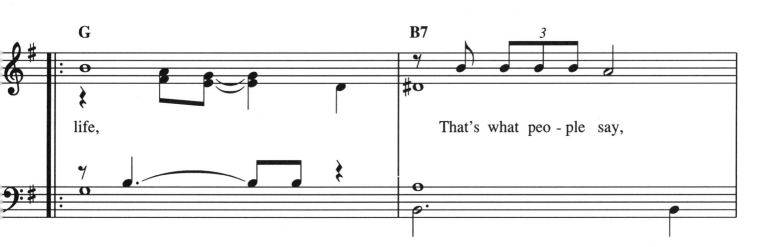

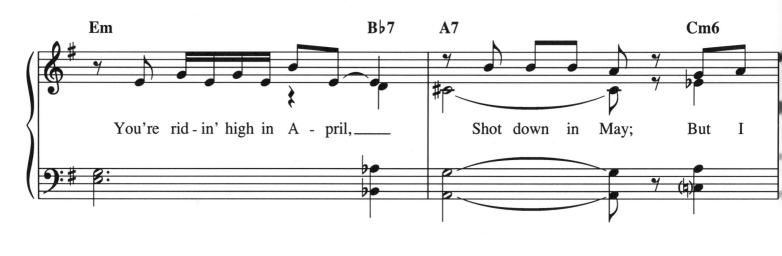

You're rid-in' high in A - pril,_____ Shot down in May; But I

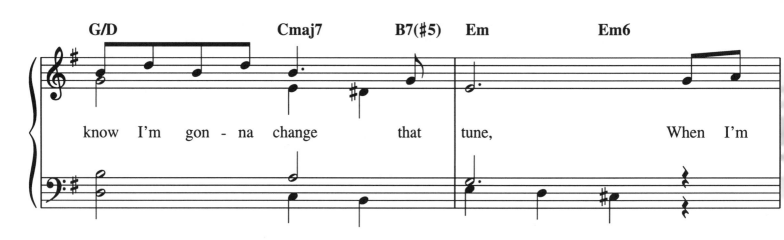

know I'm gon - na change that tune, When I'm

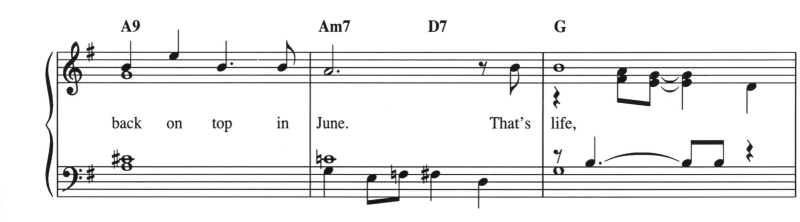

back on top in June. That's life,

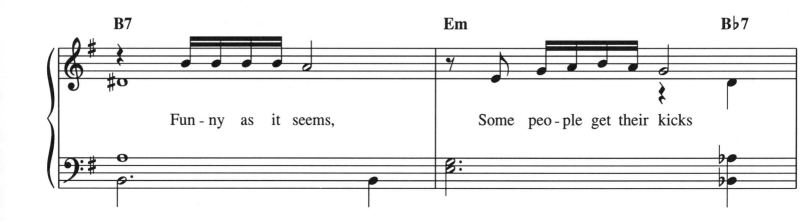

Fun - ny as it seems, Some peo-ple get their kicks

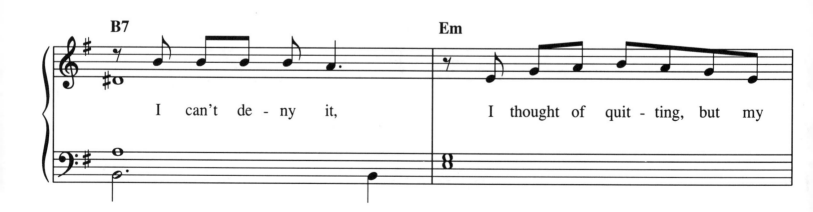

THERE'S A SMALL HOTEL
(From "ON YOUR TOES")

Words by LORENZ HART
Music by RICHARD RODGERS

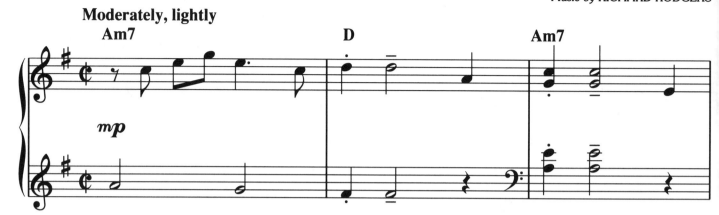

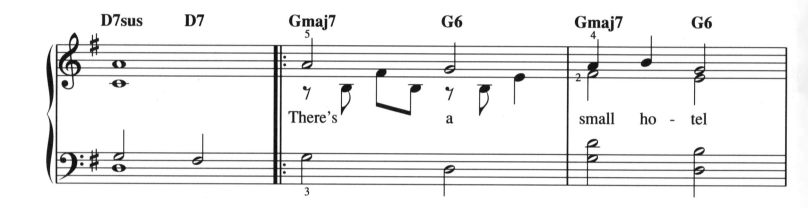

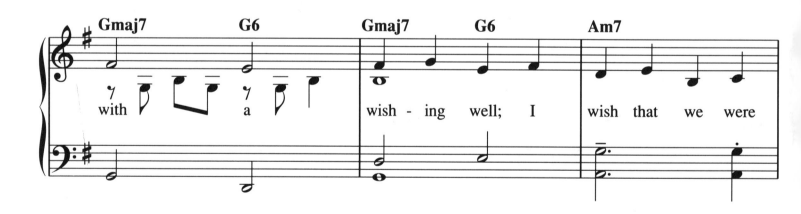

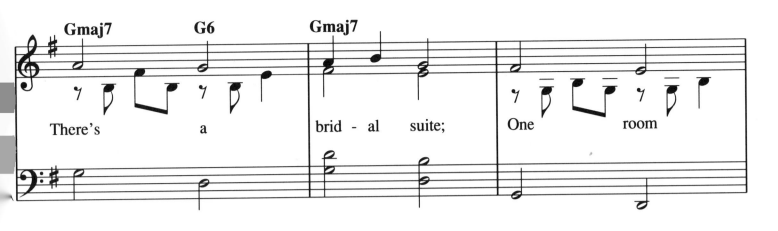

There's   a   brid - al   suite;   One   room

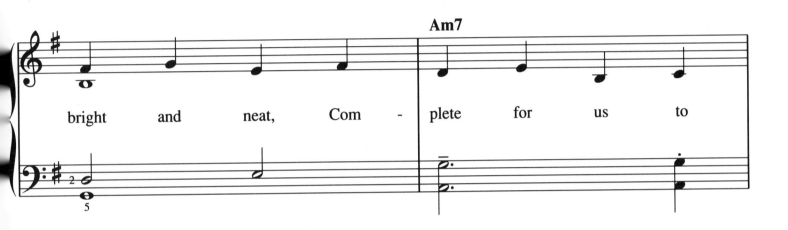

bright   and   neat,   Com -   plete   for   us   to

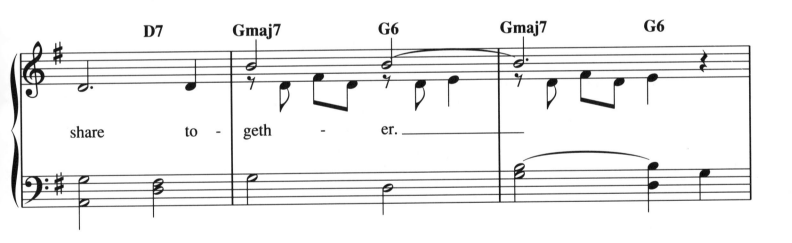

share   to - geth   -   er. _____

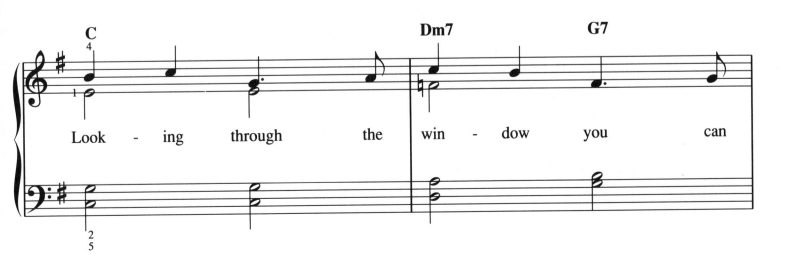

Look - ing   through   the   win - dow   you   can

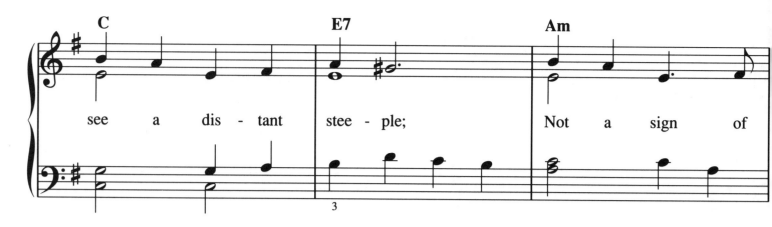

see a dis - tant stee - ple; Not a sign of

peo - ple, Who wants peo - ple?

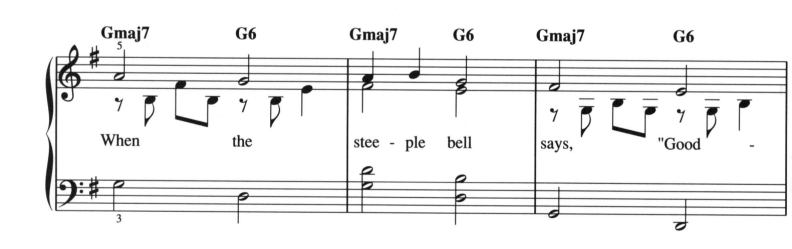

When the stee - ple bell says, "Good -

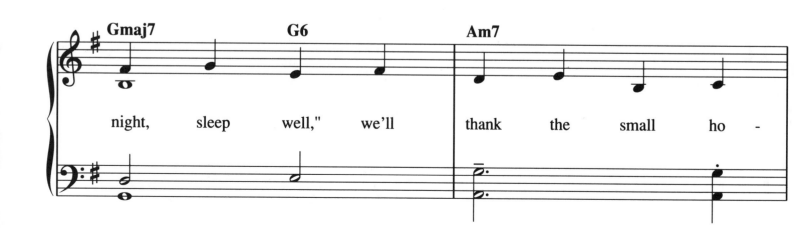

night, sleep well," we'll thank the small ho -

THEY CAN'T TAKE THAT AWAY FROM ME

(From "THE BARKLEYS OF BROADWAY")

Music and Lyrics by GEORGE GERSHWIN
and IRA GERSHWIN

The way you haunt my dreams,

F C+ F9

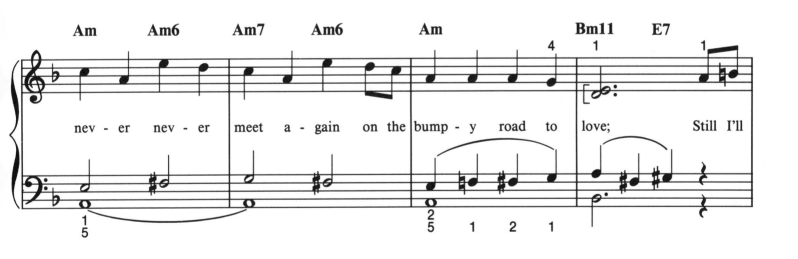

F6 C+ F9 B♭ C13-9 F6

smoothly

No, no, they can't take that a-way from me We may

Am Am6 Am7 Am6 Am Bm11 E7

nev-er nev-er meet a-gain on the bump-y road to love; Still I'll

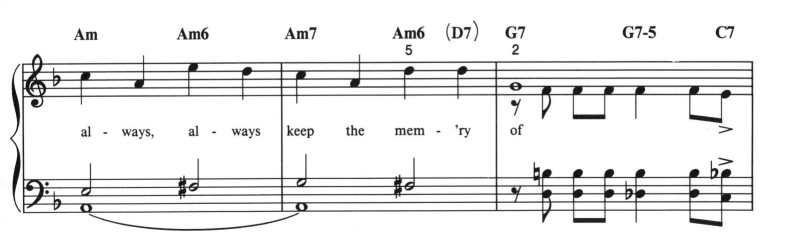

Am Am6 Am7 Am6 (D7) G7 G7-5 C7

al-ways, al-ways keep the mem-'ry of

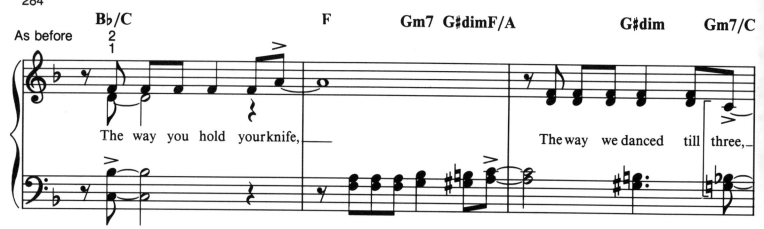

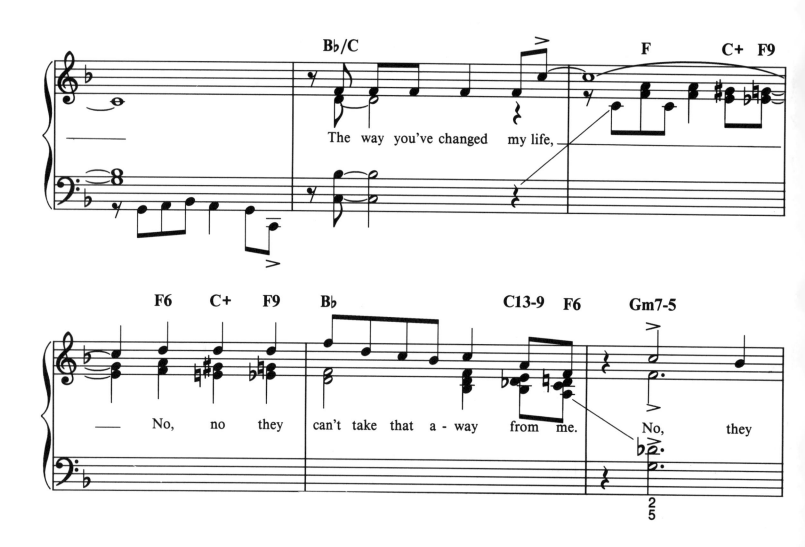

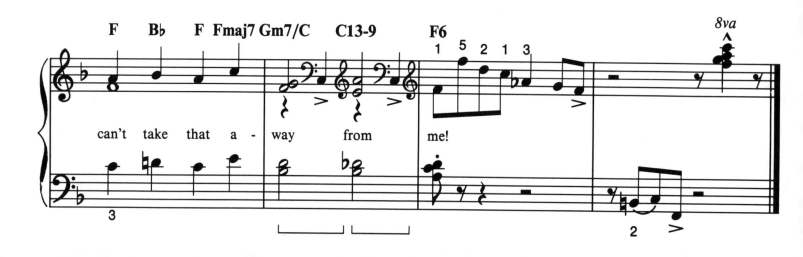

THE THINGS WE DID LAST SUMMER

Words and Music by SAMMY CAHN
and JULE STYNE

The

boat rides we would take, the
mid - way and the fun, the

moon-light on the lake, the
kew - pie dolls we won, the

way we danced and hummed our fav - 'rite
bell I rang to prove that I was

song.
strong.

The
The

things we did last sum - mer I'll re -
things we did last sum - mer I'll re -

286

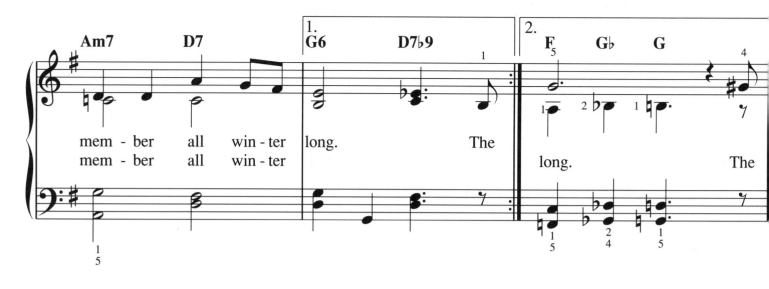

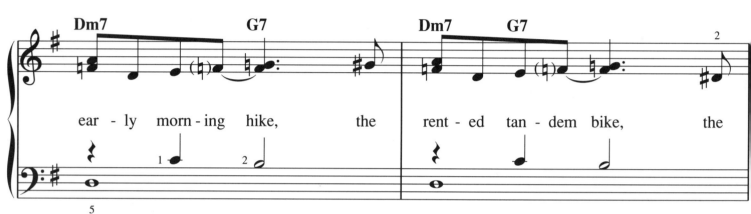

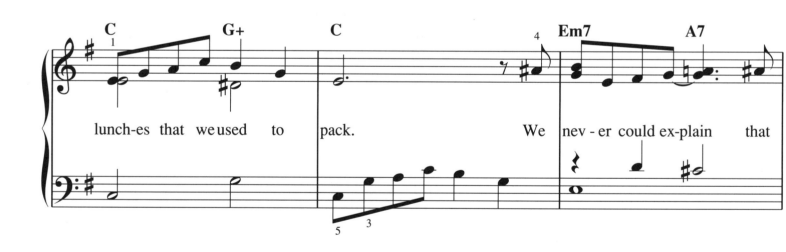

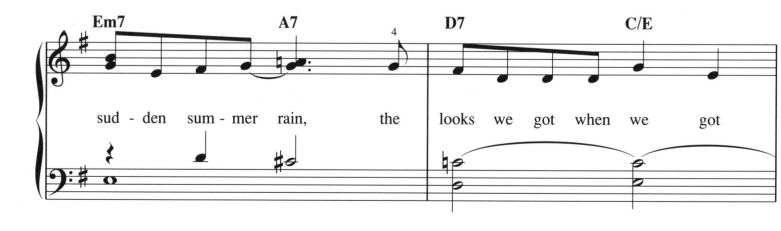

TIME AFTER TIME

(From The Metro-Goldwyn-Mayer Picture "IT HAPPENED IN BROOKLYN")

Words by SAMMY CAHN
Music by JULE STYNE

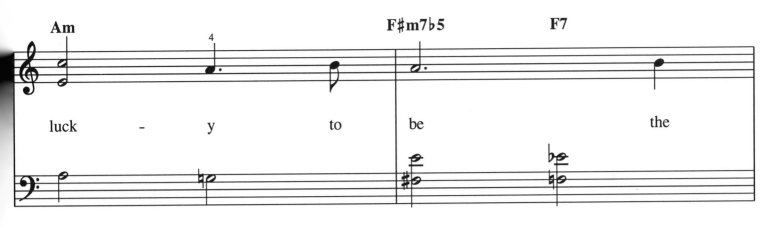

luck - y to be the

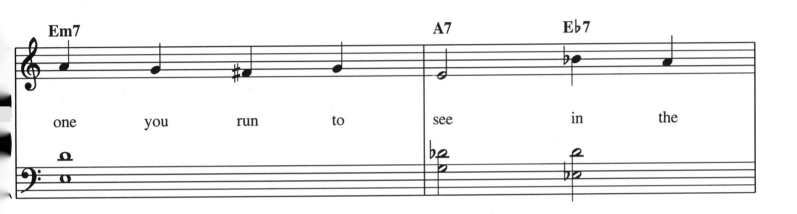

one you run to see in the

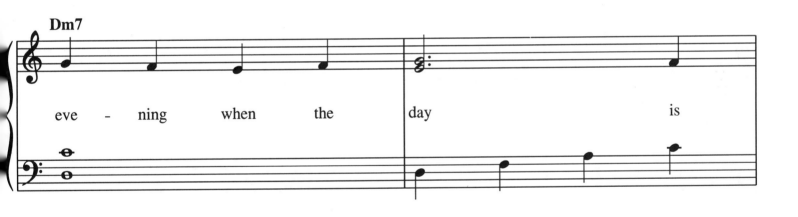

eve - ning when the day is

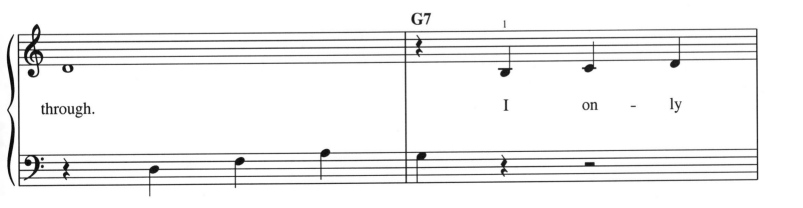

through. I on - ly

290

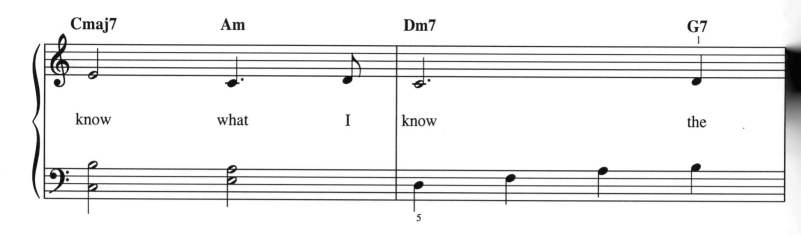

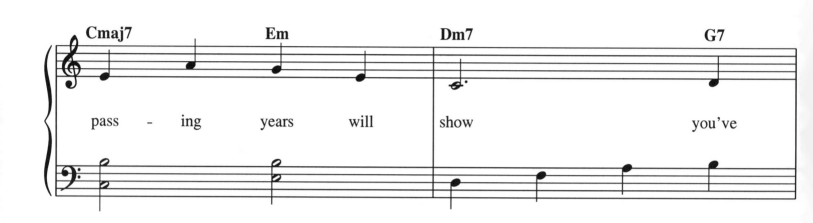

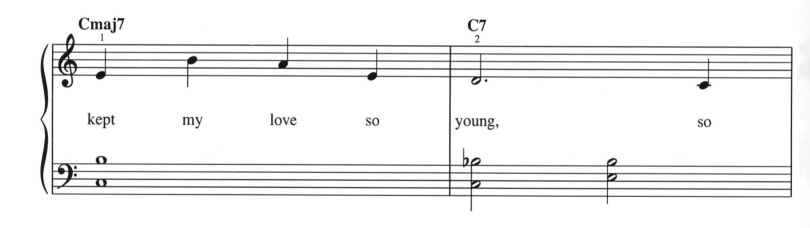

WATCH WHAT HAPPENS

English Words by NORMAN GIMBEL
French Text by JACQUES DEMY
Music by MICHEL LEGRAND

Slow Beguine tempo

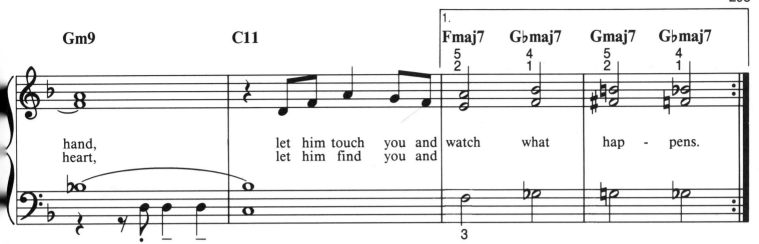

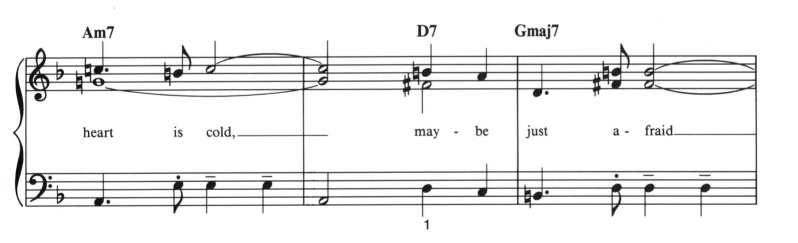

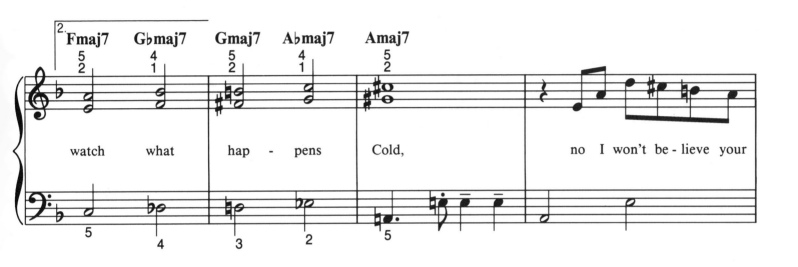

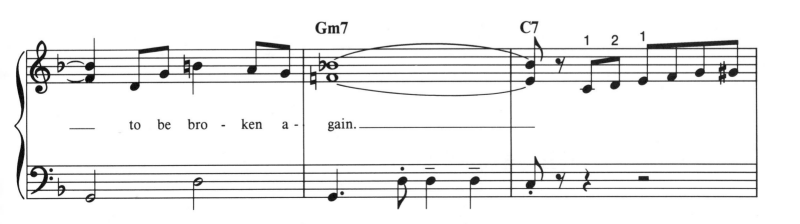

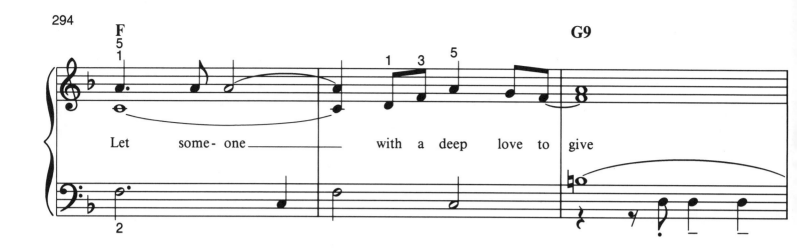

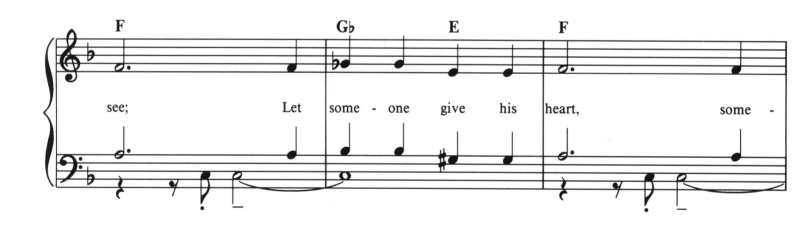

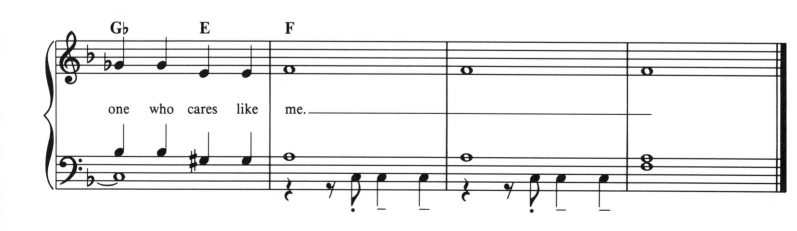

WHAT IS THIS THING
CALLED LOVE?

Words and Music by
COLE PORTER

No pedal - Finger legato bassline

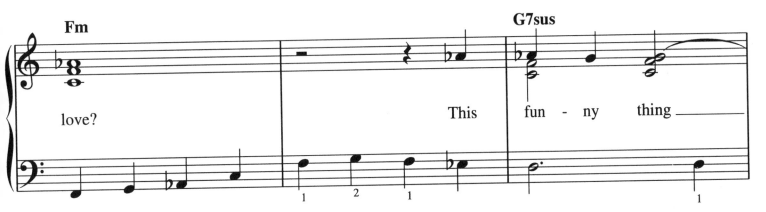

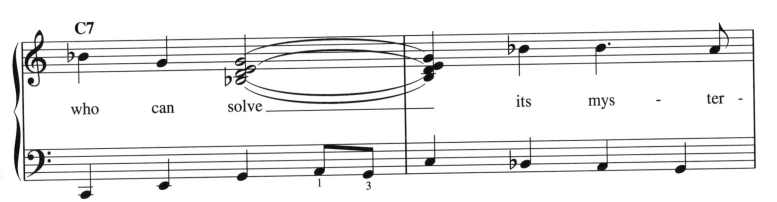

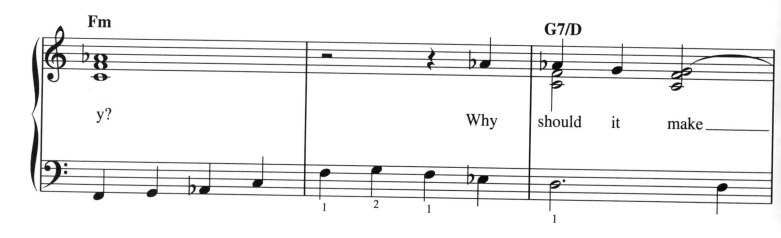

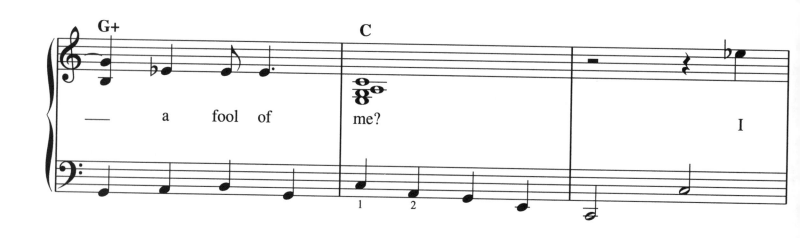

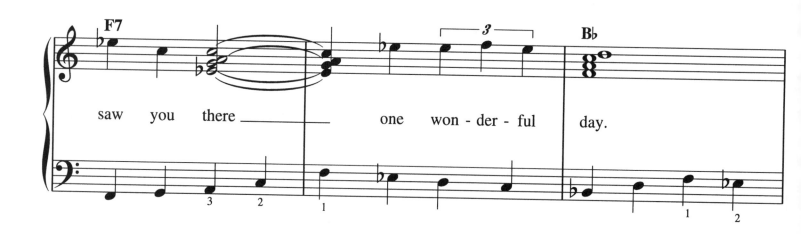

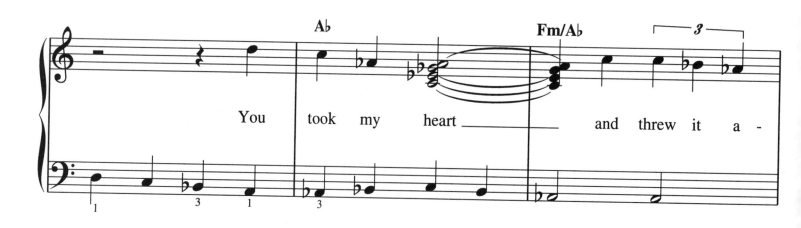

WHAT A DIFF'RENCE A DAY MADE

Lyric by STANLEY ADAMS
Music by MARIA GREVER

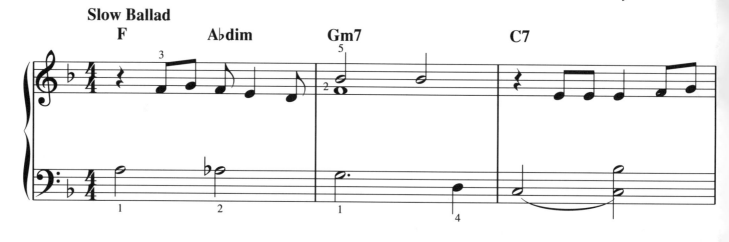

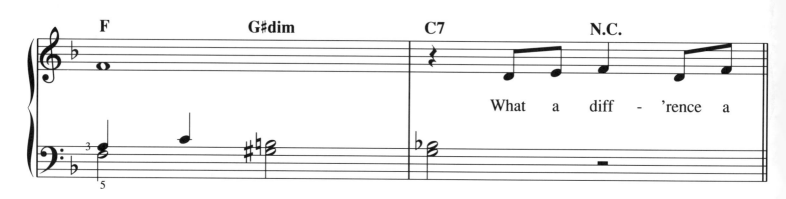

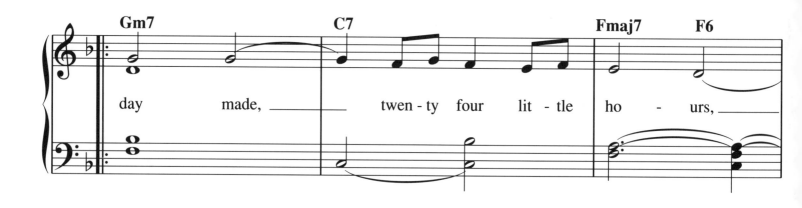

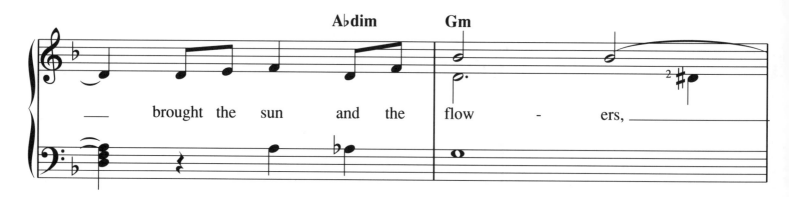

299

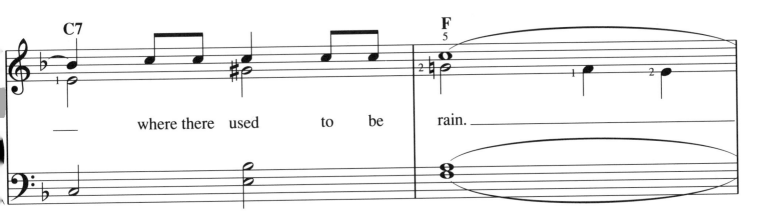

where there used to be rain.

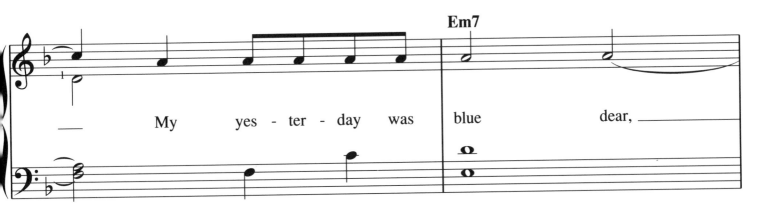

My yes - ter - day was blue dear,

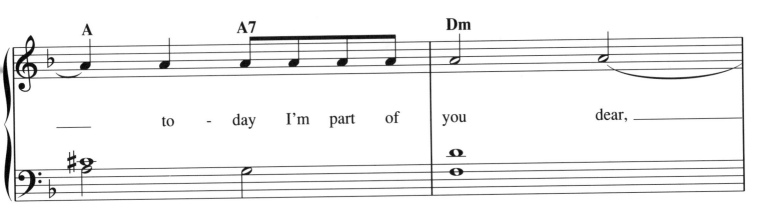

to - day I'm part of you dear,

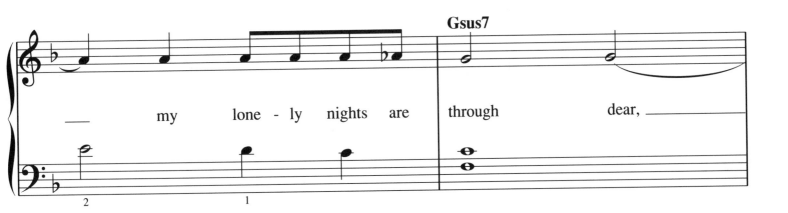

my lone - ly nights are through dear,

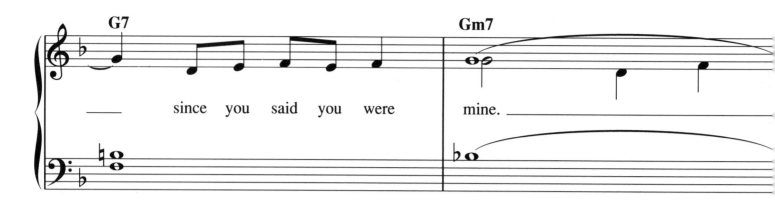

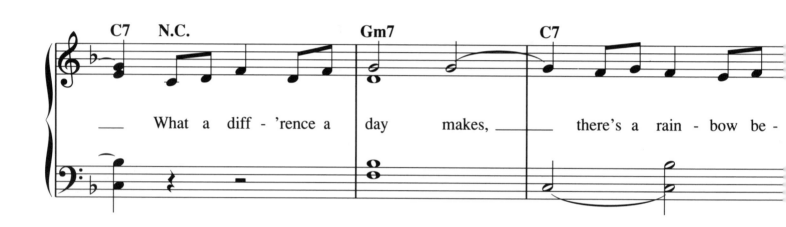

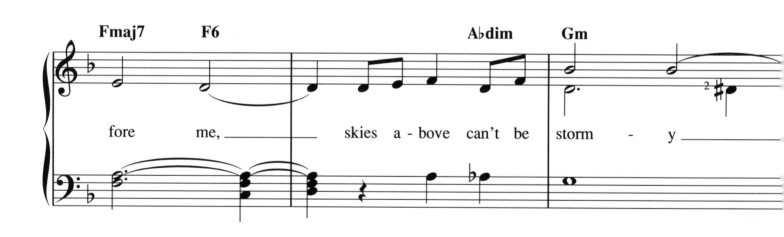

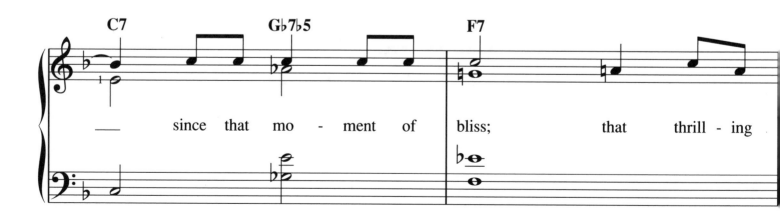

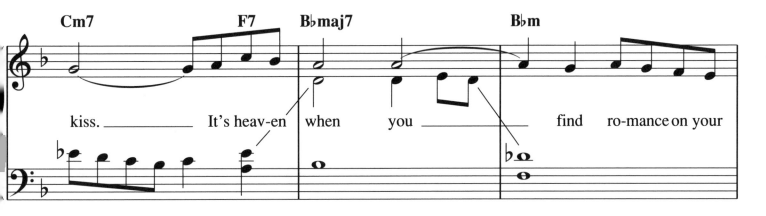

kiss. _____ It's heav-en when you _____ find ro-mance on your

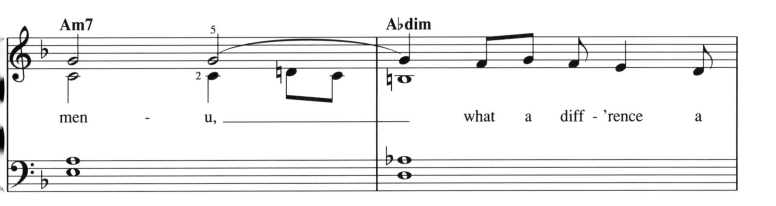

men - u, _____ what a diff - 'rence a

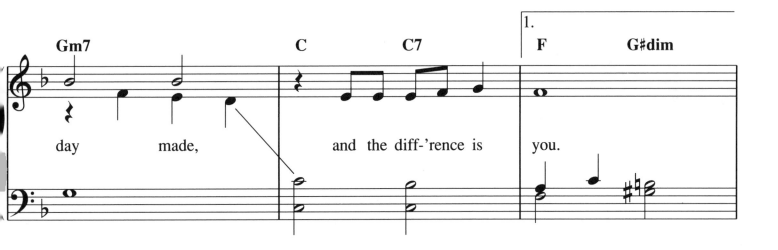

day made, and the diff-'rence is you.

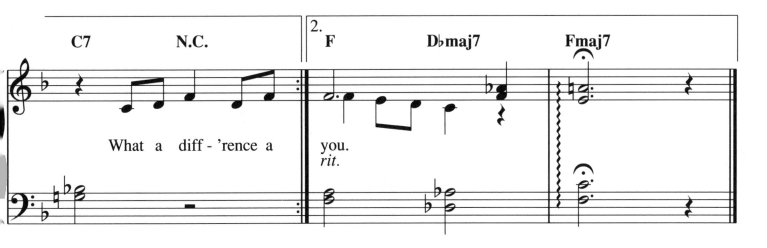

What a diff - 'rence a you.
rit.

WILLOW WEEP FOR ME

Words and Music by
ANN RONELL

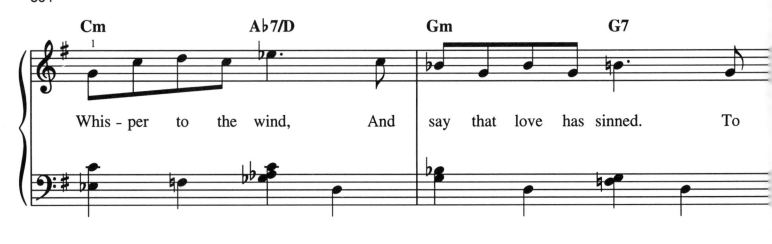

Whis - per to the wind, And say that love has sinned. To

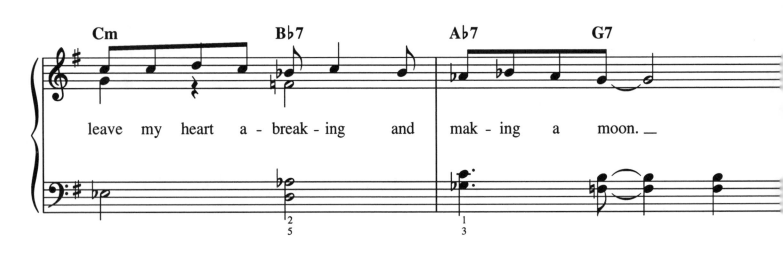

leave my heart a - break - ing and mak - ing a moon. __

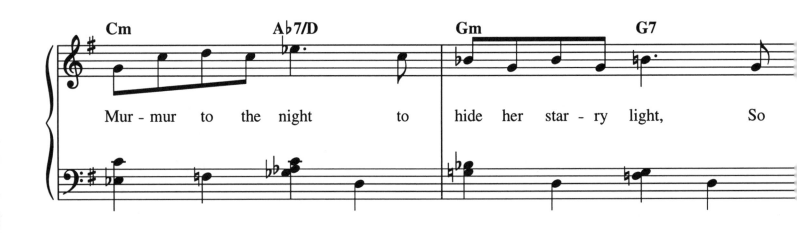

Mur - mur to the night to hide her star - ry light, So

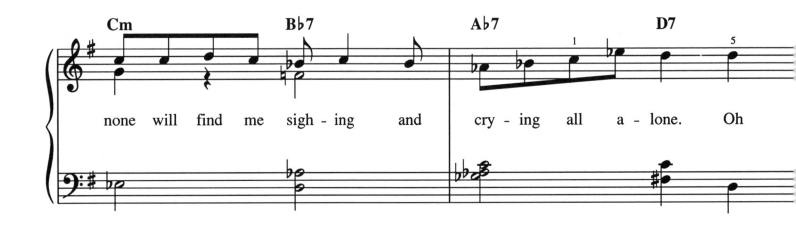

none will find me sigh - ing and cry - ing all a - lone. Oh

305

YOU'D BE SO NICE TO COME HOME TO
(From "SOMETHING TO SHOUT ABOUT")

Words and Music by COLE PORTER

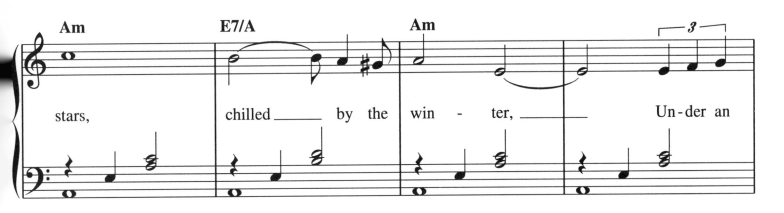

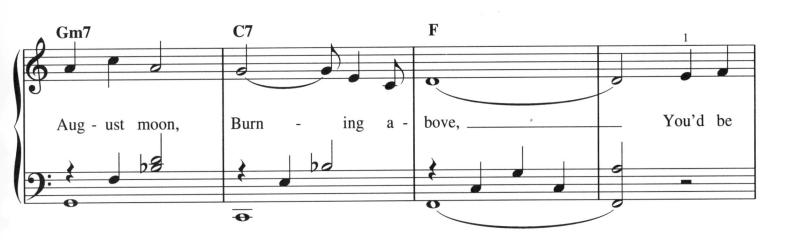

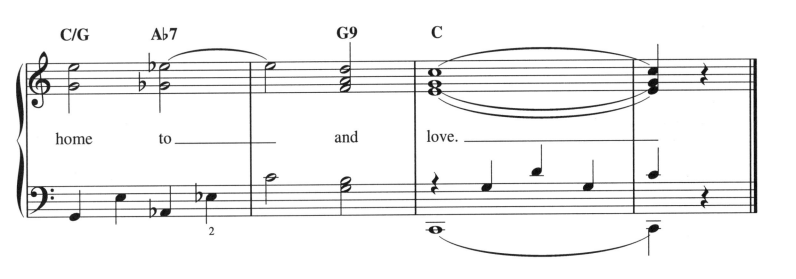

WHEN I FALL IN LOVE

Words by EDWARD HEYMAN
Music by VICTOR YOUNG

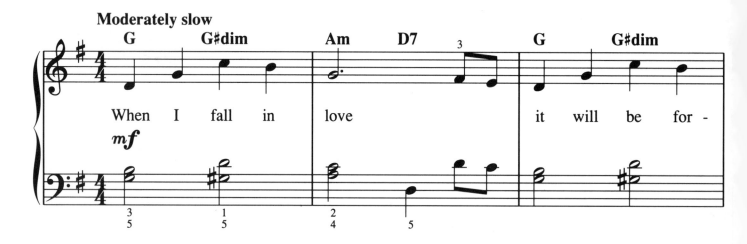

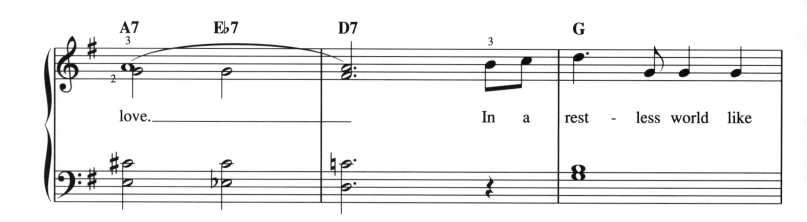

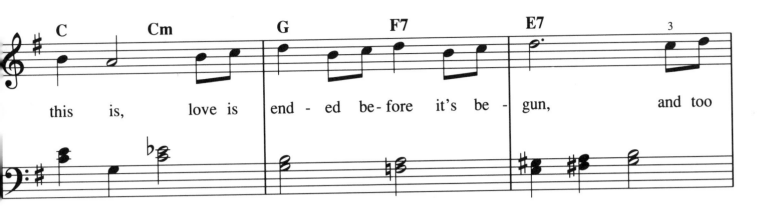

this is, love is end - ed be-fore it's be - gun, and too

man - y moon-light kiss - es seem to cool in the warmth of the
rit.

sun. When I give my heart
a tempo

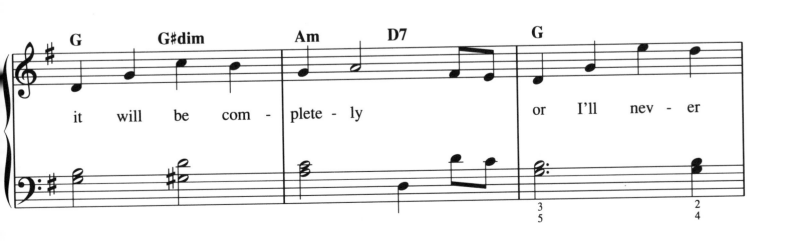

it will be com - plete - ly or I'll nev - er

give my heart._____ And the

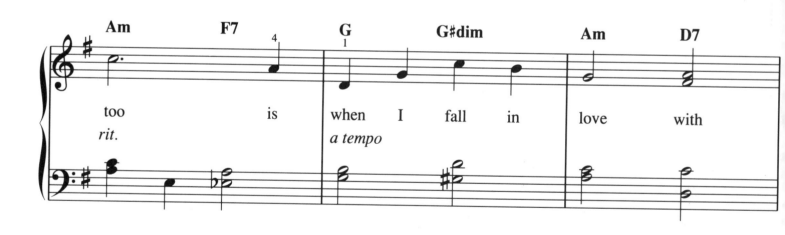

mo - ment I can feel that you feel that way

too is when I fall in love with
rit. *a tempo*

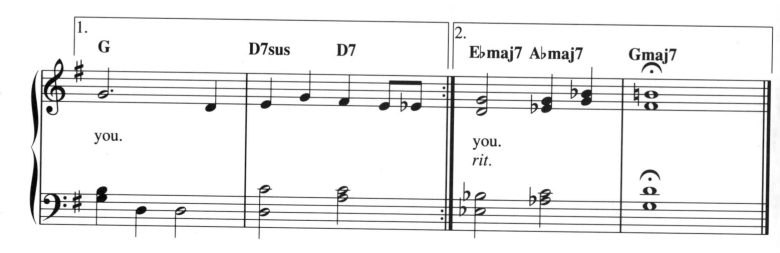

1. you.

2. you.
rit.